ESSAYS PRESENTED TO
EGON WELLESZ

EGON WELLESZ

ESSAYS PRESENTED TO
EGON WELLESZ

Edited by

JACK WESTRUP

CLARENDON PRESS
OXFORD
1966

Oxford University Press, Amen House, London E.C.4

GLASGOW NEW YORK TORONTO MELBOURNE WELLINGTON
CAPE TOWN SALISBURY IBADAN NAIROBI LUSAKA ADDIS ABABA
BOMBAY CALCUTTA MADRAS KARACHI LAHORE DACCA
KUALA LUMPUR HONG KONG TOKYO

*Printed in Great Britain
by Spottiswoode, Ballantyne and Co. Ltd.,
London and Colchester*

PREFACE

EGON WELLESZ has won equal distinction as a composer and as a scholar. His eightieth birth-day on 21 October 1965 was celebrated by performances of his compositions in several cities in England and on the Continent. The present volume is a tribute to his scholarship. It is offered to him with the good wishes and affection of his friends and colleagues in many parts of the world,

In order to give the volume some consistency it was decided to restrict it to two subjects which Dr. Wellesz has made peculiarly his own: Christian chant and opera. I am grateful to Albi and Maud Rosenthal and John Bergsagel for invaluable help in proof-reading.

J.A.W.

[v]

CONTENTS

LIST OF ILLUSTRATIONS

PART ONE

CHRISTIAN CHANT

THE REDISCOVERY OF BYZANTINE MUSIC

H. J. W. Tillyard (Cambridge)

IN APRIL 1905 a *Times* correspondent was in Athens to report on the first Archæological Congress. He heard a service at the Cathedral and declared that the chanting of the priest was often out of tune and that the choir sang steadily in four parts, without accompaniment, but that the music was the cheapest and most vulgar modern stuff, without any merit whatever.

The Cathedral and the great Church of St. Irene were trying at that time to unite two opposing movements. On the one hand there was the nineteenth-century tradition, resting upon the vocal system of Chrysanthus (published in 1821); and against this were ranged those singers who had come under European and Russian influences and were ready to drop the older method, as a remnant of Turkish supremacy and Oriental chromaticism. I. Th. Sakellarides, precentor of St. Irene's and afterwards of the Cathedral, was a gifted musician with an excellent voice; he composed the music for *Antigone*, which (and not Mendelssohn's, as *The Times* stated) was given at the grand performance in the Stadium during the time of the Congress. He was an advocate of the more European manner of singing, and some of his published specimens are harmonized in three or four parts. He was my teacher in 1905 and took me to hear the choir of the Girls' High School (*Arsakeion*) sing part of the Good Friday service (*Epitaphios*) and also the *Acathistos*, early in Lent. This is the opening stanza in his version:

[3]

Sakellarides was an enthusiast. When invited to tea at the hostel of the British School of Archaeology, he stood up at the table and sang this hymn and others in a ringing voice. He told us that he had come to Athens penniless and had sung in the streets for a living.

Meanwhile the monasteries and the smaller churches held fast to the Chrysanthine tradition. The Orthodox churches of Roumania and Bulgaria had also taken it over. Outside Greece this was regarded as the true Byzantine music; and some Greeks declared that it had come down unchanged from Apostolic times. In England Hatherly's treatise, the settings in J. M. Neale's *Hymns of the Eastern Church*, together with an uncomplimentary allusion in Athelstan Riley's *Athos*, made the sum total of most people's knowledge.

Chrysanthus, a Greek archimandrite, seeing the low state into which church music had fallen, had two chief aims: (1) to simplify the notation, which at that time few singers could read; and (2) to classify the modes and increase the number of chromatic signs. In (1) he was successful; for his notation, using fewer interval-signs and aided by a newly invented sol-fa, was easily printed, and learned without much difficulty. But in (2) he failed. The fact was that Byzantine music had been invaded by the Arabo-Turkish modal system and its confusion was incurable. A slight knowledge of ancient Greek music only tempted Chrysanthus to further inconsistencies. He classified the modes by their Arabo-Turkish names; but these are omitted in the 1911 reprint of his handbook (*Theoretikon Mega*). The difficulty of singing the various chromatic and irrational progressions of Oriental music, without accompaniment, was so great that in practice the modes were usually simplified in varying degrees, without much regard to general principles. When I visited Athens in 1950 I found that the Cathedral and several other churches in Athens had gone over completely to harmonized singing on Western lines, to which the congregations listened rapturously. Even Greek folk-music, which in 1905 could be heard unadulterated in the taverns on the back streets of Athens, had by that time been so much affected by European influence (chiefly conveyed by Italian gramophone records) that its true character had almost disappeared.

Nevertheless the conservative side had stalwart champions in Dr. Psachos and later Dr. Karas, who not only opposed the corrupting elements in choral singing, but also declared war on the European students of medieval Byzantine chant. The axiom 'Only Greeks can understand Greek music' was readily swallowed by ignorant writers in Western Europe, partly because it saved musicologists from the duty of studying the evidence of Byzantine liturgical manuscripts. This task was first undertaken outside Greece by Fleischer, Thibaut, Gaisser and Gastoué early in the twentieth century. All these did useful work, but were hampered by *a priori* theories. Still more so was Riemann, whose confident exposition is a sad example of misdirected ingenuity. At this juncture there seemed to be little hope of agreement among the rival theorists. But Egon Wellesz, who had ampler material at his disposal and was already known as a musician, began in 1914 the long series of articles and books that soon put the whole undertaking on a logical and scientific basis. In particular, he early discovered the correct interpretation of the rhythmical and accentual signs in the classical period of Byzantine music (twelfth to fifteenth centuries). Carsten Höeg in 1922 gave a rational account of the origin of the Byzantine modal system. Hence by 1931 such an understanding had been reached that a conference held at Copenhagen was able to inaugurate the *Monumenta Musicae Byzantinae*, since grown to a long series of facsimiles, transcriptions, and treatises, in which, besides the founders, many younger investigators have taken

[4]

part. Wellesz's discoveries have provided the standard for rhythmical interpretation. He has also attracted a zealous band of disciples and fellow-workers, especially from Greece, America, and the Slavonic countries.

The total results show that the musical notation began about the tenth century, but, like the early Gregorian and Russian neumes, it did not give the melodies note for note, but only a general guide to the singer, who was obliged to learn the tune by heart from his master's lips. In the twelfth century, however, a complete system of interval-signs was evolved, so that every step of the melody was clearly and exactly indicated. By careful comparison with the more archaic manuscripts we can now trace, with fair exactitude, the course of the earliest known musical versions. The results show that Byzantine music was diatonic and resembled Gregorian and Mozarabic chant. An important offshoot of Byzantine music survives in the so-called Italo-Grecian hymns, sung by the Albanian churches in Sicily and Southern Italy. These hymns were brought over by the Christians from Epirus, who, fleeing from the Turks, were granted shelter in the West and were allowed to keep their own Greek rite, on condition that they accepted the rule of the Roman Church. Until the present century these hymns were handed down unwritten, but several collections have since been issued. These show clearly the Byzantine foundation, but also Sicilian, Chrysanthine, and perhaps Saracenic, influences and are more tuneful and romantic than genuine Byzantine music.

If Byzantine hymns are to be sung in this country, they ought to be rendered by a single voice or a small choir in unison. But a simple accompaniment is useful, if the music seems unfamiliar; and it also takes the place of the rich echo of the domed churches of the East, which prevents any feeling of emptiness; or else the drone, which accompanies the melody in some Greek churches, may be held on an organ or harmonium. If the singers are unused to Greek, it is easy to make a Latin version; only a few more slurs are sometimes needed. Already more than a thousand Byzantine hymns have been published in European notation, and many more have been deciphered.

Besides his contributions to the *Monumenta* Wellesz also wrote many articles on Eastern Church music, including Serbian, Armenian, and Abyssinian. He dealt conclusively with the stenographic theory of Greek music, propounded, though not applied, by Chrysanthus, and revived by Psachos, Karas, and Georgiades in recent years. This theory—that Byzantine music can be sung only by the light of a tradition, confided exclusively to groups of Greek singers—sounds plausible when repeated to inexperienced learners, but when put in print the absurdity soon becomes evident.

Before 1914 the student of Byzantine music was an adventurer over untrodden paths. By mule or camel or small coastal steamer, he made his way to the monasteries, not knowing what treasures they might reveal or what reception awaited a visitor from the West. Nearly always the Greek monks (and here I include Grottaferrata) were generous with their hospitality and ungrudging of access to their shelves. So in an improvised dark-room the slides were loaded and then the heavy camera unpacked and every exposure made singly and usually developed on the spot. Now all is changed. Hundreds of manuscripts at Sinai and elsewhere have been photographed by experts with modern apparatus. The student need only order the film-strips that he requires, and all his research may be done in his own study or college library. His reward is a university degree; but in the old days we had wider hopes, for, in view of the revival of Gregorian music

[5]

in the nineteenth century, we dreamed of an equally glorious reconstruction of medieval Byzantine chant, based on a thorough-going recension of the most important manuscripts. Today, however, most of the churches affect the popular and the vernacular. Nevertheless a musicologist, who is also a composer, may find, amid the relics of a neglected and half-forgotten hymnody, a source for new creations to be the delight of our own age and of many audiences yet unborn. So now I join with my fellow-contributors in offering warmest congratulations to Egon Wellesz and in wishing him long life in the enjoyment of his fame.

BYZANTINE COMPOSERS IN MS. ATHENS 2406

Miloš Velimirović (New Haven)

LITTLE, IF anything, is known about composers of Byzantine music and it is quite likely that a large number of them may for ever remain simply names in a list of Byzantine musicians. One of the bits of unfinished business seldom tackled in the study of Byzantine music is a bio-bibliographical index-list of composers. There are a number of reasons for the delay with such a project, the main one being the fact that the body of Byzantine chants is extremely vast and that, owing to their functions and their variety, the texts and individual melodies are widely distributed in a large number of Greek-Orthodox liturgical books[1] and manuscripts; and the latter have not yet been fully listed and catalogued. The difficulties one encounters in an attempt of this kind are often out of all proportion to the results obtained.[2]

By the mid fifteenth century Western Europe had already produced composers such as Perotinus, Machaut, and Dufay (not to mention scores of others), but even musicologists would feel hard put to it if they were asked to name Byzantine musicians of repute for the same period. It would truly be fascinating to know how many musicians and composers were known either by name or by their works to a professional church-singer in Constantinople before the Turkish conquest of the city and the fall of the Byzantine Empire on 29 May 1453. It appears that a good answer, without any pretensions to completeness, to such a hypothetical question may be found in a manuscript, No. 2406, to be found in the National Library in Athens, which was written in that same year in the monastery of St. John Prodromos near Serres (north-east of Thessaloniki in Northern Greece). In it the fall of Constantinople has been duly recorded by the scribe.

---

[1] Egon Wellesz, *A History of Byzantine Music and Hymnography* (Oxford, 1961[2]), pp. 133–45.

[2] The earliest attempt by a Western scholar in this direction may have been that by Leo Allatius in his *De libris ecclesiasticis Graecorum* (Paris, 1646) [inaccessible to me at the time of writing]. Allatius' list was reproduced with some bibliographical additions by Fabricius in *Bibliotheca Graeca* (Hamburg, 1737), pp. 130–9. Of the more recent studies, the work by G. Papadopoulos, Συμβολαί εἰς τὴν ἱστορίαν τῆς παρ' ἡμῖν ἐκκλησιαστικῆς μουσικῆς (Athens, 1890) contains useful data for the last three centuries, though, for the medieval period it is, unfortunately, almost worthless. Much more ambitious and systematic was the unfinished project of Dom Casimir Émereau, published in instalments in *Échos d'Orient*, Vols. 21 (1922)–25 (1926). A list of musicians with summary references to some types of their works in manuscripts on Mount Athos was compiled by Sophronios Eustratiadis in an appendix to his *Catalogue of Greek Manuscripts in the Library of the Laura on Mt. Athos* (Harvard Theological Studies, Vol. XII, Cambridge, Mass., 1925), pp. 444–61. Another of Eustratiadis's lists appeared in his article 'Θρᾶκες μουσικοί', Ἐπετηρὶς Ἑταιρείας Βυζαντινῶν Σπουδῶν XII (1936), pp. 46–48. I have been given to understand that Mr. Ilia Hourzamani of Athens, Greece, is currently engaged in a similar project.

This manuscript is a type of anthology which is most frequently referred to as 'akolouthia',[1] and of those written before 1453 there are perhaps two dozen copies still in existence. Their number continued to grow after the fall of Constantinople and they were still extensively copied late in the eighteenth century. What distinguishes the *akolouthia* manuscripts from the *sticheraria* and *hirmologia* of the same period, besides their basic differences in content and repertoire, seems to be the fact that *akolouthia* manuscripts contain many attributions and names of composers, a feature which by that time appears to be rather an exception for other types of manuscripts. It is because of this that manuscript Athens 2406 may serve as a good starting-point toward the compilation of a catalogue of Byzantine composers which could, ultimately, contain a master-index of all compositions by each composer, and serve as a checking point for the validities of attributions in manuscripts of later centuries. Yet before a discussion of composers listed in Athens 2406 a few words about this manuscript are needed.[2]

In its present shape this manuscript is fairly complete, with only a small number of folios missing[3]. It is in fact an exceptionally large manuscript and in all probability was compiled to serve as a comprehensive anthology. There is no doubt about its date and also about the fact that the copying must have started before the fall of Constantinople.[4] This is most vividly documented in the acclamation to the Emperor, Constantine XI, the last Byzantine emperor, which appears at its regular place within the frame of the liturgy. Furthermore, the scribe must have known that the Emperor was not married at that time, and—probably having heard rumours about negotiations concerning his marriage—he left empty space for the name of the then non-existent empress in the acclamation.[5] It may also be argued that this manuscript represents a collection bound at a later date, since the colophon is not at the end of the manuscript but in the middle. On the basis of the numbering of quires it would seem that there is nothing against the assumption that the colophon was written under the shock of the news, and that the compilation of the rest of the manuscript may then have proceeded as originally planned. Because of the presence of the inscription recording the year 1453 in the middle, this manuscript may serve as a good example

[1] For one of the best descriptions of this type of manuscript see Kenneth Levy, 'A Hymn for Thursday in Holy Week', *Journal of the American Musicological Society*, XVI (1963), p. 155.

[2] This manuscript has not yet been described in a published catalogue, although it has been used by Trempelas, as well as by me, in, e.g., my studies: 'Liturgical Drama in Byzantium and Russia', *Dumbarton Oaks Papers* XVI (1962), p. 354, n. 18, and *infra*, n. 4 and p. 11, n. 8. Since Professor Linos Politis of the University of Thessaloniki is currently preparing for publication a full catalogue of all the manuscripts from Serres in the National Library in Athens, I shall not discuss the contents of this manuscript but restrict myself to a discussion of titles of musicians and to prosopographic remarks. I wish to use this opportunity to express my deep gratitude to Mr. A. Athanasopoulos, curator of manuscripts in the National Library in Athens, for numerous courtesies extended to me during my stay in Athens, and to Professor Politis my deepest thanks for having placed at my disposal some codicological data about the manuscripts in Athens.

[3] The manuscript now consists of 468 folios. On the basis of quire signatures it is easy to determine that 29 folios in the beginning are missing, and it seems that between folios 460 and 461 some eleven additional folios are missing.

[4] The colophon on fo. 291 r. was published by André Guillou, *Les Archives de Saint-Jean-Prodrome sur le mont Ménécée* (Paris, 1955), p. 190. As I have already indicated in my article Ἰωακεὶμ μοναχὸς τοῦ Χαρσιανίτου καὶ δομέστικος Σερβίας, *Recueil de travaux de l'Institut d'études byzantines*, VIII/2, *Mélanges G. Ostrogorsky*, II, Belgrade, 1964, p. 452, n.3), toward the end of the colophon the word ὅσαι should be corrected to read οὐαί.

[5] Folio 218 r. Constantine was twice a widower at the time he became Emperor. About considerations and even negotiations for his third marriage perhaps the fullest account is that by S. Lampros, Ὁ Κωνσταντῖνος Παλαιολόγος ὡς σύζυγος ἐν τῇ ἱστορίᾳ καὶ τοῖς θρύλοις, *Νέος Ἑλληνομνήμων* IV (1907), pp. 417–66.

of the vast repertoire of chants (still by no means a collection of all the chants for all the services) in use in the Greek churches when the Byzantine Empire came to an end.

A survey of the contents and of the inscriptions in this manuscript shows that although written at Serres, a city which had been taken by the Turks some seventy-odd years earlier[1] and thus not properly belonging to the territory of the shrunken Byzantine Empire, the scribe had an extensive knowledge of the chants in use in Constantinople, specifically in the 'Great Church' (i.e. Hagia Sophia). The nearness of Thessaloniki makes it no surprise that this manuscript contains a great number of pieces in variants which are indicated to be versions sung in that city. The proximity of Mount Athos also accounts for the inclusion of a number of musical variants which are labelled as having originated either with a monk from one of the monasteries on Mount Athos, or are listed as sung in one of the monasteries there.[2] One of the distinguishing traits of this scribe is that he clearly indicated the variants of the same chants and it is this feature which enhances the musical value of the manuscript. As one might expect, the scribe was also patriotic enough to enter a peculiar local variant of a few melodies as they were sung in Serres, adding at that point 'nowhere else can these be found'.[3] The meticulous care one encounters in remarks of this kind inspires confidence that one has here a reliable source of information, and this feeling becomes strengthened as one follows the references to authors. Few are the pages containing the often frustrating reference to the composer as τοῦ αὐτοῦ (of the same), referring to a composer whose name may (or sometimes may not) appear on one of the preceding pages. With an almost scholarly care the scribe recorded diverging opinions concerning attributions, or when uncertain referred to others as his source of information.[4] In view of all these features it is rather remarkable that this manuscript can now be utilized for a variety of approaches in studies of Byzantine music as it was practised, albeit at the very end of the existence of the Byzantine Empire.

Perhaps one of the greatest surprises in the mere attempt to index the names of Byzantine composers mentioned in this manuscript is the fact that they number more than one hundred. Actually this number is obtained from a simple listing of names and titles. It is quite possible that some of the titles and some of the names may be coupled, and this number could be reduced.[5] Yet even so, one still has to reckon with a list of more than seventy composers and poets, assuming

[1] G. Ostrogorski, *History of the Byzantine State* (New Brunswick, N.J., 1957), p. 485.

[2] For instance, fo. 446 r.: τὸ πάρον . . . ἔστι δε ποίημα κ. Δωσίθεοῦ ἱερομοναχοῦ ἀπὸ τὴν Λαύρα τοῦ Ἁγίου Ἀθανασίου τῆς ἐν τῷ ὄρῃ τοῦ Ἀθωνοι. Or for singing in Vatopedi, fo. 236 r.: ἕτερον ἀσματικὸν ὁ ψαλλεταῖ ἐν τη ἱερᾳ Μονῇ τοῦ Βατοπαιδίου. It may be of interest to point out here that the name of the scribe of Athens was Matthew, and that in the book by M. Vogel and V. Gardthausen, *Die griechischen Schreiber des Mittelalters und der Renaissance* ('Beihefte zum Zentralblatt für Bibliothekswesen', Leipzig, 1909), p. 298, there is a Matthew *domestikos* who in 1440 wrote a manuscript in Vatopedi. Could this have been the same person writing later, who remembers variants from a monastery in which he resided some years earlier?

[3] Fol. 215 v.: οἱ παρόντες στίχοι τοῦ ἀμώμου ψάλλονται εἰς κοιμηθέντας μοναχοὺς ἐν τῇ πόλ[ει] Σερρῶν ὡς οἶμε [= οἶμαι] γοῦν εἰσὶν ποιήματα τῆς αὐτῆς πόλεως διὰ το ἀλ[λ]αχόθεν οὐχ

εὑρίσκονται εἰμὴ εἰς τὴν δηλωθεῖσαν πόλιν καὶ ἴδη [= ἤδη] γράφω τὰ καὶ ἐγὼ ἐνταῦθα.

[4] As an example of a piece attributed to Koronis, yet also to a certain Christophoros, see fo. 47 v.: ἕτεροι γράφουσιν ὅτι τὸ πάρον ἔστιν ποίημα τοῦ δομεστικοῦ κ. Χριστοφόρου. For example of a reference, i.e., to sources from Thessaloniki see fo. 207 v.: ἄλλαγμα παλαία Θεσσαλονικαῖα. οἱ Θεσσαλονικοῖς γράφουν ὅτι εἰσι τοῦ μοναχοῦ Κορνηλίου. Finally, for an example in which the scribe indicated that he 'did not find the author', there is fo. 24 v.: οὐκ εἶδα τὸν ποιήτον.

[5] Specifically in the case of Andreas the priest, listed as author on folios 212 v, 213 r, and 213 v. On fo. 214 v. the author is listed as Andreas *domestikos*, and the proximity of these references makes it plausible to assume that this may be the same person. The names of Gerasimos, Theodoulos, Markos, and Christophoros may involve similar possibilities, as may be inferred from the appendix.

that some twenty-five per cent. of the original listing can be re-attributed or connected with an already listed name or title. The difficulty of reconciliation with such a large number may be partially removed if one accepts the probability (and in some instances certainty) that not all of these names were contemporary musicians.[1] It is on this basis that the appearance of a large number of works by a John Koukouzeles or a Xenos Koronis in comparison with the other composers may be explained, as may be seen in the Appendix to this essay.

While lists of composers recorded in manuscripts can be compiled relatively easily and concordances eventually obtained, solutions for the problems of chronology[2] and of the identity of these composers cannot be offered. For only a few Byzantine composers are there sufficient data to place them within a specific period of time or to illuminate some of their movements with recorded facts. It is the purpose of this study to examine some of the names and titles recorded in Athens 2406, and to suggest some possible identifications in this as yet uncharted area of Byzantine musicology.

Among the titles and professions recorded, those of μοναχός and ἱερεύς do not require particular attention. Their meaning of 'monk' and 'priest' is clear, as is that of ἱερομόναχος. The title δομέστικος refers to a choir-leader, and so does πρωτοψάλτης.[3] The frequency with which one encounters the title maïstor makes it an almost Pavlovian reaction to associate it with the name of John Koukouzeles, and it is quite possible that Byzantine scribes reacted in much the same way. Yet within this manuscript there are three other composers who have the same designation. It appears towards the end, in a few instances with the name of Manuel Chrysaphes and in isolated instances with the names of Demetrios Redestinos and Manuel Argyropoulos.[4] It has been this writer's assumption that in these cases the scribe may have been carried away with the artistry of these men and added a title which when used alone almost invariably implied that the work in question was by Koukouzeles. Perhaps a similar instance of enthusiastic reaction is to be discerned in the addition of the epithet λαμπρότατος (most brilliant) to the name of a certain Grigorios. Whether this one is identical with three other composers, all named Grigorios in this manuscript, is not clear. The title of λαμπαδάριος[5] appears only with two names, those of Manuel Chrysaphes and John Lampadarios of 'the imperial choir'. The latter in all probability is the person elsewhere recorded as John Kladas.

The term ferentaris, used on only two occasions, might possibly be a corrupted form of ῥεφερενδάρις.[6] Designations of other titles not connected with the Church may also be found. Such are

[1] A parallel may be seen in our own days in an album of piano pieces which could contain works of composers from the last three centuries. As the works of Haydn, Mozart, and Beethoven may dominate such an anthology, the names of some Byzantine composers from the thirteenth and fourteenth centuries may assume a disproportionately large place in a manuscript written in the mid fifteenth century.

[2] Some ideas about chronology have already been expressed by Levy, op. cit., p. 156, n. 47.

[3] Documentation for these as Church singers was assembled by K. M. Rallis in his two studies: 'Περὶ τοῦ ἐκκλησιαστικοῦ ἀξιώματος τῶν δομεστίκων', Πρακτικὰ τῆς Ἀκαδημίας Ἀθηνῶν XII (1937), 294–6, and 'Περὶ τοῦ ἀξιώματος τοῦ πρωτοψάλτου', ibid. XI (1936), pp. 66–69.

[4] See below, Appendix. Manuel Chrysaphes is one of the few Byzantine musicians about whom something has been written in this century. Cf. the article by A. Papadopoulos-Kerameus in Vizantiĭskiĭ Vremennik VIII (1901), pp. 526–45.

[5] Cf. K. M. Rallis, 'Περὶ τοῦ ἐκκλησιαστικοῦ ἀξιώματος τοῦ λαμπαδαρίου', Πρακτικὰ, IX (1934), pp. 259–61.

[6] Δ. Β. Βαγιακάκος,' Ἡ ἐκκλησιαστικὴ γλῶσσα καὶ ἡ μεσαιωνικὴ καὶ ἡ νεοελληνικὴ ὀνοματολογία', Ἀθήνα 63 (1959), p. 224. This excellent study contains an exhaustive list of titles with up-to-date bibliographical data.

orfanotrofos (in charge of an orphanage) and *protostrator* (master of the stable, or leader of cavalry),[1] the latter unfortunately without his first name. At least one more unusual profession appears in the case of *ampelokypiotis*, which would seem to designate a 'vineyard-guardian', unless this is the geographic name of a settlement, in which case it would imply the composer's origin.[2] Instances of the type of name designating provenance, or at least residence, abound and need no particular elaboration. This is obviously the case with *aghioretikos*, which clearly indicates origin from Mount Athos (in Greece invariably called Ἅγιον Ὄρος) or for that matter *aghiosofitikos*, which is more specific in that it describes either a chant in use in the church of Hagia Sophia or a person associated with it.

With a touch of local pride the scribe recorded the name of Antonios, *domestikos* in the city of Serres.[3] In the case of Demetrios Redestinos, his place of origin can be identified as Raidestos on the shores of the Marmara Sea, not far from Constantinople. Incidentally, this place seems to have provided a number of singers in later centuries.[4] In the same geographical area of Eastern Thrace (now European Turkey) can be found the settlement of Kallikrateia, from which a certain Theodoros apparently came.[5] One wonders about Nikolaos Rentakinos whether he was a resident of Ryndakos, a settlement on the coast of Asia Minor.[6] As for the designation of a certain Phocas as ὁ πολίτης perhaps it is possible that the scribe had in mind a Phocas from Constantinople in order to distinguish him from Phocas who was a protopsalt on the island of Crete.[7] For John Laskaris, who was a Constantinopolitan by origin, a stay on Crete has been documented and one can understand why he was referred to as 'from Crete.'[8]

Among musicians from other Greek islands the scribe indicated that Nikolaos Kamateiros was from Chios and a certain Sgouropoulos from Rhodes.[9] The identification of a protopsalt from Cyprus, in the manuscript simply written as *kas*, depends on whether this represents an abbreviation or not. From Eustratiadis's catalogue it was already known that a certain Nikolaos Asan is identified as being from Cyprus,[10] and in Athens 2406 one may encounter a Konstantin Asan in addition to Nikolaos, who also appears, but without any other identification as to the place of his origin. Could it be that *kas* represents an abbreviation for *K*(onstantin) *As*(an)? This is, admittedly, a conjecture without any more foundation at this moment, and the validity of such an assumption will have to be tested when more data for a catalogue of composers are available. Our manuscript also contains a work by an unnamed monk from Sinai.[11]

[1] For *orphanotrofos* see H.-G. Beck, *Kirche und theologische Literatur im Byzantinischen Reich* (Munich, 1959), p. 104. For *protostrator* see R. Guilland, 'Études de titulature et de prosopographie byzantines: le protostrator', *Revue des études byzantines* 7 (1949), pp. 156–79.

[2] There is an area in Athens today known as Ampelokypoi and it is likely that there are a number of similarly-named localities in other parts of Greece.

[3] See Appendix.

[4] See the Index in Papadopoulos, op. cit., also in Eustratiadis's study in the Supplement to the third volume of Θρᾳκικά (1931), pp. 224–5.

[5] For the location see Ἐγκυκλοπαίδικον λεξικόν, Vol. VII (Athens, Eleftheroudaki, 1929), p. 117.

[6] V. A. Mystakidis, 'Λασκάρεις', Ἐπετ. Ἑταιρ. Βυζ. Σπ. V (1928), p.141, n. 2.

[7] See Appendix.

[8] Cf. my study 'Two Byzantine Composers—John Vatatzes and John Laskaris', *Aspects of Medieval and Renaissance Music* ('Festschrift Gustave Reese') New York, 1965.

[9] In the case of the work of Sgouropoulos it is not clear whether the inscription contains some nickname of his or whether it may designate a title of the work. It is also possible that it should be transliterated 'Tramountanis, tou fournou', in which case it means something like 'North wind, from the furnace'; yet what connection this has with the following clear statement, 'from the island of Rhodes', remains something of a mystery. I have taken it to mean that Sgouropoulos was from Rhodes.

[10] Eustratatiadis, *Catalogue*, p. 457.

[11] See Appendix.

The number of names of musicians who were either of Constantinopolitan origin or simply lived there and were employed in one of the local churches is quite large. It is interesting to note that only one musician is mentioned as having been associated with the 'imperial' choir (or clergy), and that is John Kladas, a *lampadarios*.[1] Specific references about being in the service of the Hagia Sophia appear for the deacon, John Sgouropoulos, who is listed as having been a *domestikos* of the 'Great Church', and for John Doukas, also a *domestikos* of the same church (the latter had also the title of *laosynaktos*).[2] By implication Manuel Chrysaphes also must have belonged to the same august body of musicians; and although Athens 2406 does not spell it out, it would appear that the names of John Glykys, Koukouzeles, Demetrios Dokeianos, Georgios Kontopetris, and perhaps Xenos Koronis,[3] should be considered as having been at least candidates for that choir, if they were not actually in it.[4]

Four other musicians can be linked directly with some of the monasteries in the city of Constantinople. These are: Joakeim of the monastery Χαρσιανίτης, who also had the title of '*domestikos* of Serbia';[5] two other monks, Gabriel and Mark, are known to have belonged to a monastery which was referred to by the name of the family which either built it or reconstructed it—τῶν Ξανθοπούλων—and this family is known to have produced some rather famous personalities;[6] finally, *domestikos* Theodoulos was in the monastery τῶν Μαγγάνων which can be identified as the monastery of St. George, about which a substantial amount of information is available.[7] In this same monastery, in 1360, a monk with the family name of Gavras was recorded.[8] It remains doubtful whether this monk was the same person as the Konstantin Gavras listed in Athens 2406 and it would appear plausible to assume that the latter may have been another member of that influential family.[9]

In addition to those identifying professions and origin, a good many names preserved in our manuscript appear to be family names. In at least one instance the inscriptions reveal several members of one family as having been musicians by listing Manuel as the son of Xenos Koronis; and in the case of Agathon Koronis there are records of his being a brother of Xenos.[10] Another most interesting—and so far unique—reference may be inferred from a note about a daughter of John Kladas (another woman besides Cassia) who appears to have been known as a singer, if not also as a composer.[11] Other names which could be either family names or names of monas-

---

[1] Papadopoulos, op. cit., p. 274, lists Kladas as *lampadarios* of Hagia Sophia.

[2] Cf. Beck, op. cit., p. 114. What Beck considers a corrupt form—*laosynaptis*—is the standard spelling in Athens 2406.

[3] The name Koronis raises another problem. It could, conceivably, designate origin from Koroni in Southwestern Peloponnese. However, there was a church in Constantinople known as Koronis. Cf. R. Janin, *La géographie ecclésiastique de l'empire byzantin*, Part I, vol. 3: *Les églises et les monastères* (Paris, 1953), p. 200. The difficulty of associating Koronis with that church is that it is known only from a single document in the tenth century.

[4] Data about the life of Koukouzeles are a mixture of facts and legends. Yet owing to his renown it may be assumed that he would at least have been invited to participate in services. For Dokeianos, Eustratiadis lists him as a pupil of

Koukouzeles (cf. *Catalogue*, p. 449), and if that is correct the same assumption would be valid for him. For Koronis, Papadopoulos states that he was a protopsalt in Hagia Sophia (op. cit., p. 266). Papadopoulos links Chrysaphes with the same church (ibid., p. 292), while Papadopoulos-Kerameus (see *supra*, p. 10, n. 4) considers him a member of the 'imperial' choir.

[5] See *supra*, p. 8, n. 4.

[6] Cf. Janin, *La géographie . . .*, p. 393. See also Beck, op. cit., pp. 705-7.

[7] Janin., op. cit., pp. 75-81.

[8] Ibid., p. 77.

[9] Janin, *Constantinople byzantin* (Paris, 1950), p. 328.

[10] Eustratiadis, *Catalogue*, p. 444.

[11] Folio 258 v. Besides the Kladas problem, there is that of the relationship of the two musicians designated as Glykys. For John Glykys it seems plausible to assume that he is

teries are Argyropoulos, Moschianos, Magoulas and also perhaps Panaretos.[1] The Cretan family Gavalas seems also to have had a musician recorded in this manuscript.[2]

The case of Grigorios Alyates is highly interesting as he appears to have been not only a musician but a scribe as well, and the dates of the manuscripts which he copied and signed indicate that his activity was closely related in time to that in which Athens 2406 was compiled and executed.[3] In the case of Koukoumas, who, Papadopoulos suggested, was identical with John Plousiadenos,[4] the problem consists in reconciliation with dates now assumed for his lifetime. If he was born about 1429 he must have been a rather precocious composer to have written his works not later than the age of twenty and to have his compositions acquiring sufficient reputation to be copied by the middle of the fifteenth century; whilst this is not impossible, it serves as a warning against rash identifications.[5]

One of the curious problems lies in the label *latrinos* attached to a *polyeleon*.[6] If it is to be assumed that this term was derived from Latros, the name of the monastic settlements in the vicinity of Miletos,[7] this leaves an implication that there may have existed a peculiar local variant of singing, and the question of its transmission creates a different problem. The difficulty lies in the recorded information that the settlements at Latros were nearly abandoned in the fourteenth century, and one of the last known personalities to have spent some time in the Latros group of monasteries and later to become prominent in Constantinople was the Constantinopolitan Athanasios I, who was patriarch twice, first from 1289 to 1293 and again from 1303 until 1310 (a period which places him in close proximity to John Glykys.)[8] It is conceivable that such a man could have contributed to the introduction to Constantinople of the *latrinos* variant, and that this variant remained popular enough to be copied in the following century; yet in the absence of a chronological catalogue of references to the various titles and names this is still only a hypothetical explanation.

A problem of a different kind involves the personality of John Koukouzeles, probably the most famous and most frequently cited Byzantine composer. Opinions about the date of his life vary from the tenth century to the late fourteenth century.[9] It is obvious that a new and critical reappraisal of all the sources is called for to narrow down the limits of the possible period of his

---

identical with John XIII, patriarch of Constantinople (cf. Levy, op. cit., p. 156). It is known that he had two sons: cf. R. Guilland, *Correspondance de Nicéphore Grégoras* (Paris, 1927), p. 336. Yet neither of these had the name Grigorios. In Athens 2406 there are two pieces, one by each, John and Grigorios, on folios 206 v. and 210 v., and both of these pieces have an added word 'Thessalonian', but it is impossible to decide whether this designation implies that the two Glykys were by origin from Thessaloniki or whether the pieces were written down in versions as sung in Thessaloniki.

[1] The family name Argyropoulos is a well-known one in Crete and in Constantinople. The most famous member of that family seems to have been John Argyropoulos, who settled in Italy. Cf. N. Iorga, *Byzance après Byzance* (Bucarest, 1935), p. 15 foll. The name Moschianos appears in Constantinople, cf. Janin, *Constantinople byzantine*, p. 365. The names Magoulas and Panaretos are also known there. Cf. Janin, *La géographie*, pp. 324, 400.

[2] Cf. E. Gerland, 'Histoire de la noblesse Crétoise au Moyen Âge', *Revue de l' Orient Latin* X (1905), pp. 220-1. There was a monk in that family in 1443.

[3] Vogel-Gardthausen, op. cit., p. 92. The dates are between 1433 and 1446.

[4] Papadopoulos, op. cit., p. 258.

[5] Cf. M. Manoussacas, 'Recherches sur la vie de Jean Plousiadènos', *Revue des études byzantines* XVII (1959), pp. 28–51.

[6] Folios 90 v.–99 v.

[7] *Lexikon für Theologie und Kirche*, VI (1961), cols. 821–2.

[8] Beck, op. cit., p. 692.

[9] Papadopoulos, op. cit., pp. 261–5, places him in the eleventh century. Mme. Braschowanowa, in *MGG*, VII (1958), cols. 1888–90, thinks he lived in the second half of the fourteenth century. My student, Mr. Edward V. Williams, has undertaken to study the life and works of Koukouzeles in his doctoral dissertation, now in progress.

activities, besides a stylistic analysis of his compositions to determine the aesthetic factors which may have made him so popular.

On the basis of these few data it appears that the manuscript Athens 2406, with its repertory and detailed inscriptions, represents one of the crucial sources for a substantial part of the preserved body of Byzantine chant. Among the points which emerge clearly from its contents is the fact that Constantinople unquestionably still represented one of the main centres of musical activities, in spite of the hardships the Byzantine Empire was enduring at that time. Another point worthy of particular attention, and hitherto seldom taken seriously into consideration, is the emergence of a vast repertory of musical variants of the chants which are associated with the city of Thessaloniki. Furthermore, the wide distribution of musicians mentioned in this manuscript—Crete, Cyprus, Chios, Rhodes, not to mention Mount Athos—indicates the vigour with which Byzantine music was being practised and enriched with new works, besides testifying to its dissemination at a time when the Byzantine Empire was reduced to the city of Constantinople and some isolated areas on the Peloponnese. Of singular significance also is the fact that this manuscript was written in an area under Turkish domination, and in the compilation of the contents the scribe not only used the traditional melodies attributed to composers of a preceding century but included more recent compositions, implying religious contacts and a flow of music from a besieged Constantinople, as well as from other Orthodox centres. This fact alone may serve as a stimulus for additional investigations of Byzantine music at that critical juncture of its historical development. One can only hope that through a collaboration with the historians of Byzantium and Byzantine literature and a more searching study of both published and unpublished archival data new light may be thrown on some of the Byzantine musicians whose identities are still hidden and who have been hitherto but names.

APPENDIX

Catalogue of Names of Composers and Authors of Texts in MS Athens 2406.

THIS appendix contains lists of pages on which composers' names appear. It does not reflect the number of compositions by any one of them.

Ἀγάθων Κορώνης, μοναχὸς   24 v., 265 v.

Ἀγάθων μοναχὸς   45 v., 127 r., 128 r., 129 r., 140 r., 245 r.

Ἀγαλλιανὸς   36 r., 36 v., 43 r., 91 r., 94 r., 96 v., 99 r., 117 r., 117 v.–118 v., 120 v., 140 r., 140 v., 233 r., cf. Μανουὴλ Ἀγαλλιανὸς, δομέςτικος.

Ἀθανάσιος μοναχὸς Ἁγιωρήτικος   464 r.

Ἀλέξιος ἱερεὺς τοῦ Ἀγάλωνος   111 v.

Ἀλυάτης   Cf. Γρηγόριος Ἀλυάτης.

Ἀμπελωκηπιώτης   460 r., cf. Μανουὴλ Ἀμπελωκηπιώτης, ἱερεὺς.

Ἀναπαπαρδᾶς   242 r.

Ἀνδρέας   92 r., 93 v., 115 v., 127 v., 128 r., 212 r., 290 r.

[15]

Λέων Δεσπότης   453 r.–457 v. (heothina).

Λογγῖνοσ μοναχὸς   279 r.

Μαγουλᾶς   Cf. Κωνσταντῖνος.

μαῖστωρ   Cf. Ἰωάννης ὁ Κουκουζέλης.

Μακρόπουλος   37 r.

Μανουγρᾶς   192 v., 200 r., 201 v., 203 r., 206 v., 207 r.

Μανουὴλ   Cf. Θυβαϊκος κὺρ Μανουήλ.

Μανουὴλ Ἀγγαλιανὸς,   243 r., cf. Ἀγαλλιανὸς.

Μανουὴλ Ἀργυρόπουλος, μαῖστωρ   267 v., 271 v., 462 v.

Μανουὴλ Ἀμπελωκηπιώτης, ἱερεὺς   259 r., cf. Ἀμπελωκηπιώτης.

Μανουὴλ Βλαστύρος   269 v.

Μανουὴλ Κορώνης, υἱὸς τοῦ Ξένου Κορώνη   263 v.

Μανουὴλ Κούρτεσης   102 r.

Μανουὴλ ὀρφανοτρόφος   186 v., 187 v.

Μανουὴλ Πανάρετος, ἱερεὺς   185 v., 188 v.

Μανουὴλ Χρυσάφης, λαμπαδάριος   252 r., 255 r., 257 v., 260 v., 262 r., 270 r., 274 r., 274 v., 286 r., 288 v., 337 r.,
    448 r., 449 r., 450 r., 450 v., 451 v., 462 r., 462 v., 464 r.

Μάρκος ἱερομόναχος   185 r., 254 r., 287 v., 288 r.

Μάρκος ἱερομόναχος ἐκ τῆς μονῆς τῶν Ξανθοπούλων   51 v., 246 r., 260 r., 268 v.

Μιχαὴλ Ἀνεώτης, δομέστικος   138 r., 236 v., cf. Ἀνεώτης.

Μιχαὴλ ἱερεύς τοῦ Πρώπολα   257 v.

Μιχαὴλ ὁ Μυστάκων   28 r., cf. Μυστάκων.

Μοσχιανὸς, δομέστκος   31 v., 46 r., 55 v., 253 v., 259 v., 264 v., 268 v., cf. Γεώργιος and Κωνσταντῖνος.

Μυστάκων   91 r., 91 v., 93 r., 121 r., 124 r., 201 r., 202 v., 214 r., 458 r., cf. Μιχαὴλ and Χριστοφόρος.

Νικηφόρος ὁ Ἠθικός   (N.B.: This entry contains also all references to Ἠθικός only):   116 v., 131 v., 139 v.,
    184 v., 189 r., 195 v., 210 v., 229 r., 231 r., 231 v., 280 r., 281 v., 283 r., 309 r., 321 v., 365 v.

Νικόλαος Ἀσάν   130 r., 130 v., 258 v.

Νικόλαος Καματεῖρος πρωτοψάλτης Χίου   32 r.

Νικόλαος ὁ Κλωβᾶς   357 v. (as he sings a piece by Koronis).

Νικόλαος πρωτοψάλτης τοῦ Ρεντακίνου   333 v.

Νίκων μοναχὸς   23 r., 29 r., 103 v.

Ξανθοπούλος   Cf. Γαβριὴλ and Μάρκος.

Ξένος Κορώνης, πρωτοψάλτης,   3 r.–16 r. (methodos), 25 r., 26 r., 26 v., 28 r., 28 v., 30 v., 34 v., 36 r., 37 r.,
    39 v., 41 r., 41 v., 42 r., 46 r.–47 v., 49 r., 65 r., 66 r., 67 r., 77 v., 78 r., 91 r.–92 v., 93 v.,–94 v., 97 v., 105 r.,
    106 v., 109 r., 110 r., 111 v., 112 r., 113 r., 113 v., 116 r., 117 r.–119 r., 120 r.–122 v., 125 r.–126 v., 132 v.–
    138 v., 139 v.–140 r., 141 r.–142 v., 155 v., 170 r., 174 r., 175 r., 176 r., 178 r., 185 r., 187 r., 194 v., 203 r.–
    203 v., 214 r., 219 v., 222 r., 234 r., 244 r., 249 r., 250 r., 261 v., 263 v., 265 v., 267 r., 271 r., 284 v., 290 v.,
    296 r., 304 v., 307 r., 313 v., 314 v., 315 v., 316 v., 318 r., 319 r., 323 r., 332 v., 335 v., 341 r., 342 r., 345 r.,
    349 v., 350 v., 351 v., 357 v., 360 v., 361 v., 369 r., 371 r., 379 v., 381 v., 383 r., 389 r., 393 v., 394 r., 398 v.,
    399 r., 404 v., 405 r., 406 r., 406 v., 408 v., 410 r., 410 v., 411 v., 415 v., 417 r., 417 v., 418 v., 419 v., 420 r.,
    444 r.

Ξενοφώντος   115 r., 117 v., 119 v.

Ξηρὸς   34 r., 37 v.

Πανάρετος   22 r., 42 r., 93 r., cf. Γεώργιος and Μανουὴλ.

Πατρίκης   48 v., 130 v.

Πλαγίτης   101 r., 103 r.

πρωτοστράτωρ   130 r.

Σγουρόπουλος   27 v.

Σγουρόπουλος Τρακουντάνης ἐκ τοῦ νησιου Ρόδου   334 r., cf. Ἰωάννης and Γεώργιος.

THE GENESIS OF THE LITURGICAL SANCTUS

Eric Werner (New York)

IT WILL be my task to trace the textual development of the Sanctus in Judaism and Christianity up to its final redaction in the respective liturgies. I shall also attempt to find a sort of melodic *Urlinie* for certain musical traditions of the Sanctus, though by no means for all. For terminological reasons I shall distinguish between the Hebrew (and Aramaic) *Kedusha* (henceforth ĸ), the *Tersanctus* or Thrice-Holy (henceforth s), and the *Trisagion* or *Aius* (henceforth т, the periphrastic variant of s, which found its way into both Eastern and Western liturgies.

I. *The Earliest Forms of the* Kedusha

The synagogal ĸ has a long history. Its nuclear cell, Isa. vi. 3, has in the course of time undergone many variations. I shall not deal with these variants, as they are of peripheral importance for our quest.[1] The scriptural verse is nowhere alluded to in later books of the canonic Old Testament; yet there are abundant references to it in the apocryphal and pseudepigraphic literature between the Old and the New Testaments. Of these numerous citations a few may be listed here: Apocalypse of Abraham, xvii. 7; I Enoch (Ethiopic version), xxxix. 12; II Enoch (Slavonic text), xx; Testament of Adam, i. 4; Testament of Isaac, viii. 3. To these long-known texts two most significant additions can be made now; they are contained in the Dead Sea Scrolls (DSS)—in Hymns of Thanksgiving XVI, and in the so-called 'Angelic Liturgy'. All the works listed are intertestamentary, that is, they were written in pre-Christian times; indeed, some of them were known to St. Paul. Some of them were later altered in a Christological sense.[2] In all of them the Jewish angelology is fully developed.

The earliest texts of the synagogal ĸ exist in three forms; they are all intrinsically connected with angelological conceptions. They are most evident in the *K-Yotzer* of the morning service, less pronounced in the *K-'Amida* of the eighteen benedictions, and of the same strength in the *K-Sedra* ('of the Academy'). All three have two Scriptural passages in common, Isa. vi. 3 and Ezek. iii. 12, which are juxtaposed; the surrounding framework differs, however, quite considerably. As every ĸ has a framework of its own, I shall quote here the essential phrases of *K-Yotzer* and *K-'Amida*, both before and after the Isaiah verse itself in their ancient order. I shall italicize the significant phrases.

[1] These deviations are treated in A. Baumstark, 'Trishagion und Qeduscha', *Jahrbuch für Liturgiewissenschaft* iii (1923), pp. 18 foll.; also by E. Werner in *The Sacred Bridge* (New York & London, 1959), pp. 282 foll., and in the same author's *Doxology in Synagogue and Church* (HUCA, 1945).

[2] Cf. G. Kretschmar, *Studien zur frühchristl. Trinitaetslehre* (Tübingen, 1956).

K-Yotzer

The chiefs of the hosts are holy beings that exalt the Almighty and *incessantly* declare the glory of God and His holiness. Be Thou praised, O our Rock . . . Creator of holy beings . . .; Creator of ministering spirits, all of whom stand in the heights of the Universe, and proclaim with awe *in unison* (in one voice) aloud the words of the living God and everlasting King. . . . All of them open their mouths in holiness and purity, with *song and psalm*, while they adore and extol, glorify and sanctify and ascribe sovereignty to—

The Name of the Divine King, the great, mighty, and dreaded One, . . . and they all take upon themselves *the yoke of the Kingdom of Heaven* one from the other . . . in tranquil joy of spirit, with pure speech and holy melody, they all respond *as one* and exclaim with awe: Holy, holy, holy. . . . And the *ophanim* ('wheels') and the holy animals with a noise of great rushing, uplraising themselves towards the Seraphim, thus over against them offer praise and say: Praised be the Glory of the Lord from His (its?) place . . .[1]

K-'Amida

True and firm, established and enduring . . . good and beautiful is Thy word for us for ever and ever . . . Yea, faithful art Thou to quicken the dead. Praised be Thou, O Lord, who quickenest the dead.

Reader: We will sanctify Thy Name in the world even as they sanctify it in the highest heavens, as it is written by the hand of Thy prophet: "And they *called one unto the other* and said: Holy, holy, holy. . . . (Congreg.)

Reader: Those over against them say "Praised".

Congr.: Praised be the glory of the Lord from His (its?) Place. . . .

Reader (in silent prayer): *Thou art holy, and Thy Name is holy* and holy beings praise Thee daily. (Selah). Praised art Thou, the holy God.

The Isaiah passage early became the subject of Christological interpretation, owing to the three-fold 'Holy'; later Church fathers also discussed the synagogal K.[2] The resemblances to the Preface and s of the Latin rite, with the anaphora of the Eastern rites, were likewise noticed during the Middle Ages.

In the relatively recent discipline of liturgiology the question of the age of K and s has elicited a bulky literature. Of the differing views the three main ones are:

(a) The K antedates both s and T; the latter forms were created under the influence of K.

(b) Both s and T arose independently of K; K itself is post-apostolic.

(c) Elements of K were used by the earliest Judaeo-Christians, though not by Judaism in general, in apostolic times; from these sectarian rites the Church took over the basic elements and reshaped them in various versions.

Before examining these three conceptions and their respective arguments we shall have to consider the angelological background of K, s, and T.

The doctrine of the angels, fairly well established in Judaism at the time of the Maccabean revolt, became one of the most beloved tenets of the people. While the aristocracy, the Sadduceans and Hellenized hierarchy, frowned or smiled at these 'aberrations', the Hasideans and Pharisees fervently championed it. The idea that God delegates authority to inferior spiritual beings, who may, in turn, be held responsible for mishaps, as imagined by a Jewish observer, served to solve at least partly the unsolvable problem of theodicy. The scriptural verse, Deut. xxxii. 8–9: 'While the Most High gave to the nations their inheritance, when He separated the children of man, He set the bounds of the peoples according to the number of the children of Israel. For the

---

[1] The word *ophan* (wheel) has undergone a remarkable change of meaning, so that in later mystical literature it stands for 'musical modes' or 'melodies'.

[2] Cf. G. Kretschmar, op. cit.

Lord's portion is Israel, Jacob the lot of His inheritance', gave some authority to such ideas. Instead of reading 'according to the number of the children of Israel' the Septuagint (LXX) reads here κατὰ ἀριθμὸν ἀγγέλων Θεοῦ, 'according to the number of the angels of God'—which may have been a then current variant of the Hebrew text.[1] Upon this verse and its variegated nationalistic, ethical, and theological interpretations rests perhaps the entire structure of Jewish angelology until the end of the Talmudic age. The idea was again elaborated upon in Revelation, where not only every nation but each of the Seven Communities has an angel of its own.

The picturesque idea of the interaction between the angels' liturgy and that of mortals originated in these post-Maccabean times, and has left many traces in both Judaism and Christianity. Particularly important here are the passages I Enoch, xxxix. 9–13, which I quote, and the DSS fragments of the so-called 'Angelic Liturgy':[2]

Before Him there is no ceasing. He knows what the world is before it was created, and generation unto generation that shall arise: Those *who sleep not* bless Thee; they stand before Thy glory and bless, laud, and extol, saying: 'Holy, holy, holy, is the Lord of Spirits; He filleth the earth with Spirits'. And here my eyes saw all those who sleep not, how they stand before Him and bless, and say: 'Blessed be Thou and blessed be the Name of the Lord for ever and ever'.[3]

Here the second constituent element of κ, Ezek. iii. 12, is replaced by a short doxology from the Psalms. Yet the Ezekiel passage is again a vision of angelic worship, part of the immortal image of the heavenly throne-chariot (*Merkaba*). The lasting impression of that vision is best described in G. Scholem's classic book *Major Trends in Jewish Mysticism*, where a quarter of its contents consists of the *Merkaba* mystic alone. A characteristic portion of this angelic worship has been retained, in a relatively mild paraphrase, in the *K-Yotzer*. The apocalyptic literature of pre-Christian Judaism thrived on these passages, sometimes in a wildly fantastic spirit. Some elements of the vision entered also into Catholic theology: the four personages with the countenances of the bull, the eagle, the lion, and the πρόσωπον ἀνθρώπου became later the emblems of the four evangelists. In Judaism that fourth enigmatic person was later identified with Metatron, highest prince of angels, and second only to God.[4]

Let us now consider the juxtaposition of the passages from Isaiah and Ezekiel in the two Kedushas quoted above. The strong angelological bent was characteristic of Essenic and, to a lesser degree, Pharisaic thinking during the last 150 years B.C. and the first century A.D. It must have been during these 250 years that the pattern of the κ was set and canonized. That the Sadduceans, who held jurisdiction in the Temple, mocked angelology is well known also from Christian sources,[5] just as the miracle-hungry masses of Judæa loved it. At least an archetype of a κ must have evolved in the synagogues of that time, since a later inclusion of so significant a portion of

[1] It almost appears as if in this instance the LXX was based upon a better text, because among the DSS we encounter the passage 'according to the number of the sons of God'. On this point see G. F. Moore, *Judaism*, i, pp. 227 foll.; M. Burroughs, *The Dead Sea Scrolls* (1956), p. 319; E. Werner, 'Midrashic Elements in the Prima Clementis', in *Festschrift H. A. Wolfson* (New York, 1965); and D. S. Russell, *The Method and Message of Jewish Apocalyptics* (Philadelphia, 1964), pp. 248 foll.

[2] J. Strugnell, 'Angelic Liturgy at Qumran', in *Congress Volume* (Oxford, 1959), pp. 318–45.

[3] Translation after R. H. Charles' edition of the Ethiopic text (Oxford, 1893), p. 117.

[4] The etymology of Metatron is a most controversial subject among the scholars. Cf. H. Odeberg, *III Enoch* (Cambridge, 1928), pp. 125–46, containing a full analysis of the question; also G. Scholem, op. cit., pp. 67 foll. and 366.

[5] Cf. Acts xxiii. 8.

the liturgy would not have been possible without leaving definite and argumentative traces in early rabbinic sources, such as *Mishna* or *Tosefta*. There, however, the K is already taken for granted. This is no more than an *argumentum e silentio*; but there is more positive evidence to be found.

The *K-'Amida* has come down to us in a Palestinian and a Babylonian version. The Babylonian redaction of the eighteen benedictions, of which the K is today an integral part, already contains in its earliest form this reference to a preceding K:

Thou art holy, and Thy Name is holy, and holy beings praise Thee daily [third benediction], and:

. . . unto all generations. From generation to generation we will declare Thy greatness.

This verse alludes to the preceding 'from generation to generation' of Psalm 146, which was also contained in the *K-'Amida*. The Palestinian version, on the other hand, included the recitation of the *Shma'* (Deut. vi. 4–9), which was hidden in the *ad hoc* inserted K, because of the Roman prohibition against pronouncing the *Shma'* in its original setting.[1] The Roman suppression of the *Shma'* is well documented. These and other historical reasons indicate that the *K-'Amida* came into being during the persecutions of Domitian and Hadrian; the total collapse of Bar Kokhba's revolt in A.D. 135 closed that period.

The case lies somewhat differently with the *K-Yotzer*. Here we are in possession of a source dating from the first Christian century, which formally states the existence of interplay between angelic and human worship:

'When the morning stars sing all together' [cf. Job xxxviii. 7] . . . this relates to the praises offered by Israel, and also 'when the sons of God sing' [ibid.] . . . this relates to the angelic worship.[2]

We may recall the earlier occurrence of that idea in I Enoch. Thenceforth, and in many variations, the idea of that interaction became a well-established tenet of rabbinic theology. By the discovery of the DSS an older analysis by K. Kohler has been vindicated. Long before some of the pseudepigrapha were published, and sixty years before the Qumran literature made its impact on our knowledge of the intertestamentary theology, Kohler had in a most intuitive study attributed the *K-Yotzer* to the liturgy of the Essenes.[3] Certain ideas reported as Essenic by Philo occur often in the DSS, thus justifying Kohler's views.

All these analyses prove the pre-Christian existence of *K-Yotzer* and the apostolic age of the *K-Amida*. Most modern scholars have accepted these arguments as cogent. Yet there are a few authors who continue to cast doubt on both rabbinic and DSS evidence. As they are responsible students, we are obliged to heed, and, if possible, to refute their arguments. A. Baumstark

[1] The arguments listed above were for the most part collected and cogently put forth in L. Finkelstein's study 'La Kédouscha et les bénédictions du Schma', in *Révue des Études Juives* (Paris, 1932), pp. 3 foll.

[2] Cf. Sifre, *ad Deut.*, 306 (No. 132).

[3] K. Kohler, 'Ursprünge und Grundformen der synag. Liturgie', *Monatsschrift für Geschichte und Wissenschaft des Judentums* (Breslau, 1893), pp. 447 foll. Kohler shows there quite clearly the parallelism between the Hebrew prayers of the earliest Christian times and the liturgies of books VII and VIII of the Apostolic Constitutions, the so-called Clementine liturgy. Much later the gist of this pioneering study was 'written out', not to say copied, by W. Bousset in his 'Eine jüdische Gebetssammlung in der Clement. Liturgie', in *Sitzungsber. der Göttinger Akademie der Wissenschaften, phil. hist. Kl.* (1925–6).

has, in two publications, discussed both ᴋ and ꜱ and their hypothetical relationship.¹ He was not familiar with the midrashic quotation above, nor could he anticipate evidence of the ᴅꜱꜱ. Thus two essential testimonies to the ᴋ in pre-Christian literature escaped his knowledge. None the less, weighing all documents and arguments available to him, he reached the conclusion that a hypothetical 'primal version' of K-Yotzer antedated all others: this redaction might be traced to the first century. He was well familiar with Christian and many Hebrew sources.

This cannot be said for C. W. Dugmore's book *The Influence of the Synagogue upon the Divine Office*², in which he states: 'The original form of the ᴋ has been shown to have borne no resemblance to that early Christian prayer [the ꜱ in Clement of Rome, *Epistle to the Corinthians*, chap. 34]'. The author refers here (in a footnote) to an earlier passage of his book; however, the cited pages contain no such refutation. He accepts and uses the conclusions reached by Finkelstein, and nowhere does he go beyond these findings, much less against them, but ignores the most important point: the existence and greater age of the K-Yotzer and its connection with Essene, Hasidean, and apocalyptic conceptions and practices. He could not, of course, anticipate the evidence of the ᴅꜱꜱ, the discovery of which has altered many ideas hitherto considered axiomatic. A much more cautious attitude is taken by J. Jungmann, S.J., in his standard work on the history of the Mass.³ He assumes the existence of the K-'Amida in early Christianity, again ignoring the K-Yotzer. I shall return to Jungmann's point of view in connection with the relation of ꜱ-ᴋ-ᴛ. Recently Kenneth Levy has offered his views on the question of the ᴋ.⁴ In his solid and well-reasoned musicological essay he touches on our subject only twice in passing. Unfortunately he has not applied the same care to Jewish liturgy as to other subjects under discussion. He relies blindly upon the findings of Dugmore concerning the age of the ᴋ. While he otherwise distinguishes between ꜱ and ᴛ, no such refinement is applied to the ᴋ. Like Dugmore, he ignores the K-Yotzer; in general he is unaware of the existence of any new material since 1942.

The Judaeo-Christian liturgy had been neglected for a long time, in spite of Kohler's emphasis on its importance for the formation of the Mass and the Office. This aspect was thrown into sharp focus by recent studies of E. Peterson, J. Schoeps, J. Daniélou, S.J., and most lately by D. Flusser, who has perhaps the widest knowledge of Jewish and Christian sources. This sectarian church amalgamated some of the Hasidean and apocalyptic ideas and practices with the new Christian theology, thus forming a liturgy, fragments of which have survived to this day. In reviewing the New Testament framework of ꜱ and ᴛ I shall recall the Judaeo-Christian contributions to the development of the *anaphora*.⁵

---

¹ A. Baumstark, op. cit., and *Liturgie Comparée*, 3rd ed. (1953–4). Baumstark makes an error by identifying R. Yehuda as the rabbi of the same name, called the Prince (fl. A.D. 190). Actually the rabbi mentioned was R. Yehuda ben Il'ai, who lived at least one-and-a-half generations before the Prince: cf. H. L. Strack, *Introduction to Talmud and Midrash* (Philadelphia, 1931), p. 115.

² London, 1944. The author confuses the third benediction of the eighteen benedictions with the ᴋ itself and argues from that erroneous position. Cf. my *Sacred Bridge*, p. 308, n. 64 and 66.

³ Joseph A. Jungmann, *Missarum Sollemnia* (Vienna, 1949–50), esp. II, pp. 157 foll.

⁴ Kenneth Levy, 'The Byzantine Sanctus and its Modal Tradition in East and West', *Annales de Musicologie* (Paris, 1964), pp. 7–67.

⁵ Mr. Levy apparently knows the VIIth and VIIIth books of the Apostolic Constitutions; is he unaware of the attention drawn to them in modern research, which asserts that the Clementine Liturgy exerted a distinct influence on the Byzantine *anaphora*?

[23]

II. *The Confluence of* Sanctus, Kedusha, *and* Trisagion

The first literal quotations of Isa. vi. 3, the seraphic hymn, in New Testament literature occur in Clement's *First Epistle to the Corinthians*, and in Rev. iv. 8. We know fairly well the date of the former document (96–100); of the latter we have at least a *terminus post quem* in the testimony of Papias, who was Bishop of Hierapolis in Phrygia during the early part of the second century. He must have known at least parts of Revelation.[1] All of this evidence points to the end of the first century as the time when canonical and apostolic authors began to make use of the seraphic hymn. Recently D. Flusser has offered a most interesting, almost revolutionary, hypothesis: he suggests that a certain verse of the Gloria (Luke ii. 14) is virtually a paraphrase of the *K-de Sedra*.[2] This conjecture would put a paraphrase of the κ right into the text of the synoptic Gospels. Flusser juxtaposes the Greek with the Aramaic text of the *K-Sedra*:

Δόξα ἐν ὑψίστοις
Θεῷ καὶ ἐπὶ τῆς
γῆς εἰρήνη ἐν
ἀνθρώποις εὐδοκία.

Holy is He in the highest heavens, the place of His divine abode;
holy upon earth, the work of His might . . .
the whole earth is full of the radiance of His glory.

Whatever one may say against this bold conjecture, the fact remains that the *Targum* to Ezek. iii. 12 corresponds in its phraseology with both I Enoch and the αἰνούντων καὶ λεγόντων in Luke.[3] Yet in spite of a host of learned references and allusions Flusser's conjecture is—to this writer—not fully convincing.

Further early references to s are found in St. Ignatius, Eph. iv. 2 and in the writings of Clement of Alexandria. We may compare these concrete testimonies with the liturgical function of s in early Christianity:

(1) Clement of Rome, I Cor. xxxiv. 6, 7:
'Ten thousand times ten thousand waited on Him, and a thousand thousand served Him and cried: "Holy holy, holy is the Lord of hosts, the entire creation is full of Thy glory." And we, guided by our conscience, gathered together in our place, cry to Him *constantly as with one voice*; so that we become sharers in His great and glorious promises.'[4]

(2) Rev. iv. 8:
'And the four living creatures, each of them with six wings, are full of eyes all around and within, and day and night they *never cease to sing*: "Holy, holy, holy is the Lord God Almighty (παντοκράτωρ), who was and is, and is to come."'[5]

---

[1] Cf. B. F. Westcott, *The History of the Canon of the New Testament*, 5th ed. (Cambridge and London, 1881–5), pp. 69, 77, and 121 foll.

[2] David Flusser, 'Sanktus und Gloria', in *Festschrift für Otto Michel* (Leiden and Cologne, 1963), pp. 129 foll.

[3] On this similarity Flusser writes: 'The resemblance of the Gloria and the *Targum* of Isa. vi. 3 is neither accidental nor indirect; it flows from the direct dependence of the Gloria on the κ, where words from prophetic books are introduced.'

[4] Best critical ed. by J. B. Lightfoot, *The Apostolic Fathers*, rev. ed. (London, 1890); see also A. v. Harnack, *Das Schreiben der Römischen Kirche an die Corinthier* (Leipzig, 1929); W. C. van Unnik, 'I. Clement 34 and the Sanctus', *Vigiliae Christianae*, v (Amsterdam, 1951), pp. 214 foll.; and recently E. Werner, 'Midrashic Elements in the Prima Clementis', *Festschrift H. A. Wolfson* (New York, 1965).

[5] The redactor of Revelation has managed to combine the two visions of Isaiah and Ezekiel in one verse. The s

(3) Clement of Alexandria, *Stromata* vii. 12:

'. . . and let him teach his son . . . in a way . . . so that he would always praise God, just as the praising beasts do, of whom Isaiah speaks allegorically . . .'[1]

(4) Ignatius, Ad Eph. iv. 2:

'. . . this is why in the symphony of your concord (ὁμονία) and love the praises of Jesus Christ are sung. But you, the rank and file, should also form a choir, so that, joining the symphony by your concord, and by *your unity* taking the keynote from God, you may *with one voice* through Jesus Christ sing a song to the Father . . .'[2]

(5) An allusion to the s by Tertullian:

'. . . cui illa angelorum circumstantia *non cessat dicere*: sanctus, sanctus, sanctus Deus . . . proinde igitur et nos angelorum, si meruimus, candidati, jam hic caelestem illam in Deum vocem et officium futurae claritatis ediscimus'.[3]

(6) An early Martyrology, *Passio SS. Perpetuae et Felicitatis*:

'. . . et introivimus et audivimus *vocem unitam dicentem* (φωνὴν ἡνωμένην λεγόντων) 'Agios, agios, agios' *sine cessatione* (ἀκαταπαύστως) . . . et in dextera et in sinistra *seniores quatuor* . . .'[4]

In order to evaluate the elements common to all allusions to the κ–s *before* the first appearance of a consistently arranged and articulated eucharistic prayer, as attributed to Hippolytos (*c.* A.D. 215), I shall add a few remarks on the standing or recurrent phrases:

(1) 'Constantly as with one voice' occurs already in I Enoch xxxix. 11, and I Enoch lxi. 11.
(2) 'Four living creatures', cf. Ezek. i.
(4) 'Your keynote from God (χρῶμα Θεοῦ)' is another example of St. Ignatius' preference for musical similes.[5]
(5) 'Iam hic caelestem . . . vocem'. Tertullian stresses the need of preparing oneself on *earth* for the angelic adoration.

In every case the angelic choir serves as a kind of worship which all Christians ought to emulate on earth. The question lies near when the Old Testament passage of the s was understood in a christological, especially in a trinitarian, sense, which the Thrice-Holy is bound to suggest. Nor was this idea neglected by early Christian authors. Origen, Jerome, and Victor of Vita, to name only three, interpreted the s in a strictly trinitarian way. The link between the Old and New

goes back to Isaiah; the 'four living creatures', and the conception of them as holy beasts covered with eyes, stems from Ezek. i. 5–19. The appositive clause 'The one who was and is', etc. is an attempt to christologize the Hebrew *tetragrammaton* JHVH.

[1] *Stromata*, vii, cap. 12, ed. O. Staehlin, in *GCS* 12, 2nd ed. (Leipzig, 1939). Clement speaks of beasts, not of angels; although he mentions Isaiah by name, he avoids the expression 'seraphim'. Is a mixture of the two visions the reason of this strange phraseology? A quotation of the Apocalypse of Zephania by Clement is known (*Stromata*, v, cap. 11, 77), which seems to indicate his familiarity with Jewish angelology and alludes to the κ.; see also Clement Al., *Excerpta ex Theodoto*, ed. Casey (1934), No. 78, where the Alexandrinian refers to the *Merkaba*-vision as *pleroma*.

[2] St. Ignatius, *Ad. Eph.*, in Lightfoot, op. cit., i, p. 30, and ii, pp. 40 foll. The term ὁμονία is a favourite expression of Clement of Rome. The old legend that Ignatius introduced the custom of antiphonal singing in the Church (Socrates, *Hist. Eccl.* vi. 8) was often repeated and can even today be found in some books. Lightfoot adds to this (more than seventy years ago): 'A tradition which appears so late does not deserve consideration . . . Antiphonal singing indeed did not need to be suggested by a heavenly vision . . . It was practised with much elaboration of detail in the psalmody of the Jews, as appears from the account given of the Egyptian Therapeutes by Philo.'

[3] Tertullian, *De oratione*, chap. 3 (*CSEL*, vii, p. 70).

[4] 'Passio SS. Perpetuae et Felicitatis', ed. I. M. I. Beek, in *Florilegium Patristicum* (Bonn, 1938), pp. 40–42.

[5] Here 'scale', or 'hue' of God; so also Aristides Quint. *De musica*: λευκοῦ καὶ μέλανος χρῶμα, and Clement of Alex. on the 'forming of a choir': ἡ ἐκκλησία Κυρίου ὁ πνευματικὸς ἅγιος χορός (*Stromata*, vii, 14).

Testaments, between synagogal and ecclesiastic worship, was preserved exactly by the angelological framework, common to both institutions.[1]

Shortly after 200 Hippolytos' *Apostolic Tradition* was written, containing *inter alia* the first rudimentary formula of a eucharistic prayer-service. This document does not contain a s nor a reference to it.[2] Moreover, all allusions to angelic worship are avoided, as in general Hippolytos' angelology is negligible.[3] Closest in time to Hippolytos are the *euchologion* of Serapion of Thmuis (fl. 335) and the oldest strata of the liturgy of Jerusalem, reconstructed after St. Cyril's *catechesis*.

The prayer of Hippolytos appears to represent a tradition totally different from that of the Serapion or St. Cyril formulae. Not only is the s absent, but the entire angelology. The Serapion ritual and St. Cyril's description, on the other hand, have quite a few standing phrases in common. If we deny the continuity of tradition running from Clement of Rome to Hippolytos, Serapion, and Cyril, we should assume that the inclusion of the s in the latter two liturgies originates in another, thus far unknown, Christian source. Or could the interplay between angelic and human worship, so characteristic of the Jewish apocalyptic writers and the first versions of the κ, have been introduced in the spirit of catholic liturgy as late as the third century?[4] This is most improbable in view of the frequent instances quoted above, and their insistence on the very point. Moreover, both Serapion and Cyril introduce not only the pertinent passages from Isaiah, but allude to Dan. vii and to Ezek. i and iii. This combination of three Old Testament passages can hardly be a coincidence.[5] Hippolytos' disinclination for any angelology may—at least partly—account for the absence of the s.

The addition of the Hosanna to the s marks the turning point in the unfolding of the eucharistic prayer. It occurs almost simultaneously in the Syrian and Greek liturgies, though one may not consider it a really new element in Christianity. Apart from the passage in Matt. xxi. 9, the Hosanna acclamation occurs first in the *Didache*, although not in connection with the s, but in

---

[1] Cf. Origen, *Hom. in Is. i-vi* (*GCS*, viii, pp. 244 foll.); also *De principiis*, iv, 3, 14; and Victor ep. Vitensis (*Hist. Persec. Afr. Prov.*, ii, p. 100 (*CSEL*, vii. p. 70); see also Jerome, *Epist.* 18, 6 (in *CSEL*, 54, p. 73). Origen's *De principiis*, ed. G. W. Butterworth (London, 1936), p. 32, contains the significant words: 'And my Hebrew master used to say that the two six-winged seraphim in Isa. vi. 3, who cry one to another and say "holy, holy, holy . . ." are the only-begotten Son of God and the Holy Spirit. And we ourselves think that the expression in the song of Habakuk "In the midst of two living creatures Thou shalt be known" is spoken of Christ and the Holy Spirit.'

[2] Cf. Gregory Dix, *The Shape of the Liturgy* (Westminster, 1949), pp. 158 foll.; for an opposite view see H. Engberding, 'Das angebliche Dokument römischer Liturgie aus dem Beginn des 3. Jahrhunderts', in *Miscellanea Liturgica in honorem C. Mohlberg*, i, pp. 47–71.

[3] The remarks of the great patrologist Bardenhewer (in his *Patrologie* [Freiburg, 1894]) on Hippolytos are still true: 'Hippolytos is, in his exegesis, much more down-to-earth than Origen; . . . he loves the allegorical method. . . .'

[4] Between the version of Hippolytos and that of Cyril lie about a hundred years. On the lacunae in Cyril's descrip-

tion see Brightman, *Liturgies Eastern and Western* (Oxford, 1896), p. 469, n. 9. One may not assume that Cyril was familiar with the Clementine liturgy, although some identical phrases appear to stand out; the Apostolic Constitutions and their liturgy are known as a remnant of the Judaeo-Christian Church, yet Cyril was, next to St. John Chrysostum, the most fanatical Jew-baiter and -hater in the garden of patrology.

[5] Hippolytos knew this tradition well himself. In his *Apostolic Tradition*, iv, he admonishes all faithful Christians to worship at midnight, for at that moment 'stars and trees and waters stand still with one accord, and all the angelic host does service to God by praising Him, together with the souls of the righteous . . .' This is, of course, pure Jewish doctrine, and Hippolytos refers to it as 'the tradition taught to us by the elders', i.e. of Apostolic origin. The recent editor, B. S. Easton (New York, 1934, pp. 67–70, 76 foll., 95, 99, 101–3) adds: 'The ancient Law is still fully binding'. 'Many prayers have a distinct Jewish background'. He proves conclusively that the entire section on presbyters and their prayers is completely dependent upon the Hebrew Mishnaic tradition.

a Judaeo-Christian version of the grace after meals.[1] The passage reads: 'Let grace come and this world perish [or "pass away"]. Hosanna to the Son of David'. The Hosanna in this context, as in Matt. xxi. 9, is used in an erroneous sense, as I have proved elsewhere in detail.[2] It is clear that the Hosanna had assumed the significance of a triumphal acclamation long before the third century. I surmised at first that owing to its inclusion in the s the entire prayer S-Hosanna-(later Benedictus)-Hosanna was called the ὑμνὸς ἐπινίκιος, the victory-hymn.[3]

The term ἐπινίκιος has both a classical Greek and a biblical connotation. In classic literature the terms stands for a triumphal celebration or hymn, from Pindar on to Nonnos Dionysius.[4] Τὰ ᾄσματα ἐπινίκια are hymns after a battle has been won, or encomia on a victor at the games; the word reaches into the Hellenistic period.[5] In this very sense Symmachus, the translator of Scripture, uses ᾄσματα ἐπινίκια in Isa. vi. 3; also for the Psalm-superscription *lam'natzeah*, usually —and falsely—translated as 'to the music master' or 'choirmaster' in Psalms iv. 1; viii. 1 and elsewhere.[6] Why, then, does the s carry such an almost military epithet? As far as I was able to trace this designation, it seems that St. John Chrysostom used it first in a specifically liturgical sense, usually with the byword ἀκαταπαύστως (incessantly).[7] Thereafter it occurs quite frequently in the Eastern liturgies. Who is conquered? The epithet *epinikios* seems to allude to the Hosanna (during Jesus' entrance into Jerusalem, Matt. xxi. 9), yet Symmachus used it for the s in Isaiah. Chrysostom cannot mean the Hosanna either, for his description of the liturgy does not mention it as part of the s. Actually there are more ancient liturgies without the Hosanna than with it. Jungmann, who more or less derives the epithet from the Hosanna, is refuted by the abundance of Sanctus-passages in early liturgies without Hosanna, yet bearing the term *epinikios*.[8] Perhaps it conveys merely the idea of a praising hymn, Symmachus' version of the Isaiah passage. Be that as it may, when we consider the next and last of our liturgies, the *anaphora* contained in the seventh book of the *Apostolic Constitutions*, we are the more perplexed; for that liturgy, a Judaeo-Christian relict, neither contains the Hosanna nor uses the term *epinikios*.

A. Baumstark and J. Jungmann (and their disciples) have repeatedly stressed that the *Apostolic Constitutions* are unique in juxtaposing, just as in the κ, the verses Isa. vi. 3, and Ezek. iii. 12. It is true that the texts, in which we observe a mixing of the two visions, were not always related to human worship. Baumstark and Jungmann emphasize the point that the verse from Ezekiel was too narrowly nationalistic in a Jewish sense—interpreting the passage 'from His place' as the Temple in Jerusalem—and became for this very reason unacceptable to Christianity in general, to be eventually dropped altogether. However, both scholars are mistaken, and their explanation is untenable. For the juxtaposition of Isa. vi. 3 and Ezek. iii. 12 did occur at least twice long after

---

[1] Cf. *Didache*, ed. K. Lake, in *The Apostolic Fathers* (London and New York, 1930), end of chap. 9.

[2] E. Werner, 'The Hosanna in the Gospels', in *Journal of Biblical Literature* (New Haven, 1946).

[3] This term for the s and its additions seems to occur in S. Gregory of Nyssa's *De Baptismo* (P.G. 46, col. 421) and *In Christi resurr.* (P.G. 46, col. 654).

[4] Cf. Sophocles, *Dictionary of the later Greek Language*.

[5] Cf. Pauly-Wissowa, *Realenzyklopaedie des klassischen Altertums*, art. ἐπινίκιος.

[6] Cf. Gregory of Nyssa, *Oratio de occursu Domini* (in P.G. 44, col. 1140 foll.), where reference is made to 'quocumque carmine, quo Deus celebratur' (τὰ ἐπινίκια).

[7] See Brightman, op. cit., pp. 479, n. 20, 480, 536: 15, where the verse is called ἁγιαστικὴ δοξολογία=κ.

[8] Cf. J. Jungmann, op. cit. ii, p. 164. Yet the expression *militia exercitus coelestis* has a somewhat militaristic connotation, just as the Hebrew *S'ba'oth*. See J. M. Hanssens, S.J., *Institutiones liturgicae*, iii, pp. 402 foll.

the spread of the *Apostolic Constitutions*: in Ps.-Dionyius Areopagita, and in the writings of Asterius the Sophist.[1] Ps.-Dionysius, *De caelesti hierarchia*, vii. 4:

Therefore the theology of Scripture has transmitted to us men of the earth the hymns, in which the loftiness of their illumination (ἐλλάμψεως) is revealed in a most holy manner. For like the 'rushing of the waters' . . . the one group of this hierarchy exultantly exclaims:

'Praised be the Glory of the Lord from His place'. The others respond in loudly sounding that often-celebrated praise of God (δοξολογία) in great piety:

> Holy, holy, holy is the Lord Sabaoth,
> Full is the whole earth of His Glory.

I have described these supreme laudations (ὑμνολογίας) of the spirits of the highest heavens according to my best ability in my book 'On the divine hymns' . . . Hence it behoves us . . . to praise the supreme divinity.[2]

M. Richard: *Asterii Sophistae Commentatorium in Psalmos quae supersunt*:

Ps xviii: again we encounter the juxtaposition of Isa. vi. 3 and Ezek. iii. 12.[3]

The recent studies of E. Hammerschmidt dealing with Ethiopic and Coptic liturgies show again the combination of these two texts. They occur in the Ethiopic *Normal-anaphora* and in the Syrian *Basilios-anaphora*.[4] Hammerschmidt arrives at the conclusion that 'all elements of the preambles before the s can be traced to either biblical or late Jewish (mishnaic) concepts and phrases'. These sources and their historical interpretation definitely refute A. Baumstark's, C. W. Dugmore's, and their disciples' assumption that s and k are not necessarily related to each other, because the Ezekiel passage had allegedly to be dropped by the Christian authors.

Before summarizing our results, I shall briefly discuss the origin of the T. According to Brightman the T was 'supernaturally revealed' during the pontificate of St. Proclus (434–46).[5] The

[1] In fairness to the memory of Professor Baumstark it must be said that he modified his original conception expressed in the article quoted above (see p. 19, n. 1, *supra*). His *Liturgie Comparée* (3rd ed. by Bernard Botte, O.S.B.) stresses anew the importance of the *K-Yotzer* and links it with the Apostolic Constitutions and their Judaeo-Christian worship. Had he, who eagerly expected new findings in early Christian liturgies, lived to examine the DSS, we might have benefited greatly by his views of the Qumran literature and its impact on the early Church.

[2] My own translation after Ps.-Dionysius, *De caelesti hierarchia*, ed. P. Hendrix (Leiden, 1959), p. 17. On the Hebraisms of that text see J. Stiglmayr, S.J., 'Dionysius and Severus', in *Scholastik*, iii (1928) and vii (1932); also the German edition of Dionysius' work on the heavenly hierarchy edited, translated, and annotated by Hugo Ball (Munich, 1955). As these authors have demonstrated, the Areopagite was quite familiar with Hebrew expressions, also with Gnostic and Jewish mysticism. He was probably the one Church Father, who was, without rancour, fully aware of the synthesis of Judaism and Hellenism in Christianity. Hence his neo-Platonic interpretation of Jewish angelology comes close to later Hebrew philosophy. Cf. Leo Baeck on the 'Book of Creation' in *Monatschrift für*

Geschichte und Wissenschaft des Judentums, 70 (1926), pp. 371–6, and 378 (1934), pp. 448 foll.

[3] Oslo, 1956, pp. 233 foll.; see also M. Richard, on the same topic, in *Symbolae Osloenses* (1952), pp. 24–33, 93–98.

[4] Cf. E. Hammerschmidt, in *Texte und Untersuchungen*, vol. 80 (Berlin, 1962), pp. 59–61, where all sources and references are given. See also the same author's *Die koptische Gregoriosanaphora* (Berlin, 1957), pp. 112–28. He is fully aware of the great impact of the Synagogue's *Yotzer* prayer upon the early liturgies: 'In the West Syrian anaphoras of Gregory Nazianzenus, of Jaqub of Saruǧ, and of Gregory Bar-Hebraya we find still the *ophanim* (wheels) and the divine chariot (*Merkaba*) of the Jewish morning service.' As to Hammerschmidt's lengthy discussion of the attributes of God—indescribable, invisible, without origin, etc.—which he ascribes to Hellenistic influence, these negative epithets occur in almost identical order in the Apocalypse of Abraham, xvii. 8, where we read: 'Eternal powerful, . . . Self-created, impeccable, unblemished, immortal', etc. Hellenistic influence is here certainly possible in such passages, for the original scriptural attributes are mainly positive.

[5] Cf. Brightman, op. cit., p. 531, n. 2, where the first sources are quoted.

combination of the epithets 'Holy', 'strong' (or unique) and 'eternal' (or immortal) was already a standing formula of address to God in the Apocalypse of Abraham, where many instances of this address occur.[1] Quite a few Jewish apocalyptic writers took over this form, and it is difficult to believe that this particular combination of epithets arose suddenly in the Byzantine orbit; for the doctors of that church were in general quite familiar with the apocryphal and pseudepigraphic literature, as especially E. Peterson, H. Ball, and J. Daniélou, S.J., have demonstrated. It seems that the T may be considered a periphrastic form of the S, interpreted in trinitarian fashion, and not very far from the character of a litany. In this sense it is still used in the Roman Church on Good Friday.

To summarize the main points of our evidence, the established or the most probable facts are:

(a) The *K-Yotzer* contains both prophetic visions (Isaiah and Ezekiel) and elaborates upon the *Merkaba* angelology.

(b) The *K-'Amida* contains mainly Isaiah, and uses only one verse from Ezekiel (iii. 12).

It is certain that (a) existed in pre-Christian times; (b) was introduced into the Synagogue during the first Christian century. Both formulas have roots in Jewish apocalyptic literature.

(c) All Christian prefaces (except Hippolytos) contain S with angelology, and many of them add verses from Dan. vii.

(d) Most of them mention the interplay between angelic and human worship; this concept is also rooted in pre-Christian Judaism.

(e) In many cases we find a continuous parallelism, which turns from

> *Dignum et justum*
> to Angelology
> to *Sanctus*
> to *Hosanna–Benedictus–Hosanna*[2]
> to 'Holy art Thou',

the last-named being the incipit and close of the third benediction of the *'Amida* after the K.

(f) Many prefaces contain the angelological doctrine of the 'never-sleeping' spirits and their 'incessant' exaltation of God. Both conceptions are already well established in I Enoch and in early rabbinic literature.[3]

(g) Elements from Isaiah and Ezekiel are usually combined in the preface and S. The verse Ezekiel iii. 12, however, is omitted in most of them (Roman, Byzantine, Egyptian, Syrian); it is retained in the liturgy of the Apostolic Constitutions VII, the Ethiopic *anaphora*, and in quite a few angelologies of the Church Fathers.

(h) The Ezekiel verse (iii. 12) does not lend itself to a trinitarian interpretation, while Isa. vi. 3 invites it and has been so understood from the second century on. It is suggested that this fact was the real reason for the omission of Ezek. iii. 12 in the Christian liturgies.

---

[1] Apocalypse of Abraham, ed. G. H. Box (London and Cambridge, 1919), xvii. 7, 8; xx. 6; xxii. 1; xxvi. 1. In apocalyptic literature the expressions 'holy' and 'unique' (*monos*) are often interchangeable. E. Bishop, the great historian of Christian liturgy, discusses the origin of the T on the basis of information supplied by Dom Connolly; they differ considerably from Brightman's sources and indicate a possibly Nestorian origin of the T. See Edmund Bishop, *Liturgica Historica* (Oxford, 1918), p. 132, n. 3.

[2] It is well known that the passage in Matt. xxi. 9 (εὐλογημένος ὁ ἐρχόμενος κτλ.), which follows the LXX, Ps. cxvii. 26, is an erroneous translation from the Hebrew; the intent of the verse is: 'Blessed by the Name of JHWH be he, who cometh!' See E. Werner, 'The Hosanna in the Gospels', in *Journal of Bibl. Literature* (1946).

[3] I Enoch 39, 12; 12, 13, *et passim*.

III. The Musical Tradition

I have but a few observations to add concerning the musical tradition of the s; this topic has been frequently and extensively discussed during the last forty years.[1] Little is known about the early practice of performance of the κ. We know that it was chanted responsorially in a kind of simple recitative; this was necessary because the Thrice-Holy was always sung by the congregation. This fact is amply testified to in Talmudic literature.[2] No notation of the old synagogal tradition has come down to us that was written before the eighteenth century, if we set aside a κ-parody in the form of a three-part motet, which was perhaps written by a Spanish Marrano in Italy about 1460.[3] If I pursue the task of tracing an ancient tradition in spite of such formidable obstacles, it is due to Dr. Wellesz's ingenious methods, which blazed a path of investigation and have, for me at least, set a pattern and pace to follow. I shall, therefore, resort to much older, indeed to truly primary sources: to Clement of Alexandria, the Apocalypse of Moses, and to those numerous angelologies, where, as in Revelation, psalmody is coupled with the chant of the s. Clement writes:

For this reason also we raise the head and lift the hands towards heaven, and *stand on tiptoe* (τὰς πόδας ἐπεγείρομεν) as we join in the closing outburst of prayer, following the eager flight of the spirit into the intelligible world . . . and while we thus endeavour to *detach the body* from the earth by lifting it upwards along with the uttered words, we spurn the fetters of the flesh and constrain the soul . . . to ascend into the holy place.[4]

Clement refers here to a peculiar *gestus orationis*, which was well known among the Jewish mystics of antiquity: the lifting of the feet and almost jumping on tiptoe three times, exactly timed with each 'Holy' of the κ. This custom is practised even today among certain Hasidic groups. The question arises here whether Clement also alluded to the s; he says 'as we join in the closing outburst of prayer' (κατὰ τὴν τελευταίαν τῆς εὐχῆς συνεκφώνησιν), which seems to indicate at least a congregational response, spoken or chanted.

It is all but impossible to state what was the last congregational response in the Alexandrian Mass during the second century. Yet, if we may trust the sources that have come to light thus far, one may conjecture that it was either the s or the acclamation: 'One is holy . . . ('Εἷς ἅγιος, εἷς κύριος, κτλ.).'[5] If the s was the last public response, we may apply Clement's remark about the tiptoeing to it, and understand it as an observation on a more or less familiar *gestus*, which originated with

---

[1] K. Levy's study on the Byzantine Sanctus, quoted above (p. 23, n. 4) contains not only a vast list of palæographic sources, but also most of the pertinent musicological literature on the subject.

[2] The rabbis objected to melismatic chant, which they called 'hymns without words'; they feared, not without good reason, heretical influence.

[3] Cf. E. Werner, 'The Oldest Sources of Synagogue Chant', in *Proceedings of the American Academy for Jewish Research*, xvi (1947), pp. 228 foll.), and the subsequent rectification of my previous views, as described by Dr. D. Plamenac in his admirable 'Reconstruction of the French Chansonnier in the Biblioteca Colombina, Seville', in *Musical Quarterly*, xxxvii (1951), p. 524, n. 59.

[4] Clement of Alexandria, *Stromata*, vii, chap. 7, no. 40,

ed. Stählin (in *GCS* 12); translation by Oulton-Chadwick, 'Alexandrinian Christianity', ii (Philadelphia, 1954), p. 117. See also R. B. Tollington, 'Clement of Alexandria' (London, 1914), ii, p. 150: 'Standing was the usual attitude in worship, with head erect and hands raised and the heels lifted from the ground, and the face turned to the East'.

[5] This response seems to date from a time after Clement, as he nowhere alludes to it. See on this point the interesting note in Brightman, op. cit., p. 509, n. 25, 26, where St. Cyril of Alexandria is quoted as saying that the closing phrase of the *anaphora* (and Mass) was the τὰ ἅγια τοῖς ἁγίοις pronounced by the liturgists, i.e. the priest. The formula Εἷς ἅγιος is mentioned by S. Didymus, but nowhere in connection with the liturgy.

the Jewish mystics, perhaps even among the Egyptian Therapeutes, who paid considerable attention to dance-like movements in prayer, as we know from Philo.[1] We may recall also that in Revelation and in the Apocalypse of Moses the s is coupled or surrounded by psalmody and Alleluia-singing. It was the same Alexandrian Clement, who gave us, in his *Paedagogus*, a valuable description of the practice of psalmody among the Jews of Egypt. This is a lengthy, well-known passage, in which he suggests that the mode of the Jewish psalmody was a variant of the *tropos spondeiakos*.[2] Plutarch offers in his book on music a technical analysis of the *tropos spondeiakos*, so that we may—however roughly—reconstruct the skeleton of that mode.

I have closely examined this mode and Plutarch's analysis of the *tropos spondeiakos*, and its identity with the mode mentioned by Clement, in four previous publications. I may therefore refer to those without repeating the details of my investigation.[1] It will suffice if I briefly summarize the conclusions I had reached many years ago:[3]

I. The mode of psalmody mentioned by Clement is the *tropos spondeiakos*.

II. This mode consists of a hexachord based on E, in which either the F or the C, yet never both at the same time, are omitted. Sometimes a subtonal D is added.

III. To the same mode belong many melodies of the oldest strata of Gregorian chant, especially the s in the Te Deum, the Gloria XV, and passages of Gloria XIV, also the psalm-verse of the antiphon 'Postquam surrexit Dominus' on Maundy Thursday.

IV. A number of Byzantine tunes belong to the same mode; also ancient prayer-tunes of the Yemenite Jews, e.g. their Sh'ma', which is almost literally identical with the s of the Te Deum. The mode is also known in Nestorian and Syrian chant.

V. The Doric Spondaic mode (or τρόπος σπονδειακός) originated in the Hellenistic world of the Near East; its solemn ethos was acclaimed by numerous Hellenistic writers, such as Dionysius of Halicarnassus and Plutarch, to name only two eminent authors.[4]

VI. The mode is common to early Jewish chant of the first Christian centuries, as well as to the early Church; its origin in all cases lies in the Mediterranean orbit.

VII. The Sh'ma' forms an integral part of the K-'Amida; and the oldest Jewish traditions (Yemenite, Babylonian, and to a lesser extent Kurdistani) maintain the tradition of chanting the κ in the *tropos spondeiakos*.

As for the Gregorian tradition, the Sanctus XVIII is usually considered the oldest version.[5] It seems, in its present form, to be related to the *tropos spondeiakos*, though the *finalis* is different, and the emphasis upon the B is alien to the Greek mode. The final notes of the phrases of the Te Deum close with G before the verse 'Te rex gloriae', and end with E thereafter. This trait shows

[1] Cf. Philo, *De vita contempl.*, ii, 68, ed. Cohn-Reiter); also my study on 'The Musical Aspects of the Dead Sea Scrolls' in *Musical Quarterly*, xliii (1957), pp. 21 foll.

[2] Clement of Alexandria, *Paedagogus*, i, chap. 4. For a full discussion of that interesting passage see the bibliography in the next note.

[3] E. Werner: 'Notes on the Attitude of the Early Church Fathers towards Hebrew Psalmody', in *Review of Religion* (New York and Chicago), May 1943; 'The Conflict between Hellenism and Judaism in the Music of the Early Church', in *Hebrew Union College Annual*, xx (Cincinnati, 1947), pp. 427–9; 'The Common Ground in the Chant of Church and Synagogue', in *Atti del Congresso Inter-*

nazionale per la Musica Sacra, (Rome, 1951), pp. 1–15; *The Sacred Bridge* (New York and London, 1959), pp. 441–5, 366, 369, n. 51, *et passim*.

[4] Cf. Dionysius of Halicarnassus, *De compositione verborum*, 17; H. Abert, *Die Lehre vom Ethos in der griechischen Musik* (Leipzig, 1899), pp. 133 foll.; Plutarch, *De musica*, ed. R. Volkmann (Leipzig, 1856), cap. XI, pp. 14–15 and 95 foll.; also H. Riemann, *Handbuch der Musikgeschichte*, 3rd ed. (Leipzig, 1923), i, 1, pp. 49 foll.; and R. P. Winnington-Ingram, *Mode in Ancient Greek Music* (Cambridge, 1936), pp. 22 foll.

[5] P. Wagner, *Gregorianische Melodien*, iii (Leipzig, 1921), p. 456; also K. Levy, op. cit., p. 27.

close proximity to the Mozarabic 'Pater noster', to which I have drawn attention in former publications.[1] Peter Wagner already noticed this resemblance and concluded:

Occasionally such types of recitation are being connected with the Greek tetrachords. In this case the (Greek) Dorian is represented as E-F-G-A. . . . I hold these speculations to be entirely mistaken. In our tune (*Pater noster*) the Dorian tetrachord is exceeded already in the first part; and the same objection is valid for other types of recitation. This practice of recitation has nothing in common with Greek music; it comes directly from the Jewish and Christian liturgies of the Near East.[2]

In comparing the formulae of the *anaphora* with the Mozarabic 'Pater noster', the Gloria XV, the Te Deum, etc., K. Levy reaches conclusions which somewhat differ from those of P. Wagner: he successfully parallels the various occurrences of the tune under examination in the Byzantine *anaphora* with Latin traditions. Moreover, he adds to his list of parallel formulae the 'Exultet', which seems dubious to me, and the Lamentations, which P. Wagner had already compared with a Yemenite tradition quoted by Idelsohn, and which I had included in my list of Hellenistic formulae.[3] The formula for the 'Flectamus genua' (E-G-A-B-A-A) is again an all but identical variant of the ancient tune of *Nishmat* which I had included in my own list.[4] It runs: E-A-G-B-A-G-A. Thus Mr. Levy has reached, quite independently and by a different approach, exactly the same conclusions as I did. He also assumes a 'broad pre-Octoechic modal area that combines aspects of the modes on E and G'.

Musically speaking, the oldest tradition of ᴋ-s can be traced back to the second century A.D., and there is a good probability, to judge from the widespread and invariably ancient texts connected with the tunes of the Clementine *spondeiakos*, that that particular tradition had its origin in or around Alexandria. The stability of the texts, the mixture of angelologies from Isaiah, Ezekiel and Daniel, the position of the s before the *anamnesis*—the most memorable place of the liturgy—the many biblical and some post-biblical Hebraisms, the possibility of trinitarian interpretation of the s, of christological significance of the Hosanna, the *gestus orationis* in ᴋ and s, common to Jews and Christians, all these factors lead us to believe that the musical tradition of the s was established early in Christianity. The identity with the psalmody of Alexandrian Jews of Clement's time, with the primitive Yemenite tradition, with Byzantine and Gregorian patterns, make it more than likely that we have here an important example of liturgical and musical interdependence between Church and Synagogue.

[1] Cf. my *Sacred Bridge*, pp. 455, 459, 477.
[2] P. Wagner, op. cit., iii, p. 59, n.
[3] Ibid. p. 366; also *Sacred Bridge*, p. 356.
[4] K. Levy, op. cit. p. 56. I have, in similar fashion, listed a number of examples of this type of recitation, also of 'pre-Octoechic' character on the E-mode, in my *Sacred Bridge*, p. 498, Table VI.

SAKRALER GESANG UND MUSIK IN DEN SCHRIFTEN GREGORS DES GROSSEN

Higini Anglès (Rome)

ES BESTEHT zurzeit eine übertriebene kritische Tendenz vonseiten einiger Musikwissenschaftler, die Papst Gregor I. jede musikalische Tätigkeit absprechen möchten. Andere behaupten, er habe sich für die Musik überhaupt nicht interessiert, ja sie nicht einmal gekannt. Meine Ansicht als Kenner der Musik und der römischen Liturgie ist, daß man sich vor den Extremen hüten muß: man braucht ihm einerseits nicht ausschließlich die Liturgie- und Musikreform zuzuschreiben, darf ihm aber anderseits auch nicht jedes Interesse und jede musikalische Betätigung absprechen.

Die große Bewegung, die sich seit dem 8. Jh. um die Person Gregors I. bildete und die auf seinen Leistungen in Liturgie und Kirchengesang ruhte, wäre wohl ohne irgendeinen geschichtlichen Hintergrund nicht möglich gewesen. Von der Karolingerzeit bis zum XVIII. Jh. waren sich die Musiktheoretiker und Musikhistoriker darin einig, daß Gregor I. tatsächlich eine musikalisch-liturgische Reform vollzogen habe, indem er die sakralen Gesänge sammelte, ordnete und kodifizierte. Im XVIII. Jh. zeigten sich dann mehrere Versuche, Gregor dem Großen dieses Verdienst abzusprechen. Die Ansichten der zeitgenössischen Diskussion für und gegen Papst Gregor I. sind zwar allgemein bekannt. Damit aber meine kurze Auseinandersetzung richtig aufgefaßt werde und mehr objektiven Wert erhalte, möchte ich noch auf folgende Punkte hinweisen.

Gegen Ende des 19. Jh. versuchte der belgische Musikgelehrte Fr. Aug. Gevaert (1828–1908) noch einmal den Beweis zu erbringen, daß die musikalische Tätigkeit Papst Gregors des Großen nur auf Legende beruhe.[1] Der bekannte belgische Patrologe Dom Germain Morin O.S.B. (1863–1945) antwortete auf diese Rede Gevaerts 1890 sofort mit einer Verteidigung des liturgisch-musikalischen Werkes Gregors des Gr. und zwar in vier Artikeln, die in der *Revue Bénédictine* von 1890 erschienen. Zwei dieser Artikel wurden später unter dem Titel 'Les véritables origines du Chant Grégorien'[2] veröffentlicht. Die historischen Dokumente des berühmten Dom Morin stellen heute noch eine Apologie Papst Gregors d. Gr. dar. Auf diese wissenschaftlich fundierten Beweise Dom Morins hin nahm sich niemand mehr die Mühe, weitere Forschungen über diesen Gegenstand anzustellen. Erst 1925 veröffentlichte ein anderer belgischer Benediktiner, Dom Rambaut van Doren, von der Abtei Mont César (Löwen), seine Doktordissertation *Étude sur*

[1] Cf. seine *Les Origines du chant liturgique de l'Église latine* (Gand, 1890) und *La Mélopée antique dans le Chant*   *de l'Église latine* (Gand, 1895).
[2] (Desclée et C\ie, Rom-Tournai, 1904).

l'influence musicale de l'Abbaye du Saint-Gall.[1] Diese Dissertation befaßt sich auch mit dieser Frage, fußt aber auf der Theorie Gevaerts und wurde in den *Ephemerides Liturgicae*, vol. 39–40, von Dom L. David zurecht widerlegt. Eine weitere Widerlegung fand die Thesis, ebenfalls in den *Ephemerides Liturgicae* (1926), vonseiten des bekannten belgischen Liturgikers C. Callevaert und des Liturgikers und Patrologen C. Mohlberg O.S.B.

Nach einem Zeitraum von 30 Jahren hat nun noch einmal eine wahre Zerstörungswut gegen das Werk Gregors des Großen eingesetzt; der junge deutsche Musikwissenschaftler H. Hucke schrieb 1955 einen kurzen Artikel über 'Die Entstehung der Überlieferung von einer musikalischen Tätigkeit Gregors des Großen'.[2] Obwohl er die geschichtlichen Tatsachen des VII. u. VIII. Jh. anerkennt, da man in England die in Gebrauch befindlichen Liturgie- u. Gesangbücher, welche vom Hl. Augustinus und seinen Nachfolgern eingeführt worden waren, als Werk Gregors des Großen betrachtete, mißt er diesen Dokumenten keinerlei Beweiskraft zu. Vielmehr stützt er sich auf die des VIII. Jhs. aus der Karolingerzeit, da man begann, die musikalische Tätigkeit Papst Gregors I. zu verherrlichen. Er zieht aus diesen Dokumenten die Schlußfolgerung, sie seien zu späten Datums und verdienten keine Glaubwürdigkeit, weil sie das liturgische Werk Gregors des Gr. mit einem musikalischen koppelten, das von Gregor tatsächlich niemals ausgeübt worden sei. Im Kirchen-Lexikon (Herder, IV. Band, 1960) vertritt Hucke den gleichen Standpunkt. Dieser ist umso verwunderlicher, als Hucke nur ein Jahr zuvor beim Internationalen Kongreß für katholische Kirchenmusik in Wien (1954) seine Abhandlung 'Die Tradition des Gregorianischen Gesanges in der römischen Schola Cantorum' verlesen hatte. Dort heißt es: 'Von ihm [Gregor] . . . ist die Kirchenmusik zu einer Disziplin erhoben worden . . . und so trägt unser liturgischer Gesang . . . mit Recht seinen Namen, und ihm selbst gebührt es, als Vater der abendländischen Musikgeschichte angesehen zu werden.'[3]

Der deutsche Professor Bruno Stäblein ist ohne Zweifel einer der erfahrensten zeitgenössischen Wissenschaftler in der Geschichte des Gregorianischen Gesanges; wir verdanken seinen in *Die Musik in Geschichte und Gegenwart* veröffentlichten Studien das reiche Material, das er in jahrelanger Arbeit zusammentrug und das für künftige kritische Forschungen über die Geschichte und Entwicklung des Gregorianischen Gesanges stets grundlegend sein wird. In seinem Artikel 'Gregor I'. (*MGG*, v, 1956, col. 772–9) spricht er ein hohes Lob auf Papst Gregor den Gr. aus; im selben Artikel schreibt er jedoch ganz offen, daß das musikalische Werk Papst Gregors reine Legende sei, die 300 Jahre nach seinem Tode eingesetzt habe. Diese Legende, so fährt Professor Stäblein fort, begann 754, als Papst Stefan II. sich mit Kaiser Pippin traf, und entfaltete sich bis zur 2. Hälfte des 9. Jahrhunderts, da der Name Papst Gregors des Großen schon gleichsam zum Symbol geworden war. Nichtsdestoweniger steht dieses rein negative Urteil des bekannten Professors im Gegensatz zu den zwei Artikeln 'Alleluia' und 'Choral' (Bd. 2, 1952), die er ebenfalls in den *MGG*, vol. 1 (1949–51) veröffentlicht hat.

Unter den anderen Musikwissenschaftlern, die in den letzten Jahren über die Geschichte des Gregorianischen Gesanges geschrieben haben, ist noch der berühmte Byzantinist Egon Wellesz zu nennen, der soviel Schönes zu sagen wußte über den liturgischen Gesang in Rom und in der

---

[1] Cf. sein *Étude sur l'influence Musicale de l'Abbaye de Saint-Gall (VIIIᵉ au XIᵉ siècle)* (Louvain, 1925).
[2] *Die Musikforschung*, 8. Jg. (1955), S. 259–64.

[3] Cf. *Bericht des Zweiten Internationalen Kongresses für katholische Kirchenmusik, Wien, 4–10 Oktober 1954* (Wien, 1955), S. 120–3.

Ostkirche und dabei stets die größte Verehrung für Papst Gregor den Gr. zeigte.[1] Der Musikologe Walther Lipphardt verlas beim Internationalen Musikwissenschaftlichen Kongreß in Rom (1950) die schöne Abhandlung 'Gregor der Große und sein Anteil am römischen Antiphonar.'[2] P. Josef Smits van Waesberghe S. J.,Spezialist auf dem Gebiete der mittelalterlichen Musiktheorie brachte beim 2. Internationalen Kongreß für Kirchenmusik in Wien (1954) seinen hochinteressanten Bericht über 'Neues über die Schola Cantorum zu Rom'. Darin erinnert er an die großen Verdienste Papst Gregors zugunsten der Benediktinerklöster, die den liturgischen Kult in den römischen Basiliken ausübten und an seine Verdienste zugunsten der römischen *Schola Cantorum* seiner Zeit.[3] Frau Professor Solange Corbin befaßte sich im Jahre 1960 mit der Frage der römischen *Schola Cantorum* und spricht dabei von Gregor dem Großen als einem großen Liturgiker. Sie ist der Auffassung, daß die *Schola Cantorum* in Rom zum erstenmal ausdrücklich unter dem Pontifikat Sergius I. (687–701) und nicht unter dem Gregors erwähnt wird.[4]

Um einem römischen Papst eine Liturgie- und Musikreform zuschreiben zu können, braucht dieser selbst kein Liturgist und nicht einmal ein hervorragender Musiker zu sein. Es genügt, daß der Papst den Wunsch und die Absicht hat, eine derartige Reform durchzuführen und mit einem Dekret die Durchführung der Reform entsprechend seinen Wünschen anordnet. Papst Pius X. war weder ein großer Liturgiker noch ein hervorragender Musiker und trotzdem machten unter seinem Pontifikat die geschichtlichen Forschungen über die Liturgie große Fortschritte, ja sein Pontifikat wurde geradezu zu einer Epoche der Neumenforschung und des Gregorianischen Gesanges, sowie der polyphonen sakralen Musik und des Kirchengesanges im allgemeinen.

Wenn man daher von Papst Gregor als Liturgiker oder Musiker spricht, so schließt das nicht ein, daß er selbst ein großer Liturgiker oder ein großer Melodiker war. Man braucht nur seine 854 authentischen Briefe zu lesen, um zu sehen, daß er bei der Vielfalt seiner Probleme keine Zeit zum Lesen und Schreiben hatte, wie er immer wiederholt, wenn er von der großen Sorgenlast spricht, die ihm die Verantwortung als Papst verursachte. Er allein hätte also nichts unternehmen können zugunsten des römischen Kirchengesanges. Wenn daher der fränkische Autor des *De convivio* über verschiedene Päpste und auch über Gregor den Großen den 'Cantum anni circoli nobili edidit' schrieb, so können wir uns nicht vorstellen, daß der Autor dabei die Idee gehabt habe, der Papst habe persönlich den Gesang 'anni circoli' verfaßt.[5] Der *Liber Pontificalis* (ed. Duchesne, i, s. 312) erwähnt die verschiedenen von Gregor stammenden Bücher und fügt

[1] Cf. sein 'Gregory the Great's Letter on the Alleluia', in *Annales Musicologiques*, ii (1954), S. 7–26; und 'Recent Studies in Western Chant', *The Musical Quarterly* xli (1955), S. 177–90.

[2] Cf. *Atti del Congresso Internazionale di Musica Sacra*, Rom, 25–30 Mai 1950 (Desclée et Cᶦᵉ, Tournai, 1952), S. 248–54; und sein 'Die Antiphonen der Sonntagsvesper in der Altrömischen Liturgie' in *Der kultische Gesang der Abendländischen Kirche*, Festschrift für Dominicus Johner (Köln, 1950), S. 53–63.

[3] Cf. *Bericht des Zweiten Intern. Kongresses für katholische Kirchenmusik, Wien 1954* (Wien, 1955), S. 111–19.

[4] Cf. sein *L'Église à la conquête de sa musique* (Paris, 1960), S. 172–89. Nachdem Mlle. Corbin in ihrem Seminar eine Studie durchgeführt hatte über die mittelalterlichen Biographien des hl. Gregor und die Belege, die sich im *Liber*

Pontificalis, De prandio monacorum, im Liber des hl. Ildephons von Toledo usw. finden, ziet sie folgende Schlußfolgerung: 'Aucun des documents ne mentionne une activité proche du chant ou de la *musica* savante. Il est même assez invraisemblable que Grégoire ait lui-même chanté: sa santé fragile, ses perpetuelles syncopes, le lui défendaient. Pour la *musica* savante on est encore plus loin de compte ... On est donc autorisé à croire que l'œuvre musicale de Grégoire n'existe pas et que le renom lui en a été attribué pour des raisons diverses à partir de la fin du VIIIᵉ siécle. (Cf. École pratique des Hautes Études, Paris à la Sorbonne, IVᵉ section: Sciences historiques et philologiques, *Annuaire* 1963–1964, S. 171.)

[5] Cf. Michel Andrieu, *Les Ordines Romani du haut Moyen Âge*, iii (Louvain, 1951), S. 6 foll.

hinzu: 'et multa alia, quae enumerare non possumus'. Der Kopist wollte mit diesen Worten auf die zahllosen Briefe des Papstes hinweisen und auf die einzelnen liturgischen Werke, wie das *Sacramentarium* und das *Antiphonarium*, von dem in späterer Zeit soviel die Rede war. Im *Liber Pontificalis* heißt es: '*Hic* augmentavit in predicationem canonis *diesque nostros in tua pace disponas, et cetera.*' Daraus ersieht man, daß der *Liber Pontificalis* seine musikalische Tätigkeit nicht erwähnt, weil diese immer Hand in Hand ging mit der liturgischen, die er nicht im einzelnen anführt.

Andererseits muß man zugeben, daß der Römer Johannes Diaconus (geb. gegen 880) in seiner *Vita Gregorii Magni* die er 873 im Auftrag von Papst Johannes VIII. verfaßte, gewisse legendenhafte Erzählungen bringt; auch Gregor I. selbst erzählt in seinen *Dialogorum libri IV* solche legendäre Geschichten. Das darf uns nicht wundern, wenn wir an die Gewohnheiten des Altertums und Mittelalters denken. Nichtsdestoweniger bringt Johannes Diaconus, was man damals in Rom über Papst Gregor I. wußte und glaubte und was er in den Archiven darüber fand, und nicht alles, was er über das liturgisch-musikalische Werk Gregors schrieb, ist Legende. Die Liturgiker sind sich heute darin einig, daß Papst Gregor ein *Sacramentarium* geschrieben hat. Er führte auch den Gesang des 'Alleluia' für das ganze liturgische Jahr mit Ausnahme der Fastenzeit ein und fügte dem 'Kyrie eleison' der Messe noch das 'Christe eleison' hinzu; in einigen 'Communio'-Antiphonen des Proprium ersetzte er den Psalmentext mit Texten aus dem Evangelium. In der zu Rom 595 abgehaltenen Synode verbot er, daß Diakone als Solosänger in den Kirchen auftraten; nach englischen Urkunden und nach Johannes Diaconus schreibt er ein *Antiphonarium* in der Form einer ausgewählten Sammlung für die römische Liturgie. Schließlich schuf er die römische *Schola Cantorum* oder vervollkommnete sie zum mindesten und führte den Gesang der Allerheiligenlitanei in den Straßen Roms ein, indem man singend von einer Basilika zur anderen zog. All das sind geschichtliche Tatsachen, die eine liturgische Aktivität voraussetzen, welche ohne Musik undenkbar ist.

Daß Papst Gregor etwas von Musik verstand, geht aus den Ämtern hervor, die er in Rom innehatte, zuerst als Diakon, dem das *munus* des Kantors in den römischen Basiliken zustand, dann als Erzdiakon, zu dessen Pflichten es gehörte, die Diakon-Kantores zu überwachen. Ganz zu schweigen ist von der Tatsache, daß Gregor als Benediktinermönch und Gönner des Benediktinerordens etwas von Kirchenmusik verstehen mußte. Sein Aufenthalt in Konstantinopel zusammen mit seinem Freund Bischof Leander von Sevilla, — der 'in ecclesiasticis officiis idem non parvo laboravit studio . . . ; in sacrificio quoque, laudibus atque psalmis, *multa dulci sono composuit*', wie sein Bruder S. Isidor in *De viris illustribus* schreibt — in einer Zeit, da sowohl am kaiserlichen Hof als in den Kirchen von Byzanz die Musik und der sakrale Gesang eine Hochblüte erlebten. Da mußten notwendigerweise auf ihn Liebe und Begeisterung für die sakrale Kunst übergehen.

Auf Bitten Leanders begann Gregor in Byzanz seine *Moralia sive expositio in Job* und brachte sie um 595 mit einer Widmung an seinen Freund Bischof Leander zum Abschluß. Die *Regula pastoralis* schrieb er zu Beginn seines Pontifikates gleichsam als Programm für das pastorale Wirken der Priester. Die *Homiliae II in Canticum Canticorum, Homiliae in Ezechielem* und die *Homiliae XL in Evangelia* entstanden ebenfalls zu Beginn seines Pontifikates u. zwar zwischen 590 und 593. Die *Dialogorum libri IV* wurden in den Jahren 593–594 geschrieben, das *Sacramentarium* 595, d.h. im Jahre der in Rom stattfindenden Synode, in der er verschiedene liturgische Reformen einführte. Mit seinem *Sacramentarium* beabsichtigte er eine Kürzung und Angleichung an die Erfordernisse der Zeit, denn er reduziert die Präfationen und die Festembolismen im Kanon und hebt den Taufcharakter der Fastenzeit mehr hervor. Dieses *Sacramentarium* ist tatsächlich das erste und ist zweifellos das Werk Papst Gregors des Großen, wenngleich nur der 1. Teil seinem Scriptorium zugeschrieben werden kann. Allerdings ist es uns nicht in seiner ursprünglichen Version erhalten, nachdem fast alle bekannten Exemplare auf ein Modell zurückzuführen sind, das Papst Hadrian I. (772–95) gegen Ende des VIII. Jhs. an Karl den Großen schenkte. Obwohl die Entstehungszeit seines *In librum primum Regum expositionum libri VI* nicht eindeutig festliegt, haben die Spezialisten doch seine Echtheit bestätigt.[1]

Meines Wissens hat bis heute niemand die Schriften Papst Gregors daraufhin studiert, darin authentische Urteile über die Musik zu finden. Auf keinen Fall aber darf man den sakralen Gesang und die Musik im allgemeinen, die er in seinen Schriften erwähnt, übersehen und unterschätzen. Ohne diese Frage erschöpfend behandeln zu wollen, beschränken wir uns heute auf verschiedene Ausdrücke, die in seinen Büchern vorkommen und die deutlich zum Ausdruck bringen, daß er nicht nur den sakralen Gesang kannte, sondern auch im Bilde war über Zweck und Bau einiger Musikinstrumente, die in der Heiligen Schrift erwähnt werden. Wenn man derartige Ausdrücke in seinen Schriften liest, muß man immer bedenken, daß er damit gleichsam ein Bild für die geistliche Formung der Christen geben wollte; wenn er direkt über den sakralen Gesang und die Musik im allgemeinen hätte sprechen wollen, wie z.B. die Heiligen Väter des 4. und 5. Jahrhunderts, so hätte er sicherlich Schönes und Lehrreiches auch über die Kirchenmusik seiner Zeit sagen können.

In den Schriften Gregors des Großen erscheinen Sätze und musikalische Ausdrücke, die sich auf den Psalmengesang und dessen geistlichen Symbolcharakter beziehen. In seinen *Super Cantica Canticorum Expositio*, cap. I, Nr. 7, z.B. führt er die verschiedenen *cantica* an, die in der Hl. Schrift enthalten sind: 'Sciendum est etiam, quia in Scriptura sacra alia sunt Cantica victoriae, alia Cantica exhortationis et contestationis, alia Cantica exsultationis, alia Cantica adjutorii, alia Cantica conjunctionis cum Deo.'[2] In *Moralium Lib. XXVIII, Cap. xxxviii Beati Job* spricht er von der geistlichen *jubilatio* und erweitert so, was St. Augustinus über die *jubilatio* im musikalischen Sinn geschrieben hatte: 'Jubilatio quippe dicitur quum cordis laetitia oris efficacia non expletur, sed quibusdam modis gaudium prodit, quod ipse qui gaudet, nec tegere praevalet, nec explere. Laudent itaque angeli qui jam tantae claritatis altitudinem in sublimibus vident. Jubilent vero homines, qui adhuc in inferioribus oris sui angustias sustinent.'[3]

In den Kommentaren zu den *Bußpsalmen*, Vorwort zu Psalm VIII, spricht er vom Gesang der Freude und schreibt: 'Qui profecto canticum non cantat laetitiae, nec concinentium admiscetur choris, et annulo carens fidei, nec stola immortalitatis induitur, nec vituli saginati alimento satiatur.'[4] In Ps. VI 'De profundis clamavi' Vorwort erinnert er an den Symbolismus der Psalmen *graduales* und stellt heraus, daß im himmlischen Tempel Gesänge aufgeführt werden, durch die die Seele noch in dieser Welt erhoben wird zum himmlischen Jerusalem: 'Ita caeleste illud templum haec nobis cantica praeferant, per quae in Deo exsultans anima, quasi per quosdam

---

[1] Für die Bibliographie der Werke Gregors des Großen, cf. *Clavis Patrum Latinorum* von Aemilius Gaar und Eligius Dekkers, *Editio altera*, in *Sacris Erudiri*, iii (1961), S. 375 foll.; für den Text benutzen wir die Ausgabe der Mauriner von J. B. Galicciolli revidiert (Venetiis, 1768–76).

[2] *Sancti Gregorii Papae I Opera*, ed. J. B. Galicciolli, vol. xiv, S. 3; Migne, *PL*, 79, S. 475.
[3] Galicciolli, iii, S. 180.
[4] Galicciolli, xiv, S. 146; *PL* 79, S. 642.

gradus ascendat. Ascensuri ergo non corpore sed spiritu, non passibus sed affectibus, hunc Psalmum decantemus, et in eo studeamus Dei meditatione approprinquare.'[1] Im Kommentar zu Ps. IV 'Miserere mei Deus', Nr. 19 *Domine, labia mea aperies* betont er die Schönheit des Gotteslobes: 'Illi soli laudis Dei possunt sentire dulcedinem, qui peccatorum suorum meruerint percipere remissionem'.[2] Für Past Gregor ist der Psalmengesang stets mit der *compunctio cordis* verbunden, und er stärkt uns auf dem Wege zum Paradies. In diesem Sinne schreibt er in *In Ezechielem, Lib. I, Homilia I*, Nr. 15 folgendes: 'In sacrificio igitur laudis fit Jesu iter ostensionis, quia dum per psalmodiam compunctio effunditur, via nobis in corde fit, per quem ad Jesum in fine pervenitur' . . . Hinc quoque scriptum est: *Cantate Domino, psalmum dicite nomini ejus, iter facite ei*. . . . Cui dum cantamus, iter facimus, ut ad nostrum cor veniat, et sui nos amoris gratia accendat.'[3]

Es ist interessant zu beobachten, welche Sehnsucht Gregor I. nach seinem ehemaligen Mönchsleben im Kloster St. Andreas hatte, wo er in aller Ruhe beten und singen konnte; die gleiche Sehnsucht beschreibt er in verschiedenen seiner Briefe, aber *In Ezechielem, Lib. I, Homilia XI*, Nr. 6 erscheint sie noch tiefer und schmerzlicher: 'Et quidem in monasterio positus, valebam et ab otiosis linguam restringere, et in intentione orationis pene continue mentem tenere. At postquam cordis humerum sarcinae pastorali supposui, colligere se ad semetipsum assidue non potest animus, quia ad multa partitur. Cogor namque modo Ecclesiarum, modo monasteriorum causas discutere, saepe singulorum vitas actusque pensare.'[4] Die Predigten Papst Gregors, die er in den Basiliken und Kirchen Roms hielt, sind voll von Anspielungen auf den Hymnengesang des Paradieses. So liest man z.B. in *XL Homiliarum in Evangelia, Lib. I, Homilia XIV*, Nr. 5: 'Ibi hymnidici angelorum chori, ibi societas supernorum civium. Ibi dulcis solemnitas a peregrinationis hujus tristi labore redeuntium.'[5] Er erinnert mehrmals daran, daß die römische Osterfest-Feier nichts anderes sei als Festfeier der Seligen des Himmels; so heißt es in Evang. Libr. II, Homilia XXVI, Nr. 10: 'Ecce Paschalia solemnia agimus: sed ita vivendum est nobis ut pervenire ad aeterna festa mereamur. Transeunt cuncta quae temporaliter festiva celebrantur; curate, qui his solemnitatibus interestis, ne ab aeterna solemnitate separemini.'[6]

Das *canticum* der christlichen Liturgie ist ein Lied, das im Psalmen-Buch nicht vorkommt, wohl aber in anderen Bücher der Bibel. Das *carmen* der altheidnischen klassischen Poesie war ein poetisches Lied mit lyrischen Inhalt, während das mittelalterliche Carmen eine gesungene Poesie sakralen oder profanen Inhalts war, in dem ein biblisches Argument, Personen, Heilige usw. besungen wurden. So gibt Isidor von Sevilla in seiner Ethymologie folgende Definition: 'Carmen vocatur, quidquid pedibus continetur; carmina heroica, elegiaca, bucolica sive pastoralia' (cf. Migne, *PL* 82, S. 118). Papst Gregor hingegen spricht in seinem Kommentar zu 'Et scriptae erant in eo lamentationes, carmen et vae', *In Ezechielem, Lib. I, Homil. IX*, Nr. 32, von dem 'laetum carmen et lugubre carmen'. Er bemerkt, wie das *carmen* der Nacht Freude in der Trübsal bedeutet; denn wenn einer in dieser Welt leidet, so wird er durch den Gedanken an die ewigen Freuden getröstet. So lesen wir:

Carmen aliquando in bono, aliquando vero in malo dici dubium non est, quia et laetum carmen et lugubre carmen dicere possumus. . . . Carmen quippe in nocte est laetitia in tribulatione. Carmen in nocte accipimus, quando in

---

[1] Galicciolli, xiv, S. 138; *PL* 79, S. 632.
[2] Galicciolli, xiv, S. 106; *PL*, 79, S. 595.
[3] Galicciolli, iv, S. 131 foll.; *PL*, 76, S. 793.

[4] Galicciolli, iv, S. 238; *PL* 76, S. 908.
[5] Galicciolli, v, S. 797; *PL* 76, S. 1130.
[6] Galicciolli, v, S. 269; *PL* 76, S. 1130.

pressuris praesentibus de futuris gaudiis consolamur. Carmen nobis in nocte ostendebat Apostolus cum dicebat: *Spe gaudentes, in tribulatione patientes* (Rom. xii, 12). . . . Qui enim circumdari se pressuris narrat, et tamen Deum sibi esse exsultationem nominat, procul dubio carmen in nocte cantat. Quia igitur pene semper in bono carmen ponere scriptura sacra consuevit, ita a nobis etiam in hoc loco debet intelligi.[3]

In der Auffassung Gregors ist das *carmen* ein Symbol für die Freude der Heiligen, während *lamentatio* die Buße der Sünder ausdrückt. So liest man in derselben *Homilia*, Nr. 34:

Lamentationes, videlicet, quia in eo scripta est poenitentia peccatorum. Carmen, vero, quia ibi praenuntiantur gaudia justorum. Ut autem de promissione gaudii sequentis hilarescas, cognosce quae in hoc volumine scripta sunt carmina laudis aeternae. . . . Hoc nobis carmen caelestis patriae nuntiare cives ejus venerant, qui concorditer clamabant: *Gloria in excelsis Deo, et in terra pax hominibus bonae voluntatis.* . . . Cognosce ergo in hoc volumine vae, quod in eo scriptum est, atque ab animo per timorem expelle quod diligis, ut possis ex judicio carmen amare quod legis. . . . Spe caelestium gaudiorum mentem relevare desideras, ibi ad consolationem tuam invenis carmen.[4]

Gregor liebt es, die Stimme eines Predigers zu vergleichen mit dem kräftigen Klang von Bronze und Metall: *In Ezechielem, Lib. I, Homilia III*, Nr. 5: 'Aeris metallum valde sonorum est. Et recte voces praedicantium aeri comparantur, quia *in omnem terram exivit sonus eorum, et in fine orbis terrae verba eorum* (Ps. xviii, 5). Bene autem aes candens dicitur, quia vita praedicantium sonat et ardet. Ardet enim desiderio, sonat verbo.'[3]

In einer anderen Homilie will er die Tugend der *concordia* preisen und spricht dabei vom *tympanum* aus gegerbtem Fell, das einen kräftigen Ton hervorbringt, während der *chorus* sich zusammensetzt aus Stimmen, die in guter Harmonie zusammenklingen. Deshalb vergleicht Gregor das *tympanum* mit der Enthaltsamkeit, den *chorus* mit den Harmonia der Liebe. *In Ezechielem VIII*, nr. 8:

Quanta autem sit concordiae virtus ostenditur, cum sine illa virtutes reliquae, virtutes non esse monstrantur. . . . Unde psalmista quoque nullam esse abstinentiam sine concordia designans, ait: *Laudate eum in tympano et choro* (Ps. cl, 4). In tympano enim corium siccum resonat, in choro autem voces concorditer cantant. Quid ergo per tympanum nisi abstinentia, et quid per chorum nisi caritatis concordia designatur? Qui itaque sic abstinentiam tenet, ut concordiam deserat, laudat quidem tympano, sed non laudat in choro.'[4]

Das ist der Grund, warum die Heiligen des Himmels, geeint in der Liebe, dem Herrn das harmonische Lied singen können, das nie enden wird. Siehe ebenda, Nr. 9: 'Quia vero electi semper in caritate conjuncti sunt, et haec eadem eorum caritas sonum laudis reddit auctori.' Das ist auch der Grund, warum von den ersten Zeiten der Kirche an, die unter sich geeinten Gläubigen eine unbesiegbare Kraft darstellen und dem Herrn laut und begeistert ihr Lob singen können. Siehe ebenda, Nr. 10: 'Quia ergo distincti fidelium ordines ab exortu sanctae Ecclesiae usque ad finem mundi concorditer viventes, contra potestates areas dimicant, castra ambulant, et fit quasi quidam castrorum sonitus, quia in eis ad laudem omnipotentis Dei . . . sonant.'[5]

Bei näherem Zusehen staunt man, mit welcher Sachkenntnis Gregor über die Musikinstrumente spricht, ausgehend von den Saiteninstrumenten. Diese seine genaue Kenntnis half ihm, die moralischen Folgerungen für die Christen und die auserwählten Seelen zu formulieren. So lesen

[1] Gallicciolli, iv, S. 215; *PL* 76, S. 884.
[2] Gallicciolli, iv, S. 216; *PL*, 76, S. 885 foll.
[3] Gallicciolli, iv, S. 145; *PL* 76, S. 807.

[4] Gallicciolli, iv, S. 191; *PL*, 76, S. 858.
[5] Gallicciolli, ibid., S. 192; *PL*, 76, S. 858.

wir im *Moralium*, Lib. I, cap. I, *Beati Job*: 'Hi qui chordarum harmoniam temperant, tanta hac arte dispensant, ut plerumque, cum una tangitur, longe alia ac multis interjacentibus posita chorda quatiatur; cumque ista sonitum reddit, illa quae in eodem cantu temperata est, aliis impercussis, tremit. Sic ergo in Scriptura sacra plerumque de virtutibus, sic de vitiis agitur, ut dum loquendo aliud insinuat, tacendo aliud innotescat.'[1] Im gleichem *Moralium*, Lib. XX, cap. XXX, Nr. 78, kommentiert er in Vers 51 die Worte Jobs: 'Versa est in luctum cithara mea, et organum meum in vocem flentium.' Hier vergleicht er die *cithara* mit den guten Werken der Gläubigen und die Orgel mit der Predigt. Die Pfeifen der Orgel sind für ihn der Mund der Prediger. Die Seiten der *cithara* sind ihm ein Symbol der reinen Meinung. Seine gute Kenntnis der Musikinstrumente geht auch daraus hervor, daß er genau beschreibt, warum die Seiten der *cithara* gut ausgetrocknet sein müssen, wenn sie einen schönen Klang geben sollen und in welcher Weise man sie anschlagen muß, um einen guten Ton hervorzubringen. Er weiß genau, daß die Saiten der *cithara*, nur schwach angeschlagen, nicht klingen, und bei zu kräftigem Anschlag einen Mißton hervorbringen:

Quia organum per fistulas, et cithara per chordas sonat: potest per citharam recta operatio, per organum vero sancta praedicatio designari. Per fistulas quippe organi, ora praedicantium; per chordas vero citharae, intentionem recte viventium non inconvenienter accipimus. Quae dum ad vitam aliam per afflictionem carnis tenditur, quasi extenuata chorda in cithara per intuentium admirationem sonat. Siccatur etenim chorda, ut congruum in cithara cantum reddat. . . . Pensandum quoque est, quod chorda in cithara, si minus tenditur, non sonat; si amplius, raucum sonat. . . . Intueri inter haec egregium praedicatorem libet, quanta arte magisterii, fidelium animas velut in cithara chordas tensas, alias amplius tendendo extenuat, atque alias a tensione sua relaxando conservat. . . . Illas ergo chordas extenuando tendit, ne non tensae omnimodo non sonent: hanc vero a tensione temperat, ne dum plus tenditur, minus sonet.[2]

Dann kommentiert er den gleichen Text Jobs: 'Versa est in luctum cithara mea' und stellt heraus, wie der fröhliche Klang der *cithara* sich in Trauermusik verwandelt hat und die Orgel in 'Weinen', weil jene, die das Wort Gottes hätten hören sollen, es nicht hören wollten: 'Ac si aperte fateatur dicens: Pacis quidem meae tempore per alios parva more citharae, per alios vero more organi magna et sonora praedicabam; sed nunc in luctum cithara, et organum in vocem flentium versum est, quia dum me contemni conspicio, eos qui praedicationis cantum non audiunt deploro.'[3] Aus diesen Worten ersieht man, wie Gregor von der 'Pfeifenorgel' spricht, während wir keinen anderen Beweis dafür haben, daß in damaliger Zeit in römischen Kirchen bereits die Orgel verwendet worden sei. Es ist vielleicht nicht verfehlt, anzunehmen, daß er sich auf die Orgel und die anderen Instrumente bezieht, die er am Kaiserhof in Byzanz gesehen und gehört hatte.

An anderer Stelle, *In Primum Regum*, Lib. IV, cap. V, Nr. 16, kommentiert er das cap. X, 5, als Samuel nach der Salbung Sauls ihm befahl: 'Post haec venies in collem Dei, ubi est statio Philistinorum, et cum ingressus fueris urbem, obvium habebis gregem prophetarum descendentium de excelso, et ante eos psalterium et tympanum, et tibiam, et citharam.' Er will damit sagen, daß jene, die das *psalterium* tragen, das Himmelreich ankündigen; jene, die den *tympanum* tragen, predigen die Abtötung des Fleisches; jene, die die *tibia* tragen, lehren die Ihrigen zu weinen in der Hoffnung auf die ewige Freude; die die *cithara* tragen, lehren die Guten, sich bereits in dieser

[1] Gallicciolli, i, S. 21.
[2] Gallicciolli, ii, S. 316 f.; *PL* 76, S. 185 foll.
[3] Gallicciolli, 2. c., S. 317 f.; *PL* 76, S. 186.

[40]

Welt zu freuen in der gewissen Erwartung der ewigen Güter: 'Sed cum descendunt, ante se psalterium, tympanum, tibiam et citharam deferunt. Psalterium quippe habent, quia regnum caelorum annuntiant; tympanum habent, quia praedicant mortificationem carnis; tibiam habent, quia flere subditos jubent pro acquisitione aeternae laetitiae; citharam quoque habent, quia gaudere pios pro certitudine aeternorum bonorum edocent.'

Dann fährt er in seinem Kommentar, ibid., Nr. 17, fort: Da das *Psalterium* im höheren Teil klingt, ist es ein Symbol für die Verkündigung der ewigen Freuden und das *tympanum* aus Tierfellen versinnbildet die Abtötung des Fleisches. Das Evangelium berichtet uns, daß die *tibia* bei der Beerdigung teurer Angehöriger geblasen wurde; deshalb veranschaulicht sie, nach Gregor, das Weinen der guten Menschen. Die *cithara* hingegen ist ein Instrument der jubelnden Freude, weil sie die Freude der Auserwählten andeutet:

Psalterium quidem, quia a superiori parte resonat, etiam aeternorum gaudiorum praedicationem designat; quia dum superna amare suggerit, quasi a superiori parte suae dulcedinis sonum mittit. Tympanum vero, quia de mortui animalis corio tenditur, in eo non inconvenienter carnis nostrae mortificatio figuratur. Tibiam autem quia in mortuorum hominum exequiis haberi soleat, de Evangelio didicimus. . . . Quid ergo in tibia, nisi sanctorum luctus exprimitur? . . . Cithara autem valde laetum musicum est instrumentum. Quo nimirum instrumento verbum solatii electorum apte figuratur; quia velut ad sonum citharae hilarescimus, quando nos electi praedicatores inter aerumnas praesentis exilii consolantur.[1]

Aus dem Gesagten geht hervor, daß Papst Gregor seine Freude daran hatte, den mystisch-symbolischen Charakter der in der Bibel erwähnten Instrumente zu deuten; wir sehen weiterhin in Nr. 17 desselben Kapitels V, wie er das *psalterium*, das *tympanum*, die *tibia* und die *cithara*, die den Propheten vorangehen, beschreibt: Wer vor dem Herrn singt, spielt das *psalterium*; wer sich abzutöten weiß, spielt das *tympanum*; wer den Tod des Herrn zur Erlösung der Welt besingt, spielt die *tibia* und wer die Auferstehung und die Himmelfahrt Jesu Christi preist, spielt di *cithara*:

Et notandum quia psalterium, tympanum, tibiam, et citharam ante se habere Prophetae perhibentur, ut electorum praedicatorum forma videatur. . . . Sancti ergo doctores, quia itere suprnae conversationis, quod praedicant, continuo incessu boni operis servant. . . . Qui regni aeterni eum regem nominat, nobis profecto psalterium sonat. Et qui disciplinam mortificationis nostrae in eo asserit, velut tympanum ferit. Tibiam sonat, qui mortuum Redemptorem pro salute mundi denuntiat. Citharam percutit, qui eum a mortuis surrexisse et ad caelos ascendisse dicit. Sed ad tantorum organorum jucunditatem hilarescimus, si ipsum Prophetarum gregem insonantem audiamus.[2]

Im Vorwort zum 1. Psalm, *In Septem Psalmos Poenitentiales*, erklärt er noch einmal, daß das *psalterium* die betende Seele symbolisiert, da dieses Instrument in der Form eines Triangels mit 10 Saiten im unteren Teil gespielt wird und im oberen erklingt; so kämpft die Seele, die im Glauben an die Heiligste Dreifaltigkeit und in den Vorschriften des Gesetzes geschult ist, im niedrigen Teil, während der höhere zum Klingen gebracht wird:

Psalterium quoque eamdem animam spiritualibus exercitiis assuetam non inconvenienter nominamus. Sicut enim musicum illud instrumentum triangulum decem chordarum inferius quidem percutitur, superius vero sonare videtur, ita anima sanctae Trinitatis fide formata, decem Legis praecepta instructa, inferius percutitur, et superius auditur: quia cum carnem aliquis perfecte afflixerit, tunc suavissimum Deo in dulcedine melos reddit.

[1] Galicciolli, xiii, S. 234 f.; *PL* 79, S. 291 foll.   [2] Galicciolli, xiii, S. 235 f.; *PL* 79, S. 293.

4   [41]

Per psalmum ergo meditationes et laudes et gaudia de Deo in animo concepta accipimus, sicut cantum illius musici instrumenti psalmum vocamus. Hunc autem psalmum in hymnis habendum titulus adstruit, quia qui tactus dolore cordis intrinsecus peccata sua confitens, cor in poenitentia conterit. . . . Et qui pro indulgentiae desiderio iniquitates suas annuntiat, in tabernaculis justorum dulciter hymnizat.[1]

Aus diesen Ausführungen erhellt, daß Papst Gregor die hauptsächslichsten Musikinstrumente nicht nur in ihrem Bau, sondern auch in ihrem Klang und in in ihrer Eigenart gut kannte. Abgesehen von Isidor von Sevilla (560–636) kennen wir keinen Bischof des 6./7. Jahrhunderts, der über die Eigenart der Musikinstrumente so gut Bescheid wußte, wie Gregor I. In seiner *Regula Pastoralis*, Pars tertia, cap. XXII, schreibt er im Ps. cl. 4, 'Laudate eum in tympano et choro': 'In tympano namque sicca et percussa pellis resonat; in choro autem voces societate concordant. Quisquis itaque corpus affligit, sed concordiam deserit, Deum quidem laudat in tympano, sed non laudat in choro.'[2] Die Definition, die uns Gregor von dem Worte *chorus* gibt, deckt sich mit jener der Heiligen Väter und der des Isidors von Sevilla.

Auch in seinen Briefen finden sich verschiedene Ausdrücke, die auf sein großes Interesse für den kultischen Gesang schließen lassen. Wegen Raummangel muß dieses Kapitel wegfallen. Für unseren Fall wäre seine *Epistola ad Joannen Syracussanum Episcopum* von besonderem Interesse. Da aber Prof. Wellesz vor einigen Jahren diesen Brief auch auf seinen musikalischen Inhalt hin studierte, wollen wir hier von einem Kommentar absehen.

[1] Galicciolli, xiv, S. 69 f.; *PL* 79, S. 551.   [2] Galicciolli, iv, S. 75; *PL* 77, S. 551.

THE PROBLEM OF THE OLD ROMAN CHANT

Peter Peacock (Oxford)

SPECULATION OVER Old Roman Chant began with the appearance in *Paléographie Musicale*, II, 4, 1, of certain pieces of music which obviously did not show the same characteristics as the normal or general examples of Gregorian music. There are four Graduals and two Antiphonals which provide us with enough material for a fairly adequate survey of the main characteristics of the chant. These, together with a number of historical facts, have enabled scholars to present some kind of explanation for its presence; but more information from the liturgical side of the Old Roman Rite has put an even better case than would have been possible from the other sources alone. As there are about forty divergencies in Mass formularies and the Cycle of Feasts, the various Missals, Ordinals, Sacramentaries, and other volumes available from different times and places have given up many secrets that have made the task a little easier for the enquirer into the problem. The tendency for musicologists and liturgists to work apart has often resulted in delay in the presentation of essential knowledge, and it is only later, when the facts have been re-studied, that many fairly obvious conclusions have been drawn. In this particular case the background understanding of the complex liturgical situation has been of immense help in elucidating certain facts and arriving at conclusions.

The arguments may be put into three categories. Historical, Liturgical, and Musical are the headings, though perhaps the liturgical section contains an amount of necessary history as well. A number of facts have been known for a long time and others are of recent origin, but in many cases the facts have been interpreted wrongly. The Frankish King Pepin, whose earnest desire was to please and associate himself with the Pope, was visited by Stephen II in the year 753. The chant in the Frankish kingdom at this time was the so-called Gallican Chant, about which we know very little. No music exists, although it has been possible to reconstruct some of the melodies by a process euphemistically described as 'the process of elimination'. Our little knowledge of the music, the Aquitanian notation in which it was written, the importance of the School of Limoges, and the venerable if somewhat exciting person of St. Caesarius of Arles, all add up to the impression that the ultimate suppression of the Gallican Chant was nothing short of a tragedy. The Bishop of Metz, uncle of Pepin, had already been in Rome, and had returned with enthusiasm for the Roman chant—an enthusiasm which he had already imparted to his nephew, who was over- whelmed by the singing of the Papal Choir at his coronation in 754. Rome, already anxious to unify Christendom in all respects, was only too happy to help get rid of the native music, and under Charlemagne the destruction was practically complete, although in many centres the old chant survived and was incorporated, as we have seen, into Gregorian chant-books. From time to time other books were sent, as for instance those from Pope Paul I—a Gradual and an Antiphonal.

Continued efforts were made after Charlemagne's death to protect the new Roman chant, and in 825 Wala, Abbot of Corbie, went to Rome to receive an Antiphonal. Not long afterwards the Bishop of Metz, Amalar, tried to obtain yet another Antiphonal for his cathedral, and was told that none was available. Pope Gregory IV suggested that he should copy the one lately given to Corbie. Amalar found to his astonishment that the Antiphonal at Corbie was different, 'not only in the liturgical order but also in the words and in the greater number of responsories and antiphons'. These differences were more a matter of words than anything else, but undoubtedly the books had music. So much for the historical facts. Several explanations have been forthcoming about this confused situation, the most popular of which is that the original books sent to Metz were Old Roman and that the Corbie book was Gregorian. Huglo has proved, however, that the Corbie book was in fact Old Roman, which leaves us with little choice but to affirm that the Metz book must have been Gregorian. Perhaps further confirmation comes from the chance remarks of the anonymous monk of St. Gall, who tells of a singer trained in Rome at the time of Charlemagne, who was assigned to Metz, whence the chant (Gregorian) spread all over France.

The liturgical argument, although inclined to be bogged down in innumerable details, is more thorough and in some ways more convincing. This presupposes a good knowledge of the liturgical situation in Rome at the time. It is clear that before the middle of the seventh century there was no question of a number of standard different Roman Liturgies. The Popes seem to have favoured sometimes *monachi* and sometimes *clerici*, but not in any particular order, nor do they appear to have established and used one custom against another. But mention is made of Pope Vitalian (657–72), who apparently had a special body of singers with their own chants and in effect a special Papal liturgy. From this time onwards it becomes clear that there existed two main bodies: St. Peter's with its attendant monasteries and the *Sedes Apostolica* with its *clerici*, the former using the Old Roman Chant and the latter the Gregorian Chant. Medieval terms are apt to be confusing and one must treat very carefully the words *monachi* and *clerici*. References to a *clericus* might mean simply a priest, in which case a *monachus* could also be, and often is, a *clericus*. However, normally the *clericus* is a secular or diocesan priest, whereas the *monachus* will be a member of a religious order. In Rome the *clerici*, as secular clergy, administered the sacraments and said some parts of the Divine Office as well as singing the public masses. The *monachi*, who came mostly from the basilican monasteries, were dedicated to the performance of all the Office. It would appear, however, that there had to be some measure of collaboration, since the secular clergy could scarcely be expected to have experienced choirs at hand every time they had to sing Mass, and so would have to turn to the basilica choirs for help. This leaves us with one other organization which could afford to have its own choir and liturgists: the Papal Court.

Contemporary accounts of Papal ceremonies are often confusing because, although the *Schola Cantorum* performed Gregorian Chant as the normal liturgical music, there were occasions when the *monachi* and not the *clerici* celebrated, and on these occasions—and there were many of them— the Old Roman rite would be used, at the Lateran, the Vatican, and other basilicas. The demand from the Franks was for Gregorian books. But Rome at this time seems to have been particularly

[44]

short of these. She needed them herself for one thing, and they took a long time to copy. On the other hand there were a great number of Old Roman books. The comparatively large number of urban monasteries and basilicas certainly had more volumes of Graduals and Antiphonaries than the small *Schola Cantorum*. It is not surprising, therefore, that appeals to Rome for more books were met with a handing-out of some of those of the Old Roman Rite, which were more plentiful.

The Old Roman Rite was dying, even in a privileged place, and although there are traces of it up to the thirteenth century, of the four liturgical customs extant in Rome from the middle of the century not one has a real trace of the old art. St. Peter's may possibly have some remnants of the Old Roman rite, but they are not easy to pinpoint. The other three are definitely Gregorian. Much of the work of spreading the Gregorian liturgy must have been due to the fierce romanizing zeal of the Franciscans, who adopted the Papal Court Liturgy for their own use. Fr. S. J. P. Van Dijk has given us a very worthy picture of the extent of their work in maintaining the liturgy by editions and revised editions from the earliest days, and we are indebted to many of these portable breviaries and graduals for the information we have. The disappearance of nearly all the Old Roman books can be attributed to several factors, of which one of the most prominent is the reforming hand of Cardinal Orsini, afterwards Pope Nicholas III. As a Cardinal he had devised a new urban liturgy based upon a mixture of other Roman elements with Gregorian music. Many Old Roman books were then destroyed and upon his elevation to the Papal throne he finished what he had been unable to do earlier by making sure that all old books were destroyed. Only the monasteries were exempt, and this is the reason why one or two of the Old Roman books have been preserved for us. Another reason is the introduction into Italy of the square notation, which was much easier to read and much more precise. The Old Roman books were written in Beneventum notation, known as the *nota romana*. Although beautiful to look at the notes are not nearly so precise as the *nota francigena*, and with Papal propaganda, the adoption of this system by the friars, and the rapid spread of the new system, the Old Roman chant becomes less and less easy to read.

We rely therefore on a few books to help us to reconstruct something of the glory of this art. The earliest Gradual is that from the monastic church of St. Cecilia in Trastevere; but this church has also a contemporary lectionary and a Passional of a very slightly later date. However, here it is the music which is of prime interest. The date is 1071. Another is the Gradual Vaticanum Latinum 5319, whose probable date is 1100. It is thought that this was used at the Lateran, since feasts and other chants belonging to a basilica occur in it. A feature of both these manuscripts is the presence of troped Kyries, Glorias, sequences, and some Gregorian Alleluias, inserted because the Old Roman rite had comparatively few proper Alleluias. A third Gradual is later and has no Gregorian Alleluias, tropes, or sequences. All contain, or once contained, the cycles of feasts and *de tempore* settings. Various feasts of the Gregorian tradition are absent, and there is a fair amount of variation of text and a good deal of transferring of Antiphons in the Mass settings. This undoubtedly is what upset Bishop Amalar at Corbie. But the main difference lies in the chant itself, and it is this which perhaps makes the Old Roman rite such an interesting point of study. There are several theories about this music. It has some things in common with Gregorian chant and more often than not the modes of identical texts are the same, as well as the formulae of the psalm tones which give rise to the idea of a common source. But each is highly developed in its own right, with considerable melismatic passages.

Furthermore the Old Roman music has certain characteristics which lead scholars to believe that there are elements of Byzantine music present. It closely resembles the idiom of Beneventum, and is written in Beneventum notation, and undoubtedly there has always been a considerable movement of music along the Mediterranean, even if there are more important reasons for looking to the East for influences in the Western Chant. A comparison between the two Offices and the two Mass structures will give us some idea of the similarity and the divergencies to be expected.

There are two Old Roman Antiphonaries available, of roughly the same time, 1150–70. One, a Roman manuscript, is of great use because it contains a large number of directions and rubrics concerning the actual conduct of the Office, and the other is a Beneventum manuscript which is useful in confirming the remarks of Bishop Amalar in *De Ordine Antiphonari* that the Antiphons for the Benedictus and the Magnificat for the Sundays after Pentecost are not in the Old Roman Rite. It does have, however, the well-known Papal Vespers for Easter, and the so-called Double Office for Christmas Matins. The confusion over the Easter Vespers is easily explained when it is referred to the Old Roman liturgy. If the Pope were present, as normally he would be, the Vespers were sung in the basilica of St. John Lateran. They were neither from the basilican books nor from the books of the Papal Court, as the canons of the Lateran sang their own Vespers *more Romano*, after the Pope had attended Vespers and departed. Neither do they correspond to the Ordinal of the Papal Chapel but, as one would expect, to the Old Roman liturgy. This supposes that the chanting of a special Vespers *dignitate apostolica* is understood to be a very special incident not conforming to normal use. Old Roman chant was in considerable use during Amalar's visit to Rome, but even so, Vespers was a prerogative of the *clerici* and the chanting of a special Vespers for Easter was much in the nature of a local custom, where the Vatican monks were allowed to bring out their special rite as a solemnity. Similarly the idea of a double Matins for Christmas is, according to Van Dijk, a misinterpretation of Amalar's text. There were two different Matins, the one at the Vatican with the normal Gregorian three Nocturns, and the other, the Papal Matins at St. Mary Major with the Old Roman one Nocturn. Until the full analysis of the rite is made there may well be many other difficulties of this kind arising. Certainly no one can afford to look at the music alone, tempting though this may be.

Of the Office music we can say immediately that the psalm tones are usually in agreement, both initials and endings; and although the Invitatory tones are missing from Vat. Basilic. B. 79, as far as one can tell they will have been the same as all the psalm tones. One interesting point is that while the Old Roman Chant has, in the main, similar music for Antiphons, often they are used for different texts, and that the free composition which is a feature of the Gregorian style is noticeably lacking in the older chant. In the Responsories the first obvious difference is the paucity of the actual number of Old Roman examples. There are 622 of these, although this number should be reduced to about 580 because the remainder are only transferred Mass chants. Gregorian Responsories of the same period usually have about a thousand. Further proof of the antecedence of the Old Roman Chant is given by examination of the method of the Respond. This rather odd repetitive practice, that is, the repeating of the whole or parts of a verse, can be easily dated because the Roman practice of the eighth century was to repeat the whole, whereas the part repetition dates from the ninth century. It is abundantly clear that the Old Roman Chant is formulated in such a way that the partial repetition makes nonsense of the music and that it was intended to repeat the whole section—a clear indication that this music belongs to the eighth century. The Mass music is to be found in the above-mentioned Graduals. The Introits show a characteristic which, although not too prominent, is sufficiently a mark of style to warrant attention. This is the derivation of a number of the antiphons from psalm tones. The melodies have a familiar opening phrase, several words on a reciting note, and a cadence which though sometimes of greater length has affinities with the normal psalm-tone cadences. On the whole, however, there exists a good deal of melodic dissimilarity in the Introit antiphons, and those who seek to establish a strong relationship can point only to a general resemblance such as might be found in any two antiphons with a similar modal background.

One is struck by the somewhat limited nature of this chant when examining the Graduals. The lack of free composition in sections where this might have been expected and the over-frequent use of standard formulae, together with the overworking of normal modal cadences to a much greater degree than in Gregorian Chant, all give the impression of severe limitation, or at least of a stringent economy. The Alleluia and Verse is perhaps the most interesting section of the Mass to study. As in the other sections, the general form is the same as Gregorian, with the Jubilus (the Alleluia) followed by a verse and a repeat of the Alleluia. But in a number of cases the repeat of the Alleluia is extended to form an almost new version, or second Jubilus. This is a special characteristic of the Old Roman version. Of these fifty-four Alleluias, eight are used only once and the others may appear as many as thirteen times. The verses are often musically connected with the Alleluia, and as often as not the same verse melody does duty for a number of occasions, with restatement of phrases to fit the words. In the Lenten Tracts the standard procedure of using formulae is adopted, but with four phrases instead of the Gregorian three. One of the most interesting divergencies occurs in the Offertory, where the text has a great deal of either re-arrangement of standard phrases or the inclusion of new texts. If the general style of the Antiphons is practically the same as in the Gregorian Chant, the Verses differ considerably, especially in the melismas and the psalm passages. Indeed the psalm portions are very much a source of speculation. The normal reciting note is covered up by a reiterated figure, which is used almost indefinitely as the text demands. This feature, together with unusually long melismas at the end of the verses constitutes the most interesting original part of the chant.

It is fairly well established that the Old Roman Chant is the earlier of the two versions, but not necessarily for the reasons often given. It is true that this chant is more limited than Gregorian, but within its own framework it is as highly developed. It seems, moreover, that the rather obviously archaic nature of the construction and development of the music, especially when compared with contemporary Gregorian, would indicate a much more conservative care of the melodies, and that the possible changes during the successive centuries would have been much less than in the other types. For that reason a much fuller comparison between this and Ambrosian, and even Byzantine, chant is desirable.

[47]

'DE GLORIOSO OFFICIO ... DIGNITATE APOSTOLICA ...'
(Amalarius)
ZUM AUFBAU DER GROSS-ALLELUIA IN DEN PÄPSTLICHEN OSTERVESPERN

J. Smits van Waesberghe (Amsterdam)

EINES DER WERKE, das für die musikhistorischen Untersuchungen eine neue Richtung und Stimulans gegeben hat, ist das vor zwanzig Jahren von Egon Wellesz zusammengestellte Buch 'Eastern Elements in Western Chant'.[1] Was bis zu diesem Zeitpunkt (1946) über die Gesänge mit griechischen Texten in den päpstlichen Ostervespern in Rom geschrieben wurde, findet man, mit den Resultaten Wellesz eigener Untersuchungen über diesen Gegenstand, in diesem Buch.[2] Seitdem sind verschiedene Detailstudien über diese päpstliche Ostervesper erschienen.[3] Obwohl eine musikhistorische Synthese über diesen Höhepunkt liturgischer Pracht der Schola Cantorum in Rom ein Buch füllen kann, will diese Studie den Versuch machen in gedrängter Form eine Synthese-Einsicht zu geben.

Die Form dieser Ostervesper, aus der traditionellen Form der Römischen Vesper (5 Psalmen mit Antifonen, dem 'Versus' als Übergang nach dem Magnificat-Antiphon, Magnificat, Oratio) entstanden, hat historisch betrachtet drei Hauptfasen:

I. Periode der Vorbereitung, beschrieben von Amalarius ('De ordine Antiphonarii', cap. 52), mit der Reihenfolge: drei Psalmen, 'Haec dies' an Stelle des 'Versus', Magnificat, danach noch zwei Psalmen.[4]

---

[1] Oxford, 1947 (von hierab zitiert mit Wellesz, op. cit.). Siehe auch Egon Wellesz, Epilogomena zu den 'Eastern Elements in Western Chant', *Die Musikforschung*, v (1952), S. 131–7.

[2] Op. cit., S. 34–42; 64–67.

[3] Ich beschränke mich auf die Studien, in denen Melodien der Ostervesper aufgenommen sind:

"Αλληλούια, 'Ο Κύριος', Wellesz, op. cit., S. 35 f. und *Das Musikwerk: Die Musik der Byzantinischen Kirche* (1959), S. 13, Nr. 1 (nach U. Gaissner, *Rassegna Greg.* i [1902], S. 127).

'All. Dies sanctificatus', Bruno Stäblein, *M.G.G.* s.v. 'Alleluia', cc. 341–4.

'All. excita Domini', Robert J. Snow in Willi Apel, *Gregorian Chant* (Ind. Univ. Press, Bloomington, 1958), S. 497.

'All. Dies sanctificatus', Dom Louis Brou, *Revue Grég.* xxiv (1939), S. 86.

'All. Paratum cor meum', Bruno Stäblein, *M.G.G.*, s.v. 'Psalm', cc. 1688–90; Vs. 'Paratum' und 'Cantabo' auch bei R. J. Snow, op. cit., S. 498.

'All. Pascha nostrum' (ohne Vers), Bruno Stäblein, *Report of the 8th Congress of the I.M.S.*, New York, 1961, i, S. 14.

Vs. 'Priusquam montes', Br. Stäblein, *M.G.G.*, s.v. 'Psalm', c. 1689.

[4] Ed. J. M. Hanssens, iii, S. 83 f.

II. Periode des Entstehens und der Wahrung der dreifachen, päpstlichen Ostervesper, gekennzeichnet durch drei oder vier Groß-Alleluia 'cum melodiis', teilweise mit griechischen Texten für die Alleluiaverse,[1] eine Vesperkonstruktion, die Amalarius als Augenzeuge in 832 mit 'sed *dignitate apostolica* 'Alleluia' mutatum est pro eis [versibus]. Eadem re factum est ut multi versus 'Alleluia' Graeca lingua in memorato officio canantur' (ibid.) erklärte. Kennzeichnend sind ferner die Prozessionen mit den Prozessionsantiphonen ('In die resurrectionis mea', 'Lapidem quem reprobaverunt',[2] 'Vidi aquam') während des Bittgangs 'ad fontes' und zu den Kapellenaltären[3] und schließlich der Abschluß der drei Hauptteile mit dem Magnificat, mit dazugehörigem Antiphon und Gebetskonklusion.

III. Eine spätere Periode, in der der zweite Halbvers der unter II gesungenen Verse der Groß-Alleluia — insofern diese nicht während Periode II komponiert wurden — mit einer Melodie versehen wurden.[4] Daß sie aus einer jüngeren Periode stammen (dennoch höchstwahrscheinlich als ein Ganzes dem Vesperrepertoire beigefügt wurden), zeigt sich aus den folgenden Angaben:

1. Kein einziges kommt in den *Ordines Romani* des 8. und 9. Jhs. vor.[5]
2. Sie kommen ausschließlich in der Überlieferung des 11. bis 13. Jhs. vor.
3. Im Gegensatz zu den Versen der Periode I wird bei denen der Periode II die Rubrik 'Primicerius'[6] mit der Melodie der sog. *annunciatio* mitgeteilt (der Anfang des von der *Schola* zu singenden Verses mit Angabe der Tonhöhe und dem psalmodisch Moduseigenen [Musikbeisp. 1]), sowie die Rubrik 'Scola' für die hierauf folgende *Schola*-Melodie.
4. Die unter Periode III gemeinten 18 Psalmenverse (resp. Versteile) wurden alle zu derselben Melodie gesungen (Melodie I).

Aus diesen vier Punkten kann man schließen, daß, historisch betrachtet, zwei Gruppen Versmelodien bei diesen Groß-Alleluia zu unterscheiden sind; die jüngste (die der Periode III) ist, um sich der Melodie und der Texte gut zu erinnern, in den Hss. mit besonderen Hilfsmitteln notiert. Daß die 18 hinzugefügten Verse alle zu derselben Melodie gesungen wurden, weist darauf, daß sie zu *einem* Ergänzungsplan gehören und daß dies in einer Periode geschehen sein muß, in der von einer kompositorischen Kreativität keine Rede war.[7]

Beim näheren Studium dieser Verse fallen noch mehr Besonderheiten auf:

1. Sieben dieser Groß-Alleluia haben griechische Verstexte: zwischen diesen griechischen Verstexten kommen die 18 jüngeren Verstexte nicht vor, so daß die hierfür immer wieder zurückkehrende Melodie I nirgends nach oder zwischen den griechischen Texten vorkommt;
2. die 18 jüngeren Verstexte wurden, mit einer Ausnahme (nl. Nr. 15 c und d), immer als *ein* 'Vers' zwischen die Verse der älteren Periode gestellt und, mit Ausnahme von Nr. 3, wurde die

[1] Wellesz, op. cit., S. 34.
[2] Melodisch wohl von dem Versus 'Lapidem' beim Graduale 'Haec dies' zu unterscheiden.
[3] Vgl. M. Andrieu, *Ordo rom. XXVII*, iii, S. 364, N. 76; Duchesne, *Liber Pontificalis*, i, s. 242; Ant. Chavasse, *Le Sacramentaire Gélasien* (Tournai, 1958), S. 453 f.
[4] Siehe Melodie Nr. 1.
[5] Weder im *Ordo* (=*Ordo Rom. XXVII*) in dem Anti-

phonarium von Compiègne (807–80), noch in dem *Ordo* von St. Amand (=*XXX B* bei M. Andrieu) aus dem Ausgang des 8. Jhs.
[6] Andersweitig 'primus scolae', laut des *Ordo Rom. XXVII* (cf. M. Huglo, 'Le chant "vieux-romain" ', *Sacris Erudiri*, vi [1954], S. 118).
[7] Eine Übersicht der hinzugefügten Psalmverse gibt die Tabelle in der Rubrik 'Ank.' = 'Ankündigung'.

Reihe der Psalmenverse eines Groß-Alleluias (falls darin jüngere Hinzufügungen vorkommen) immer mit einem dieser Verstexte *beschlossen*;

3. mit *einer* Ausnahme und zwar 'Christus qui nos adiuvet' (Nr. 3b), die eine Akklamation oder *Laus* ist, sind alle jüngeren 17 Texte den Psalmen entnommen und zwar so, daß sie in der Regel einen ersten Halbvers des älteren Psalmenverses anfüllen, z.B. an Ps. 92, Vs. 2, 'Parata sedes tua deus', wird aus demselben Vs. 2 ,'ex tunc a seculo tu es' (Nr. 2b und 2c); an Ps. 92, Vs. 3, 'Elevaverunt flumina Domine', wird aus demselben Vs. 3 'Elevaverunt flumina voces tuas' (Nr. 2d und 2e) hinzugefügt.

Dies alles weist darauf, daß man aus irgendeinem Grund getrachtet hat, die bestehenden Melodien mit kurzen Texten anzufüllen um auf diese Weise eine ästhetisch besser verantwortete Formeneinheit des Ganzen zu bekommen; mit der Wiederholung derselben Formel für alle 18 Hinzufügungen wurde die erwünschte Formeneinheit erreicht. Musikalisch betrachtet ist der Ursache des 'irgendeinen Grundes' für diese Hinzufügungen leicht nachzugehen, denn die Modellmelodie in dem VII. Kirchenton (Siehe Melodie I) mit einer vollkommenen G-Kadenz (a-a-G) folgt auf eine bestehende Melodie, die ebenfalls auf G schließen *müßte*, doch die völlig unerwartet mit der Schlußkadenz c-h-a schließt. Der Musikologe fragt dann weiter: wie kommt es, dass viele Psalmentexte (siehe Melodie III) mit dieser c-h-a Kadenz schließen, obwohl es sich hier um G-Melodien (VII. Kirchenton) handelt? Die entscheidende Antwort hierauf ist, daß diese Melodien auf eine gregorianische Melodie (All. 'Dominus regnavit') des II. Kirchentons (D) zurückgehen, die im Altrömischen eine Quinte höher transponiert wurden; der Schlußton wurde dann a (Kadenz: c-h-a als Umbiegung von a-h-c-a) und diese wurde dann bei der Modellmelodie Nr. III gehandhabt, mit der Folge, dass die jüngere Modellmelodie Nr. I das Ganze mit einer verantworteten Kadenz a-a-G wieder einrenkt. Darum wird eine derartige Reihe Psalmenverse mit einer solchen jüngeren Hinzufügung (Musikbeisp. 2) beschloßen und wird damit vorkommen, daß die Psalmenreihe unmittelbar vor dem Alleluia-secunda mit der tonal-forcierten Kadenz c-h-a schließt.

Der Umfang dieses Beitrags macht es unmöglich alle Melodien der päpstlichen Ostervesper abzudrucken. Doch ist es, im Zusammenhang mit demjenigen was folgt, sehr erwünscht, daß dem Leser ein Eindruck von der großen musikalischen Pracht dieser Ostervesper vermittelt wird. Hierzu möge der hier folgende Verlauf der Aufführungsweise und der Musik eines dieser Groß-Alleluia[1] beitragen. Absichtlich wählte ich das erste Alleluia der Vesper zu Ostern 'Dominus regnavit' (s. Musikbeisp. 2), denn es wird sich zeigen, daß von dieser Melodie m.M. dasselbe gesagt werden kann, was H. Husmann in seinem Urteil über den 'Großaufbau der Ambrosianischen Alleluia'[2] schrieb: 'Dieser Normalform stehen verschiedene erweiterte Formen gegenüber.'

Wenn man den Eindruck bekommen hat, daß das Ganze dieser päpstlichen Ostervesper eine musikalische Pracht darstellt, die in ihrer Auffälligkeit mit dem Eintritt der großen mittelalterlichen *Ludi Paschales* zu vergleichen ist, dann kann auf die Frage übergegangen werden: was ist, musikhistorisch betrachtet, der Wert dieses Œuvres? Inwiefern ist es anderweitig entnommen, entnommen vielleicht dem byzantinischen, altmailändischen, altgregorianischen oder dem

[1] Einen guten Eindruck der musikalischen Pracht gibt auch das Musikbeisp. des Alleluia 'Paratum cor' (Nr. 11 unserer Tabelle) Bruno Stäbleins, abgedruckt in *M.G.G.*,

s.v. 'Psalm' cc. 1689–90.

[2] *Anuario Musical*, xiii (1957), S. 19.

altrömischen (bestehenden) Repertoire und inwiefern ist hier die Rede von einer neuen musikalischen Kreativität?

Betrachtet man zur Beantwortung dieser Frage an erster Stelle die gewählten lateinischen *Texte*, dann macht man die merkwürdige Entdeckung, daß ursprünglich viele nicht für den Osterzyklus bestimmt waren. Es handelt sich hier, die Dublüren nicht mitgerechnet, um 15 verschiedene Texte. Man kann sie alle in dem altgregorianischen Repertoire und darum in dem *Antiphonale Missarum Sextuplex* von Dom R.-J. Hesbert finden. Dort kommen sechs Texte für die Osterzeit vor ('Pascha nostrum', 'Te decet', 'Confitemini Domino et invocate', 'Laudate pueri', 'Cantate Domino' und 'All. Quoniam Deus magnus'). All. 'Letatus sum' (Nr. 20) ist dem 2. Adventssonntag zugewiesen; All. 'Dominus regnavit' (Nr. 2) hat den traditionellen Platz in der 2. Messe des Weihnachtstages; All. 'Adorabo' (Nr. 14) in der Mariamesse am 2. Februar; All. 'Omnes gentes' und 'Ascendit Deus' auf Vig. von und auf Ascens. Domini; die übrigen sind als zu der Rubrik 'de circulo anni' gehörend zu betrachten.

Auch die griechischen *Texte* sind nur teilweise für die Osterzeit bestimmt: Ὁ ποιμαίνων τὸν Ἰσραήλ' (Nr. 6) für das Beschneidungsfest; Οἱ οὐρανοί διηγοῦνται' (Nr. 21) für den Weihnachtstag; 'Δεῦτε ἀγαλλιασώμεθα' (Nr. 20) für 'Dominica S. Thomae' (Osterzeit); Ὁ Κύριος ἐβασίλευσεν' (Nr. 4) für den Sonnabend 'Renovationis'.[1] Ὅτι θεὸς μέγας' kommt mit der Übersetzung 'Quoniam Deus magnus' in der bekannten Reihe Alleluia (einige 'cum sequentia')[2] des Cod. Blandinensis (*Sextuplex* S. 198) vor. Ferner findet man in diesen Osteralleluia Melodien, die anderen Teilen des altrömischen Repertoires entnommen sind, aber mit einem anderen Text versehen wurden (All. 'Ostende', All. 'Excita', All. 'Beatus vir').

Auf die *Texte und Melodien* der Groß-Alleluia der altrömischen Ostervesper übergehend, bemerkt man — wie ich annehme: mit einigem Erstaunen —, daß es schwierig ist darin ursprünglich für diese Vesper entworfene Melodien zu finden. Anhand der Tabelle kann man nachgehen, wie wenig Ursprüngliches dieses umfangreiche Musik-Opus enthält.

Nr. 1, All. 'Pascha nostrum' ist, ebenso wie in dem gregorianischen Repertoire (resp. *Sextuplex*), der Ostermesse entnommen. In dem Ganzen des altgregorianischen Repertoires ist die gregorianische *Pascha-nostrum*-Melodie (mit dem Alleluia) etwas außergewöhnliches und man fragt sich, ob hier von Einflüssen der altbyzantinischen Liturgie die Rede ist. Wie es auch sei, das Kennzeichnende der gregorianischen Melodie ist auch in der altrömischen Fassung, die der gregorianischen Melodie fast auf dem Fuß folgt, vertreten.[3]

Nr. 2, All. 'Dominus regnavit', Eröffnungsalleluia der Ostervesper. Zum ersten Mal kommt es in den altrömischen Gesangbüchern in der 2. Weihnachtsmesse (mit Alleluia-secunda in Vatikan lat. 5319, fo. 13) vor und hat dort also liturgisch denselben Platz wie im Gregorianischen (resp. *Sextuplex*). Melodienbeziehungen zwischen dem altrömischen und gregorianischen Choral sind deutlich wahrzunehmen. Dies Eröffnungsalleluia (Melodie II) mit der Melodie des Verses beherrscht die altrömischen Ostervesper; die Rubrik 'Melodie' in der Tabelle zeigt dies deutlich. Es ist unnötig auf alle Verse von Nr. 2b und d (Melodie III und IIIa) mit dieser Melodienübernahme — unter denen, wie man sieht, auch einige mit griechischen Texten vorkommen — zurückzukommen,

[1] Diese Angaben verdanke ich der Gefälligkeit Michel Huglos.

[2] Stäblein, *Archiv f. Mw.*, xviii (1961), S. 1–33.

[3] Analyse des altrömischen Alleluia-prima und -secunda (ohne Vers) von Bruno Stäblein im *Kongressbericht N.Y.*, i, S. 14.

ebensowenig wie auf die jüngere Melodie I für die hinzugefügten Verse, wie z.B. hier zu 'Ex-tunc a seculo' und 'Elevaverunt flumina voces suas'. Melodie Nr. I besteht aus einem Initium motiv (h-a-c-a-G), das u.a. auch in dem Prozessionsantiphon (nach All. 'Pascha nostrum') 'In die resurrectionis' als Initium von 'et colligam regna' (fo. 85) vorkommt. Hiernach folgt gleich einem Tenor, um das Zuviel an Textsilben aufzufangen, das typisch altrömische Motiv h-c-a, worauf eine Kadenz folgt, die man auch teilweise am Schluß des Alleluia von 'Dominus regnavit' (Melodie II) antrifft und als vollständige Melodie von ungefähr 10 Versen in einer Kombination der Melodien III und I.

Nr. 3 ist eine Wiederholung von Nr. 1 mit einem eingeschobenen Vers gemäß Melodie I.

Nr. 4, All. 'Ο Κύριος ἐβασίλευσεν'. Diese Melodie des Alleluia und Vers war Anlass zu einem Mißverständnis. Da der Vers die griechische Übersetzung des 'Dominus regnavit' ist, hat man[1] erst an melodische Beziehungen mit dem gregorianischen 'Dominus regnavit' gedacht. Einige Beziehungen sind unwidersprechlich anzuweisen, aber die hat die gregorianische Melodie auch mit der gregorianischen Alleluiamelodie 'Dies sanctificatus'. Vergleicht man letztere mit der des griechischen Textes, dann sieht man, daß der Zusammenhang hier unmittelbarer ist, sicherlich in Hinsicht auf das Alleluia (Musikbeisp. 3). Da der Text des Verses 'Dies sanctificatus' (siehe auch zum Vergleich hiermit die Melodie 'Ημέρα ἡγιασμένη' bei Wellesz, *Eastern Elements*, S. 41 f.) einen anderen Inhalt wie 'Dominus regnavit' hat, sind die melodischen Beziehungen von 'Ο Κύριος' mit dem gregorianischen Vers 'Dies sanctificatus' bedeutend freier.

Bevor ich auf die Melodien der Groß-Alleluia dieser Ostervesper, die nicht die bis jetzt ange-führten Melodien (Nr. I, II, IIa, IIIa, und IIIb) unmittelbar übernehmen, eingehe, möchte ich bemerken, daß in der Hs. Rom, Vat., lat. 5319 die folgenden Alleluiaverse mit einer *melodia-secunda* vorkommen (Rom, Vat., Basilic. B 79 hat ausschließlich 'Dominus regnavit' mit Alleluia-secunda, fo. 104, Rom, Vat., Basilic. F 22 hat bekanntlich, im Gegensatz mit London, Add. 29,988, fo. 73 ff., keine Ostervesper). Dies sind:

(a) Alleluia 'Excita' (Dom. I Adv.) fo. 1. Diese Melodie kehrt zurück unter Nr. 22, d.h. Alleluia 'Laudate pueri'.

(b) Alleluia 'Ostende' (Dom. II Adv.), fo. 2. Dieselbe Melodie in Nr. 29, Alleluia 'Quoniam confirmata est'.

(c) Alleluia 'Dominus regnavit' (Nat. Dni. II), fo. 12 und 12 v. (siehe hieroben unter Nr. 2).

(d) Alleluia 'Dies sanctificavit' (Nat. Dni. III), fo. 14 r. (Alleluia-secunda nicht ausgeschrieben; siehe hieroben unter Nr. 4.)

(e) Alleluia 'Beatus vir' (S. Johannis Ev. I) fo. 16 v. Diese Melodie in Nr. 18 und 21 Alleluia 'Qui confidunt' (ohne Alleluia-secunda).

Auch hier fällt wieder auf, daß durchaus nicht das Bedürfnis ein neues musikalisches Vesper-Opus zu schaffen gegenwärtig war, aber daß man aus dem beschränkten Melodienmaterial der Advents- und Weihnachtsalleluia geschöpft hat, ohne jedoch *ein* vollständiges neues Groß-Alleluia zu kreieren. Das altrömische Messerepertoire verfügte über verhältnismäßig wenig Alleluiamelodien; man findet sie (auch in musikalischer Beziehung) in dem altgregorianischen Repertoire zurück, jedoch mit dem nicht unwichtigen Unterschied, daß die altrömischen Alleluia-verse vom ersten Sonntag des Advents ab in der Form eines hinzugefügten Alleluia-secunda beginnen, während diese Form in dem altgregorianischen Repertoire nicht vorkommt. Es ist

---

[1] Wellesz, op. cit., S. 35 und *Das Musikwerk*, S. 13.

möglich und selbst wahrscheinlich, daß diese *Form* (a–b–a) (nicht die Melodie) aus dem Osten übernommen ist, aber es ist ebensosehr wahrscheinlich, daß diese Form der Alleluia-secunda in dem altrömischen Choral für die Franken der Anlass zum Komponieren der *melodiae longissimae* war. Es ist deutlich, daß die Pilger von jenseits der Alpen, die diese päpstlichen Ostervesper mitmachten, hierfür ein besonderes Interesse hatten (darum auch das Kopieren der Rubriken und Texte). Die Bewunderung Amalarius' nach seiner Romreise in 831–2 muß für uns selbstverständlich sein: 'Alleluia canitur cum omni supplemento èt excellentia versuum èt sequentiarum' (man beachte das Zweifache: 1. *Versus*, 2. *sequentiae*, womit doch wohl die *sequentiae* des Alleluia gemeint sein werden).

Doch kehren wir zu dem, was wir bequemlichkeitshalber 'die übrigen Alleluia und ihre Verse' nennen, zurück.

Nr. 27, ῞Οτι θεὸς μέγας' (lat. 'Quoniam Deus magnus') hat eine Melodie, die, wie Musikbeisp. 4 zeigt, in starkem Masse von dem gregorianischen Alleluia mit Vers abhängig ist. Der griechische Vers auch Nr. 27 und 25.

Von einer späteren Hand ist in Vat., lat. 5319, fo. 94 r. an ein Alleluia (prima?) der griechische Vers ῾Επι σοὶ Κύριε' hinzugefügt. Es ist eine Melodie im III. Kirchenton, die stark an die Melodie zu demselben Text im Lateinischen des Gregorianischen 'In te Domine speravi', die ebenfalls im III. Kirchenton steht, erinnert. *Sextuplex* gibt dies Alleluia (Nr. 82) zum Fer. III Pasch. (Nr. 89) Dom. III p. Pasch. und (Nr. 173) Dom. I p. Pent.

Das Studium der päpstlichen Ostervesper führt nach obenstehenden Untersuchungen zu zwei voneinander abweichenden Einsichten. Die erste ist die einer unwidersprechlich großartigen musikalischen Manifestation[1]; die zweite die einer Vielheit an Melodienwiederholungen. Entwurf und Konstruktion müssen in einer Zeit stattgefunden haben, in der 1. die musikalische Schaffenskraft gering war; 2. in der man eine Vorliebe hatte, griechische Texte als Übersetzungen der lateinischen Alleluiavers-Texte zu verwenden. In Hinsicht auf die Beziehungen mit dem altbyzantinischen Repertoire steht es keineswegs fest, daß unmittelbare Beziehungen zwischen diesen Melodien und dem altrömischen resp. altgregorianischen Repertoire bestehen, was jedoch nicht verhindert, daß das letztgenannte Repertoire sehr gut melodisch mehr oder weniger von dem byzantinischen abhängig sein kann; in Hinsicht auf die Form der hinzugefügten Alleluia-secunda in dem altrömischen Repertoire, bemerkte ich schon, daß hier gut der Osten zum Vorbild genommen sein kann. Diese Form war etwas Eigenes des altrömischen und altmailändischen Repertoires, aber nicht des gregorianischen Repertoires.[2]

Das Vorhergehende führt noch zu einer anderen wichtigen Konklusion. Die Groß-Alleluia der Ostervesper — als zentraler Bestandteil — sind das Gegenteil eines neu konstruierten Werkes, sondern ein eklektisches Ganzes bestehender Melodien, meisten aus der zweiten Weihnachtsmesse ('Dominus regnavit') entnommen, der Rest — abgesehen von dem Alleluia der Ostermesse — gehört überwiegend zu den bestehenden Melodien der Advents- und Weihnachtszeit. Mit

---

[1] Amalarius (*Lib. de Ord. Ant.*, c. 52, ed. J. M. Hanssens, iii, S. 83) spricht von 'De glorioso officio'.

[2] Auch der altmailändische liturgische Gesang hatte enge Beziehungen mit den altrömischen Ostervespern. Siehe hierüber E. Moneto Caglio, *I Responsori* (Mailand, 1957), S. 541–3; über All. 'Dominus regnavit', S. 546–8; M.

Huglo, op. cit., S. 123; ders., *Fonti e Paleografia del Canto Ambrosiano* (Mailand, 1956), S. 122, 123, 136; H. Husmann, *Anuario Musical*, xii (1957), S. 17 ff. Das *Antiphonale Missarum juxta Rituum S. Eccl. Mediolanensis* (Rom, 1935) hat (ohne Alleluia-secunda) auf S. 294 'Hallelujah. Dominus regnavit' und auf S. 293 'Hallelujah. Venite, exultamus'.

anderen Worten, das Ganze ist in das schon bestehende Repertoire der Alleluiaverse der Messe verwoben. Dies feststellend, muß man konkludieren: da diese Ostervesper das *Eigene* der *Schola Cantorum* waren und dort gesungen wurden 'in ea statione' wo 'in qua apostolicus celebrat' und durch Ersatz der gewöhnlichen Verse nach den Psalmen durch die Groß-Alleluia entstanden sind; schließlich, da diese Melodien völlig mit dem altrömischen Repertoire verwoben sind (mit Namen dem Advents-Weihnachtszyklus), muß hieraus konkludiert werden, daß der altrömische und nicht der gregorianische Choral das eigene Repertoire der *Schola Cantorum* war. Solange der Zusammenhang zwischen 'den päpstlichen Ostervespern' und dem altrömischen Repertoire nicht deutlich war und man an ein abgesondertes Musikopus denken konnte, konnte man die Hypothese stellen, dass die *Schola* das Gregorianische sang, doch 'on exceptional occasions',[1] das Altrömische während der Ostervesper. Diese Hypothese ist für die Musikwissenschaft nun wohl durch das Vorhergehende wiederlegt.[2]

Etwas anderes ist die Frage, ob man mit diesem Ausgangspunkt weiter zur Geschichte des altrömischen Chorals und insbesondere dieser Ostervesper durchdringen kann. Die obenstehenden zitierten Texte weisen darauf, daß die *dignitas apostolica* diese besonderen Vesper entstehen liess; eine *dignitas*, die auch der Anlaß für das Einbringen der griechischen Texte war. Wann kann dies geschehen sein?

Als Antwort auf diese Frage wird im allgemeinen an N. Andrieu verwiesen, der eine zu vage Antwort gibt ('du VIe siècle au milieu du VIIIe') um damit die Vergriechung der Liturgie in diesen Vespern des *Ordo Romanus I* zu erklären. Zu einer deutlicheren historischen Abgrenzung

---

[1] S. J. P. van Dijk, 'The Urban and Papal Rites in 7th- and 8th-Century Rome', *Sacris Eruditi*, xii (1961), S. 425: "Again, no doubt is possible: some papal services were sung in Old-Roman chant"; S. 449: "The solemn Easter vespers too were exceptional occasions at which urban chant was sung in the presence of the pope", ders., 'The Old-Roman Rite', *Studia Patristica*, v (1962), S. 200: 'The Easter vespers of the Apostolicus at his patrimonium were a traditional concession to what may well have been the local custom.' Siehe ferner S. 199 über die Ostervesper im Altrömischen: '. . . but the whole set-up was exceptional; the vespers were not in accordance with the use either of the pope's chapel or his *patrimonium*. In Amalar's days the circumstances were very different, but they still suggest that even the *dignitas apostolica* was the reason why Old-Roman vespers were sung in his presence. An exception was made for that feast in favour of a long-standing tradition.' Ich bemerke hierbei: Amalarius erklärt wohl die besondere liturgische Form und die griechischen Texte in diesen Ostervespern mit der *dignitas apostolica*, aber über die Musik spricht er nicht; folglich ist die These, daß diese *dignitas* sich auf die 'exception' altrömisch zu singen bezieht, nur eine Interpretation.

[2] Es wundert nicht, daß man schon im 9. Jh. für dieses 'Gloriosum Officium' der päpstlichen Ostervesper durch das Abschreiben dieses *Ordo Romanus* jenseits der Alpen, vor allem wegen der griechischen Alleluiaverse, großes Interesse hatte. Vorkommend in 'gregorianischen' Antiphonaria oder Gradualia werden sie niemals mit gregoria-

nischen Melodien wiedergegeben (vgl. M. Huglo, 'Le chant "vieux-romain"', S. 120, N. 1 und J. Gajard, '"Vieux-romain" et "Grégorien"' in *Études Grégoriennes*, iii [1959], S. 14–15). Daß diese Vesper bei den Franken gesungen wurden, ist vor allem wegen des 'memoratum cursum celebramus' von Amalarius wahrscheinlich. Daß sie gesungen werden *konnten*, folgt aus der Tabelle. Daß eine Schola, die das gregorianische Repertoire sang, Ostervesper mit altrömischen Melodien zu Texten, welche auch im Gregorianischen ihre Melodien hatten, entwerfen und singen würden, ist zu ungereimt um Hypothese sein zu können. Da diese Ostervesper jenseits der Alpen mit Musiknotation (also ohne gregorianische Melodien) nicht vorkommen (man denke hierbei an die im Gregorianischen fehlenden Alleluia-secunda und die selten vorkommenden griechischen Verse) erachte ich es als wahrscheinlicher, daß man sie mit den für die Franken merkwürdigen altrömischen Melodien sang — insofern sie gesungen wurden! — genauso wie man für die *Missa Graeca* und eine Anzahl byzantinischer Melodien Interesse hatte (vgl. Wellesz, op. cit.). Die Überlieferung weist jedoch darauf, daß dies Singen der Ostervesper (oder ein Teil davon) nur sporadisch und regional oder lokal stattgefunden hat. Noch eine Bemerkung hinsichtlich der Meinung Gajards im Zusammenhang mit dem Tonarium von St.-Riquier: dieses Tonarium (vor 795) hatte sowohl das altrömische wie das gregorianische Repertoire als Quelle. Es ist hier nicht am Ort darauf näher einzugehen.

für das Entstehen dieser Vesper (den Terminus ante quem formt *Ordo Rom. XXVII*, Mitte 8. Jh.) kommt man nach dem Studium der politischen und religiösen Geschichte zwischen Rom und Byzanz im 7. Jh. Durch den Monothelismus standen Rom und Byzanz sich in der ersten Hälfte dieses Jhs. wie zwei Länder im Krieg gegenüber. Man erinnere sich an die schwache Haltung des Papstes Honorius I (625–38), die Martern in Konstantinopel und die Verbannung des Papstes Martinus I (645–55?). Kaiser Constantius II (641–68) wünschte die Residenz des byzantinischen Kaiserreichs nach Rom zu verlegen und die Macht des Papstes zu brechen. Wie ein Wolf im Schafspelz besuchte er Rom in 663, eignete sich da mit kaiserlicher Selbstverständlichkeit die nötigen Kostbarkeiten an und wird von Papst Vitalianus (657–72) mit großen Ehren empfangen.[1] Der Kaiser ist zufrieden mit dem Papst, aber wird kurze Zeit danach ermordet. Erst unter Papst Agatho (678–81) ist von einem redlich guten Verhältnis mit dem Kaiser von Byzanz die Rede: der Monothelismus konnte verurteilt werden ohne daß dies zu einem Bruch mit Byzanz führte; der Papst macht jedoch das Ende des öcumenischen Konziliums in Konstantinopel nicht mehr mit. Seine Nachfolger, Leo II (682–3), Benedictus II (684–5), Johannes V (685–6), Conon (686–7) lebten zu kurz um Vorteil aus diesem verbesserten Verhältnis zu ziehen. Dies konnte erst unter und durch Sergius I (687–701), den ersten Papst des 7. Jhs., der sich als Papst über den Kaiser Justinianus (685–95; 705–11) zu stellen wußte und ihm in religiösen Angelegenheiten seinen Willen auflegte, geschehen.

Er hatte den Vorteil aus dem Osten zu kommen. Syrier von Geburt, kam er als Erwachsener von Sizilien nach Rom. Er wünschte in den geistlichen Stand aufgenommen zu werden und es lag auf der Hand, daß er in einem griechischen Kloster in Rom herangebildet wurde[2]. Papst Adeodatus (672–6) ließ ihn jedoch — laut dem *Liber Pontificalis*[3] — 'wegen seiner Begabtheit für das Studium und seiner Musikalität' die Seminaristenausbildung in einem der Basilikaklöster von St. Peter folgen.[4] Seine 'Karriere' verlief außerordentlich flott: 675 Beginn der Ausbildung;

---

[1] *Lib. Pont.*, i, S. 343.

[2] G. Ferrari, *Early Roman Monasteries* (1957), S. 37–40; 283 f.

[3] 'Quia studiosus erat et capax in officio cantilenae' (*Lib. Pont.* i, S. 371).

[4] Dies geht aus dem in Marmor gravierten Text zu einer Gabe für die Kirche der Hl. Susanna (*Lib. Pont.*, i, S. 371) hervor; die Verweisung in Nr. 2 von Duchesne nach Note 37 muß lauten: 38. Auf s. 375 der (mutilierte) Text laut M. de Rossi ('Nutritoris nostri principis apostolorum').

Es ist hier am Ort die Entwicklungsgeschichte der Römischen Schola Cantorum zur Sprache zu bringen. Sowohl A. Chavasse (*Le Sacramentaire Gélasien* [1957], S. 86) als S. J. P. van Dijk (*Ephemerides Liturgicae*, lxxvii [1963], S. 343) weisen darauf, daß Gregorius I (*Lib. Antif.*, i, 312) die tägliche öffentliche Messe in den Basilikakirchen des St. Peter und St. Paul einführte. Van Dijk schließt hieraus, daß es damals eine *Schola Cantorum* gegeben haben muß, die diese Dienste versorgte. Wenn man annehmen würde, daß zur Zeit Gregorius I das gregorianische Messerepertoire schon bestand, jedenfalls das im neumatischen Stil der Messe-antiphone, dann ist Van Dijks Folgerung berechtigt. Doch dies kann man ohne weiteres nicht annehmen. Annehmlicher ist es, daß die Römischen Cantores-Solisten, für die Gregorius für die Zukunft das Gebot des Diakonats abweist, die solistischen Partien, auch in der neu eingeführten täglichen Messe, sangen, doch daß die übrigen Messegesänge von den *clerici circumstantes* gesungen wurden.

Anders wurde dies bei der Reformation des Kirchengesanges, die in dem gregorianischen Choral ausmündete, eine Reformation, die ich den Mönchen der Basilikaklöster des St. Peter rund 650 zuschreibe. Dadurch kann man eine *monachi-schola* annehmen, wie auch einen *archicantor*, so wie man ihn in der Person des Johannes archicantor (668–70) kennt. Bei der Einführung der Reformation des Gesanges zu den altrömischen Ostervespern (wahrscheinlich unter Vitalianus [657–72]) war wiederum eine *schola* nötig, bestehend aus Cantores-Solisten und den *pueri* (anfänglich die Waisen aus dem Orphanotrophium). Diese päpstliche *Schola Cantorum* lag in der Nähe der St. Johannes von Lateranen. So gesehen hatte Joh. Diaconus rund 885 nicht unrecht, wenn er über den *status* der beiden *Scholae Cantorum* in Rom spricht, nl. die von St. Peter und die von St. Johannes von Lateranen.

Da ich die Aufmerksamkeit auf Johannes archicantor lenke, ist es vielleicht dienlich hinsichtlich seiner Sendung bei den Angelsachsen daran zu erinnern, daß er laut Beda

683 Priesterweihe (es gab damals sehr wenig Priesterweihen); 687 zum Papst gewählt.[1] Auf dem Gebiet der liturgischen Erneuerungen verknüpft das *Liber Pontificalis* seinen Namen mit dem Fest der Kreuzerhöhung,[2] an die Prozessionen auf den Mariafesten[3] und der Einführung des 'Agnus Dei' in die Messe;[4] letzteres ist kennzeichnend für seine Charakterfestigkeit, denn das 'Agnus Dei' (bei den östlichen Kirchen immer noch ausschließlich in den syrischen Kirchen vorkommend) war, wegen der Symbolisierung von Christus als Lamm, von dem Konzilium 'in Trullo' (681) verurteilt worden, aber Papst Sergius störte sich nicht an dieser Kanonbestimmung.

Stellt man die Frage, wann ein Papst die Messeliturgie (*Ordo Rom. I*) und die Ostervesper (*Ordo Rom. XXVII*) in byzantinischem Geist und mit griechischen Texten im 7. Jh. organisiert hat, dann kann dies aus historischem Gesichtspunkt nicht vor der Regierung des Papstes Sergius I (687) liegen. Als *terminus ante quem* weist *Ordo Rom. XXVII* nach der Mitte des 8. Jhs., aber dann muß dies als ein bei den Franken schon bekannter Ritus gesehen werden. Obwohl ich es (mit anderen) wohl als wahrscheinlich erachte, daß hierbei Papst Sergius der liturgische Reorganisator war, ist es völlig verantwortbar, wenn man diese Reorganisation zwischen die Jahre 687–730 stellt, demnach auch vor die Einführung der Ostervesper. Folglich ist dies die Periode, die ich am Anfang dieses Beitrags 'Periode II' genannt habe. Wann fällt dann für den altrömischen Choral 'Periode I', die Periode in der das Jahrrepertoire der Messen zustande kam?

Ich erinnere an den Text des Radolfo de Rivo (Ende 14. Jh.): 'Et exinde apud Romanos beatus Gregorius et Vitalianus papae cantum Romanum receperunt'; an den oft zitierten Text des Ekkehard V, dessen Formulierung durchaus nicht an eine von ihm oder anderen ersonnene Geschichte denken lässt: 'Hic est ille Vitalianus cuius *adhuc* cantum *quando apostolicum celebrat* quidam, qui dicuntur Vitaliani, solent edere in praesentia eius.'[5] Auch erinnere ich an die anderweitig[6] beschriebene Rivalität zwischen den Mönchen und den sekulieren Geistlichen in der ersten Hälfte des 7. Jhs. in Rom, um die Macht an der päpstlichen Kurie zu bekommen, eine Rivalität, die in den Jahren 604–40 am größten war; hiermit im Zusammenhang ist nach dem *Ordo Rom. XIX* (Andrieu, iii, S. 224) zu verweisen, in dem eine Aufzählung (8. Jh.) eines Mönches vorkommt, der Rom besuchte und berichtete, daß nach den Päpsten Gregorius und Martinus I (649–55?) die Äbte der Basilikaklöster bei dem S. Peter die Entwicklung des Kirchengesanges in Händen haben,

einen Kirchengesang brachte 'sicut ad *Sanctum Petrum* Romae agebatur'. Es ist übrigens bekannt, daß Beda keine Gelegenheit vorbei gehen ließ zu betonen, daß der Kirchengesang bei den Angelsachsen auf Gregorius den Gr. zurückgeht und die Verbreitung außerdem über die *discipuli B. Gregorii* nach ihren *successores* verlief. Wenn er jedoch über Johannes archicantor spricht, fehlt plötzlich jegliche Beziehung mit Gregorius. Warum? Kann hier nicht die Reformation des Kirchengesanges in das 'Gregorianische' die Ursache sein?

Schließlich weise ich darauf, daß der Ausdruck *ordo cantorum* und *scola* die ältesten Mitteilungen sind. In 1954 teilte M. Andrieu mir mit, daß der vollständige Terminus *scola cantorum* zum ersten Mal in *Ordo Rom. XXIII*, (iii, 273) wahrscheinlich erste Hälfte des 8. Jhs., vorkommt: in dem *Ordo Rom. XXXVI* (Andrieu, iv, S. 195 f.) aus ca. 897 ist es die gewöhnliche Benennung.

Es ist hier nicht am Ort auf folgendes näher einzugehen:

Die Termini *scola* (*ordo cantorum*) haben an erster Stelle Beziehung auf die *infantes*, mit andern Worten auf Anstellung der *infantes* neben den *cantores viriles*; ebensowenig kann hier auf das Amt dieser *infantes* eingegangen werden, die allmählich mehr von demjenigen, was früher den *cantores viriles* zugewiesen war (der Vers des Graduale und das Alleluia), übernehmen.

[1] *Lib. Pont.*, i, S. 371, B. 1.

[2] *Lib. Pont.*, i, S. 374, 376, N. 28; Chavasse, op. cit., S. 361.

[3] *Lib. Pont.*, i, S. 381, N. 43; Hesbert, *Sextuplex*, S. lxxx–lxxxii, lxxxviii; Chavasse, op. cit., S. 376 f.

[4] *Lib. Pont.*, i, S. 376, 381.

[5] J. Smits van Waesberghe, 'The Two Versions of Gregorian Chant', *6th Congress of the I.M.S.*, Oxford, 1955, N. 11.

[6] Ders., 'Neues über die Schola Cantorum zu Rom', *Kongreßbericht 2. Internat. Kongress. f. Kirchenmusik, 1954* (1955), S. 111–19.

eine Angabe die von dem 'archicantor ecclesiae beati apostoli Petri et abbas monasterii beati Martini'[1] Johannes (gest. 680) bestätigt wird. Wenn der Streit zwischen Sekulieren und Mönchen eine unüberkömmliche Entfremdung zwischen diesen beiden Gruppen entstehen ließ, dann ist es begreiflich, daß, wenn die Mönche auf kirchenmusikalischem Gebiet — jedenfalls zeitlich — die Macht nahmen oder bekamen,[2] auch die Gegenpartei auf demselben Gebiet nicht still gesessen hat und Anlaß gab zu einem 'cantu quando apostolicus celebrat', dem altrömischen Choral der 'Vitaliani,' genannt nach Papst Vitalianus (657–72).

In diesem Zusammenhang darf es einem nicht entgehen, daß, obwohl die Meinungen über die Frage, ob das Altrömische wohl oder nicht älter als das Gregorianische ist, bis jetzt noch geteilt sind, man sich doch wohl über den Standpunkt in Hinsicht auf die Melodienunterschiede der beiden Repertoire einig ist: hier ist *bewußt* danach gestrebt nicht dieselben Melodien zu übernehmen. Dom Louis Brou schreibt hierüber: 'Partout se manifeste un parti-pris constant de cotoyer le motif grégorien (dans le 'vieux-romain' Sm.v.W.) sans jamais le reproduire purement et simplement: imiter la mélodie traditionelle, tout en la démarquant à chaque pas, telle semble être la préoccupation laquelle le compositeur a dû obéir la plupart du temps.'[3] So auch Helmut Hucke: 'Est ist ausgeschlossen, dass die eine die zersungene Fassung der anderen ist. Vielmehr liegt eine Neuformung vor und dieser Eindruck verstärkt sich beim Vergleichen der übrigen Melodien. . . . Es ist als die Weise von dem einen Repertoire in das andere übertragen worden, es sind nicht einzelne Melodien übernommen worden.'[4] Und Dr. Hans Schmidt, der u.a. darauf hinweist, daß da, wo das Gregorianische einen Intervallsprung hat, das Altrömische den Intervallsabstand 'stufenweise' auffüllt,[5] so daß er sich fragt: 'Sollte keine bewußte Absicht dahinterstehen?' Man kann in diese vergleichende Studie auch die altmailändischen Melodien mit einbeziehen. Auch dort, ebenso wie in den altrömischen Melodien ist von einem *bewußt* anders Schreiben einer selben syllabischen Grundmelodie oder einer neumatischen oder melismatischen Gregorianischen Melodie die Rede, das heißt melismatisch gegenüber syllabisch und, wenn beide Repertoire (altmailändisch und altrömisch) ebenso wie das Gregorianisch die melismatische Form haben, dann sind noch fortwährend die Unterschiede auffallend, wie z.B. der Ersatz der offenen Intervalle durch stufenweise Tonfolgen. Am kennzeichnendsten sind die syllabischen Rezitativpassagen des Gregorianischen, die nur ausnahmsweise mit den beiden anderen Repertoiren übereinstimmen, sowie die Behandlung der Tonstufenwiederholungen in dem Gregorianischen, wie z.B. *bi-* und *tristropha*, *bivirga* u.s.w.[6]

Wenn hier von einer bewußten Absicht einer Umsetzung einer bestehenden Melodie die Rede ist — eine Umsetzung gemäß bestimmter Prinzipen —,[7] dann kann eine Erinnerung an

[1] Beda, *Historia Eccl. gentis anglorum*, lib. IV, cap. 10; *Historia Abbatum*, cap. 3.

[2] Die Frage ob Johannes archicantor das Gregorianische nach Britannien brachte oder nicht, ist noch wenig untersucht worden. Daß er dort das Altrömische verbreitet haben sollte, muß, die Überlieferung und den Einfluß der Angelsachsen-Iren auf die westeuropäische Kultur im 9. Jh. in Anbetracht genommen, wohl ernstlich bezweifelt werden. Es ist hier jedoch nicht am Ort hierauf näher einzugehen.

[3] *Revue Grégorienne*, xxiv (1939), S. 86.

[4] *Archiv. f. Mw.*, xii (1955), S. 77.

[5] *Festschrift Schmidt-Görg* (Bonn 1957), S. 291.

[6] Auffallend ist im Altrömischen in den Rezitativmelodien die Verzierung der Töne E und H mit dem *torculus* E-F-D und h-c-a, während die Töne c und d resp. mit c-d-c und d-e-d verziert werden; die Alleluiaverse geben hiervon viele Beispiele.

[7] Es wurde schon bemerkt, daß im Altrömischen das Moduseigene viel weniger überzeugend als im Gregorianischen zum Ausdruck kommt. Die Finaltöne der Tabelle geben hiervon verschiedene Beispiele, namentlich Nr. 21 wo die Reihenfolge der Schlußtöne ist: F, F, G, G, a, G, F.

den Streit zwischen den Mönchen und den sekulieren Klerikern in Rom um die Macht am päpstlichen Hof vielleicht auch mit einbezogen werden: 'Having enjoyed the approval and support of St. Gregory, the monasteries of Rome during this [seventh] century must have felt the clerical reaction against them that was slowly manifesting itself. . . . This situation [nämlich Johannes IV (640–2): *pro clero*] must have continued until the reign of Adeodatus (672–6).'[1] Und was Mailand betrifft (über die altbeneventanischen Melodien haben wir zu wenig Angaben), kann man, ganz nach Wunsch, der Hypothese viel oder wenig Wert beimessen, daß dort eine, in Hinsicht auf Rom, konkurrierende Einstellung Anlaß wurde zur Formung eines eigenen Repertoirestils mit Melodien, die in jedem Fall im Wesen eine deutliche Ähnlichkeit mit denen des Gregorianischen und Altrömischen zeigen: 'Nec ipsa etiam Romani palatii basilica Mediolanensis metropolis ita in talibus ab omnibus dissidet' (Abelardus).

Wie dies auch sei, es wird deutlich sein, daß, wenn meine These einer bewußten, voreingenommenen Kontrareformation des Altgregorianischen und Altrömischen richtig ist und diese Kontrareformation ziemlich bald auf das Zustandekommen des altgregorianischen Repertoires folgte, bei vergleichenden Studien dieser beiden Repertoire hinsichtlich der Frage 'älter oder jünger' die Meinungen doch immer geteilt bleiben werden. Die vergleichende Studie an sich ist für die Lösung dieser Frage höchstwahrscheinlich nicht genügend; erst wenn man von der obengenannten These ausgeht, nämlich von einer voreingenommenen melodischen Kontrareformation, wird man sowohl diese These auf ihren Wert prüfen können, als auch zu einer befriedigenden Antwort auf die Frage 'älter oder jünger' kommen können.

Es kommt mir dann auch vor, daß das Studium der altrömischen Ostervesper uns doch zur Lösung des 'Problems des Altrömischen 'einen Schritt näher bringt. Es ist jedoch auch nötig eventuelle Einwände hinsichtlich der obenstehenden Konklusionen zu studieren. Man könnte es z.B. befremdend finden, daß—denn aus dem Obenstehenden würde hervorgehen, daß, da Pippin und vor allem Karl d. Gr. den nicht-päpstlichen Gesang in ihrem Reich verbreiten ließen — der Kaiser noch für seinen eigenen Hof, noch für sein Reich den päpstlichen Hofgesang wählte. Aber was ist die Antwort, wenn wir folgende Frage stellen: war der Kaiser in liturgischen Angelegenheiten konservativ oder progressiv? Wollte er das Beste, das Schönste *seiner eigenen* Zeit und gemäß der Wahrnehmungen in Rom, oder wünschte er für die Einführung der Liturgie auf frühere Zeiten zurückzugreifen? Der Brief des Papstes Hadrianus I (772–95), in dem der Papst die Bitte des Kaisers mitteilt, ihm ein 'sacramentarium inmixtum Gregorianum' zu senden, zu gewähren, macht es unmittelbar deutlich, daß er, mittels seines Liturgieministers Alcuinus, auf die angelsächsische Tradition der Gregoriusverehrung 'in liturgicis' seine Erneuerungen durchzuführen wünscht. Es hätte anders gehen können, aber es war Alcuinus, der den Kaiser auf das 'Gregorianum inmixtum' und die reine Liturgietradition, die gemäß Alcuinus Schulung auf Gregorius zurückging, gewiesen haben muß.[2]

Wenn man die Tatsache, daß die Musik der päpstlichen Ostervesper mit dem altrömischen

[1] G. Ferrari, *Early Roman Monasteries*, (Rom. 1957), S. 389 ff.

[2] 'In diesem Schreiben klingt irgendwie etwas von den Gesprächen nach, die Karl d. Gr. mit Alkuin und Paulus Diaconus hinsichtlich eines einheitlichen fränkischen Saktramentars geführt hat. Man scheint am Königshof wert darauf gelegt zu haben, ein Sacramentarium inmixtum nach dem Brauch der Stadt Rom (deshalb nicht des päpstlichen Hofes. Sm. v. W.) zu erhalten' (Kl. Gamber, 'Heimat und Ausbildung der Gelasiana saec. VIII', *Sacris Erudiri*, xiv, [1963], S. 128 ff.).

Repertoire verwoben ist, oder, anders gesagt, wenn man, da die Alleluiamelodien des alt-römischen Messerepertoires die Groß-Alleluia dieser Ostervesper formen, die Schlußfolgerung akzeptiert, daß dieses Messerepertoire das Altrömische und folglich das Repertoire der päpstlichen Schola Cantorum war, dann können Texte wie die von Abelardus: 'Sed sola Ecclesia Laterensis ... antiquum tenet officium, nulla filiarum suarum in hoc eam sequente':[1] oder die des *Ordo* des Hl. Johannes von Lateranen (ca. 1050) über das Fest des Hl. Johannes des Täufers: '... ex diversis terrarum partibus clerici ad serviendum Deo ibidem conveniunt, Romanorum more cantare nesciunt'[2] in ihrer auf der Hand liegenden Bedeutung — und also ohne ausführlichen Kommentar[3] — in dem Sinne, nämlich das Eigene des altrömischen Repertoires, verstanden werden. Noch andere Texte können in diesem Zusammenhang zitiert werden, doch es ist hier nicht am Ort darauf näher einzugehen.

Würde man schließlich, in Hinsicht auf meine Einteilung in drei Perioden für diese Ostervesper eine etwas genauere chronologische Einteilung wünschen, dann stelle ich Periode I in die Regierungszeit des Papstes Vitalianus (657–72). Periode II fängt aus den obenstehenden Gründe rund 690 an (Sergius I 687–701); die liturgische und musikalische Ordnung der Ostervesper muß in die Jahre 678–830 gestellt werden. Die Handhabung setzt sich zur Zeit des *Ordo XXVII, XXXB*, Amalarius und, wenn man hierbei den Datum des 'Antiphonarium von Compiègne' einzubeziehen wünscht (660–80), bis an das Ende des 9. Jhs., wenn nicht noch später, fort. Periode III überliefert uns die Ostervesper in den altrömischen Gradualia und Antiphonalia, seit dem 11. Jh. als einen eingebürgerten Gebrauch, so daß man darum annehmen kann, daß die Revision mit den Hinzufügungen im 10. Jh. stattgefunden haben wird — dies selbstverständlich weit genommen. Ich erachte es übrigens keinem Zweifel unterlegen, daß die Liturgiehistoriker durch Textvergleich-ungen der Handschriften eine genaue Chronologie dieser Einteilung feststellen werden können:

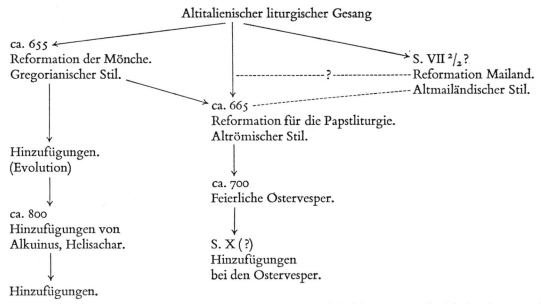

Altitalienischer liturgischer Gesang

ca. 655
Reformation der Mönche.
Gregorianischer Stil.

S. VII $^2/_2$?
Reformation Mailand.
Altmailändischer Stil.

ca. 665
Reformation für die Papstliturgie.
Altrömischer Stil.

Hinzufügungen.
(Evolution)

ca. 800
Hinzufügungen von
Alkuinus, Helisachar.

ca. 700
Feierliche Ostervesper.

S. X (?)
Hinzufügungen
bei den Ostervesper.

Hinzufügungen.

[59]

Scholion: 'Sic omnes laeti recedunt'.

An diese Studie über das *gloriosum officium*, 'un des rites les plus characteristiques de la liturgie papale'[1] möchte ich ein Scholion hinzufügen — sei es auch mit einigen Bedenken, denn der Gegenstand dieses Scholion gäbe Anlaß zum Schreiben eines selbstständigen Beitrags.

Bekanntlich werden die dreifachen päpstlichen Vesper in der Osterwoche täglich mit einem dreimaligen Leeren eines Bechers Wein in der Gegenwart des Papstes beschlossen.[2] Die *cantores* der *Schola* singen danach vor dem Weggehen, wie sie dies auch am Ende der Mahlzeit nach den Lauden am Ostertag tun. Bei letzterem wird eine Ostersequenz: 'Cantores prosam cantant quae sit conveniens Paschae', 'cantant sequentiam quae sit conveniens Paschae, modulatis organis',[3] gesungen. Am wahrscheinlichsten ist es, daß hier die Ostersequenz 'Clara gaudia festa paschalia' gesungen wurde. Sowohl diese Ostersequenz als das 'modulatis organis' — das man wieder mit den Worten, die Joh. Diakonus über Papst Vitalianus schrieb 'susceptum modulationis organum' und mit so viel jüngeren Texten, die dann wieder Papst Vitalianus mit dem Organum-gesang in Zusammenhang bringen kann — geben Anlaß zu ausführlichen Betrachtungen.[4] Dies Scholion will mit nur wenigen Worten auf die *sequentiam graecam* 'πάσχα ἱερὸν' oder *prosam graecam*, die mit der Rubrikhinzufügung: 'Sic omnes laeti recedunt', von dem *primicerius* und den *cantores* der *Schola* nach den Vespern während des Weintrinkens gesungen wurden, eingehen.

Dieser Gesangtext ist deutlich zitiert und man findet diesen Text mit einer Anzahl Veränderungen, ohne den Heilswunsch an den Papst[5] in der byzantinischen Liturgie zurück. Auch die Melodie der byzantinischen Lesart ist bewahrt[6] und Professor Oliver Strunk von der Princeton University, N.J. gab mir hiervon die Transkription.[7] Hieraus zeigt sich, daß dieser Heilswunsch an den Papst (am Ende der römischen Lesart) nicht an die byzantinische Melodie anzupassen ist; auch andere Textvarianten der römischen Lesart sind scheinbar nicht in der byzantinischen Melodienfassung vorgesehen. Das auf der Hand liegendste ist, daß der eine oder andere

Anweisungen geben. Wiederholt ist auf die griechischen Verse in den Ostervespern "written in an extremely corrupt form" (R. J. Snow in W. Apel, *Gregorian Chant*, S. 498) gewiesen. Als Musikologe kann ich darauf weisen, daß bestimmte griechische Gesänge (z.B. Nr. 8) auf ein derartiges 'Zersingen' des Textes weisen, daß die Sänger (11.–12. Jh.) den Textinhalt nicht mehr verstanden und die Silben (infolge der unverantworteten Zusammenziehungen und Scheidungen der Textsilben) nicht genau mit den betreffenden Noten verbanden.

[1] Chavasse, op. cit., S. 322.

[2] Unter Papst Zacharias (741–52) ist von einem bestehenden Brauch die Rede: 'Et post suppleta libatione' (*Lib. Pont.* i, S. 430); siehe den Kommentar von Duchesne, N. 32: 'Le jour de Pâques et toute l'octave, la libation avait lieu après les vêpres, avec une solennité spéciale. Pendant que le pape et tout le clergé vidaient trois coupes réglémentaires, la schola cantorum exécutait un hymne grec: "Πάσχα ἱερὸν ἡμῖν σήμερον".' Siehe auch *Lib. Pont.*, ii, S. 40, N. 51, 52; ferner *Ordo Rom.* (Andrieu, iii, S. 366) *XXVII*, Nr. 78–79; *Ordo Rom.* (Andrieu, iii, S. 477) *XXX B*, Nr. 82; *Ordo Rom.* (Andrieu, ii, S. 141, u. 168) *IV*, Nr. 95; A. Gastoué, *Origines*,

S. 292, 294–6; B. Andoyer, 'L'ancienne liturgie de Bénévent', *Revue du Chant Grég.*, xxii (1913), S. 108, 110; *Pal. Mus.*, xiv, S. 163–4.

[3] *M.P.L.* 78, c. 1045 (ca. 1140). Mit Weinachten findet während der *libatio* die Aufführung einer "sequentia modulatis vocibus" statt (id. c. 1135).

[4] Vgl. u. a. E. Jammers, *Musik in Byzanz, im päpstlichen Rom und im Frankenreich* (Heidelberg, 1962), S. 180 ff.; J. Handschin, *Annales Musicologiques*, ii (1954), s. 56 ff.

[5] Am Schluß muß anstelle von 'Καινὸν Πάπαν' 'Καὶ νῦν Πάπαν,' gelesen werden. Die italienische Aussprache in Anbetracht genommen, kann eine Verwechslung von νυν in -νον leicht stattgefunden haben; Καινόν hat für einen jährlich zurückkommenden Gesang keinen Sinn. Man muß dies im Sinne des 'Et nunc . . .', 'Eia dicite . . .' am Schluß der Tropen und Prosulae sehen.

[6] Michel Huglo verdanke ich ein Photo des Paris, Bibl. Nat., grec 242, fo. 207 mit der altbyzantinischen Notation dieser Melodie.

[7] Nach der jüngeren Lesart der Hs. Iviron 953 (ohne Foliation) und der Hs. Sinai 1471 (fo. 273).

griechisch gesinnte Papst (und man muß hier wohl an die Periode II und Papst Sergius denken), den byzantinischen Text übernehmen und ihn von seiner *Schola Cantorum* gemäß *ihrer* musikalischen Auffassung singen liess. Ist es nicht merkwürdig daß, wenn man die römische Textlesart unter die Melodie desjenigen Alleluia secunda (All. 'Dominus regnavit'), das den zentralen Platz in diesen Ostervespern einnimmt, setzt, sowohl die Phrasierung dieser römischen Lesart, als der Heilswunsch am Schluß sich harmonisch an diese altrömische Melodie anpassen? (siehe Musikbeispiel 5).

(Übs.: U. Schouten-Glass)

TABELLE

Liste der Abkürzungen

M = Messe
V = Vesper
★ = mit Ankündigung

+ = vollständige Melodien
/ = nur das Initium
— = Melodie nicht in der Hs. notiert

Tag	Messe/Vesper	Vat l. 5319 Fo.	Nr.	Text	Psalm	Finalton	Melodie	Ank.	Im Ms.	Der altrömischen Liturgie entnommen	Melodienparallele im Gregorianischen Choral
Dom. Paschal.	M	84 r.	1	Alleluia		G	s. Beisp. I		+	Dom. Resurr.	Idem: All. Pascha nostrum, Epulemur
			a	Pascha nostrum	(1. Cor. 5, 7)	G	idem		+		
			b	Epulemur	(1. Cor. 5, 8)	G	idem		+		
				Alleluia		G	idem		+		
	V	85 r.	2	Alleluia		G	II		+	Nat. Dom. II	Idem: All Dominus regnavit
			a	Dominus regnavit	92, 1	G	IV (III var.)		+		
			b	Parata sedes	92, 2	a	III		+		
			c	Ex tunc a seculo	92, 2	G	I	★	+		
			d	Elevaverunt flum. dom.	92, 3	a	IIIa		+		
			e	Elevaverunt flum. voces. s.	92, 3	G	I	★	+		
				Alleluia		G			+		
	V	85 r.	3	Alleluia		G	s. Beisp. I		/	Dom. Resurr.	s. nr. I
			a	Pascha nostrum	(cf. nr. 1)	G	idem		/		
			b	Christus qui nos		G	I	★	/		
			c	Epulemur		G	s. Beisp. I	(★)	/		
				Alleluia		G	idem				
	V	85 v.	4	Alleluia		D	s. Beisp. 2		+	(Nat. Dom. III)	All. Dies sanctificatus
			a	Ὁ Κύριος ἐβασίλευσεν	92, 1	D	idem		+		
			b	Καὶ γὰρ ἐστερέωσεν	92, 2	D	idem		+		
				Alleluia		D	idem				
	V	86 r.	5	Alleluia		G	IIb		+	Fer. II p. Pent. (u.s.w.)	
			a	Venite exsultemus	94, 1	G	X+IIa		+		
		86 v.	b	Preoccupemus	94, 2	G	IIa+X+II		—		
				Alleluia		G					
Feria II	M	87 r.	6	Alleluia		D	s. Beisp. 2		/	(Nat. Dom. III)	All. Dies sanctificatus
			a	Ὁ Κύριος ἐβασίλευσεν	92, 1	D	idem		—		
				Alleluia		D	idem				
	V	87 v.	7	Alleluia		G	IIa nr. 6		—	(Nat. Dom. II)	All. Dominus regnavit
			a	Domine refugium	89, 1	a	III		+		
			b	A generatione	89, 1	G	I	★	+		
			c	Priusquam fierent montes	89, 2	a	III+III	★	+		
			d	A seculo usque	89, 2	G	I		+		
				Alleluia		G	(IIb)		—		

TABELLE

Liste der Abkürzungen

M = Messe
V = Vesper
★ = mit Ankündigung

+ = vollständige Melodien
/ = nur das Initium
– = Melodie nicht in der Hs. notiert

Tag	Messe Vesper	Vat 1. 5319 Fo.	Nr.	Text	Psalm	Finalton	Melodie	Ank.	Im Ms.	Der altrömischen Liturgie entnommen	Melodienparallele im Gregorianischen Choral
	V	88 r.	8	Alleluia	79, 1	G	II		/	(Nat. Dom. II)	All. Dominus regnavit
			a	Ὁ ποιμαίνων τὸν Ἰσραήλ	79, 2	a	III		+		
			b	Ὁ καθήμενος ἐπὶ τὸν χερουβίμ		G	III+III		+		
			c	Ἄμπελον ἐξ Ἀιγύπτου	79, 9	a	III		+		
			d	Ἐξέβαλες ἔθνη	79, 9	a	III		+		
			e	Ὡδοποίησας ἔμπροσθεν	79, 10	G	III+III		+		
				Alleluia		G	(II)		–		
	V	88 r. 88 r.	9	Alleluia	113, 1	G	II^b		+	(Nat. Dom. II)	(All. Dominus regnavit)
			a	In exitu Israel	113, 1	a	III		+		
			b	De populo	113, 2	G	I		+		
			c	Facta est Iudea	113, 3	G	III^b+I	★	+		
			d	Mare vidit	113, 3	a	III^b	★	+		
			e	Convertus est		G	I		+		
				Alleluia		G	II^a		/		
Feria III	M	89 r.	10	Alleluia	94, 1	G	cf. nr. 5		/		
			a	Venite exsultemus		G			/		
				Alleluia		G			–		
	V	89 v.	11	Alleluia	107, 1	G	II		+	(Nat. Dom. II)	All. Dominus regnavit
			a	Paratum cor	107, 1	a	III+III		+		
			b	Cantabo et psalmum	107, 2	G	I	★	+		
			c	Exsurge gloria mea	107, 2	a	III+III	★	+		
			d	Exsurgam diluculo	107, 7	a	I	★	+		
			e	Ut liberentur electi	107, 7	G	I		+		
			f	Benefac domine		G	II		/		
	V	90 r.	12	Alleluia	77, 1	G	II		+	(Nat. Dom. II)	All. Dominus regnavit
			a	Προσέχετε, λαός μου	72, 2	a	III+III		+		
			b	Ἀνοίξω ἐν παραβολαῖς		G	III+III+I		+		
				Alleluia		a	(II)		/		
	V	90 r.	13	Alleluia	137, 1	G	Adorabo (II) (Kad. II)		+	All. Adorabo Dom. II p. Epiph.	
			a	Confitebor	137, 2	G			+		
			b	Adorabo	137, 2	G(?)	?		/		
			c	Super misericordiam		G	(Kad. II)		/		
				Alleluia		(G)			+		
Feria IV	M	91 r.	14	Alleluia	137, 2	G	Adorabo		/	All. Adorabo Dom. II p. Epiph.	
			a	Adorabo (cf. Fol. 24 r.)		G			–		
				Alleluia		(G)			–		

TABELLE

Liste der Abkürzungen

M = Messe
V = Vesper
* = mit Ankündigung

+ = vollständige Melodien
/ = nur das Initium
− = Melodie nicht in der Hs. notiert

Tag	Messe Vesper	Vat I. 5319 Fo.	Nr.	Text	Psalm	Finalton	Melodie	Ank.	Im Ms.	Der altrömischen Liturgie entnommen	Melodienparallele im Gregorianischen Choral
	V	91 v.	15	Alleluia		G	II (cf. nr. 5a)		/	Dom. I p. Epiph.	
			a	Te decet hymnus	64, 2	G	(cf. nr. 5a)		+		
			b	Replebimur	64, 5	G	I var.	*	+		
			c	Sanctum est templum	64, 5	G	I	*	+		
			d	Mirabile in	64, 6	(G)	I				
				Alleluia					/		
	V	91 v.	16	Alleluia		G	I		+		
			a	Confitemini . . . et invoc.	104, 1	G	III+III+I		+		
			b	Cantate et ei psallite	104, 2	G	III+III+I		+		
				Alleluia		G	(II)		/		
	V	92 v.	17	(Grad. Haec dies)		a			−	Dom. Resurr.	Grad. Haec dies
Feria V	M	92 v.	18	Alleluia		F	Beatus vir		+	Joh. Ev. I	All. Beatus vir
			a	Qui confidunt	124, 1	F			+		
				Alleluia		(F)			−		
Feria VI	M	94 r.	19	Alleluia		E			+		
			a	Ἐπὶ σοὶ Κύριε ἤλπισα	30, 2	G			+		
			b	Κλῖνον πρός με τὸ οὖς σου	30, 3	E			+		
				Alleluia		(?)			−		
	V	94 v.	20	Alleluia		G	II		+		
			a	Letatus sum	121, 1	a	III		+		
			b	In dominum domini	121, 1	G	I	*	+		
			c	Stantes erant	121, 2	a	III		+		
			d	In atriis tuis	121, 2	G	I	*	+		
			e	Rogate quae a pace	121, 6	a	III		+		
			f	Et abundantia	121, 6	G	I	*	+		
				Alleluia		(G)	(II)		−		
	V	94 v.	21	Alleluia		(F)	Beatus vir		/	Joh. Ev. I	All. Beatus vir (21+21a)
			a	Qui confidunt	124, 1	(F)	Beatus vir		/	Nat. Dom. II	All. Dominus regnavit
		95 r.	b	Montes in circuitu	124, 2	G	III+I		+		
			c	Ex hoc nunc	124, 2	G	I	*	+		
			d	Ut non extendant	124, 3	a	IIIa		+		
			e	Benefac domine bonis	124, 4	G	I	*	+		
				Alleluia		(F)			/		

[64]

TABELLE

Liste der Abkürzungen

M = Messe
V = Vesper
★ = mit Ankündigung

+ = vollständige Melodien
/ = nur das Initium
— = Melodie nicht in der Hs. notiert

Tag	Messe Vesper	Vat I. 5319 Fo.	Nr.	Text	Psalm	Finalton	Melodie	Ank.	Im Ms.	Der altrömischen Liturgie entnommen	Melodienparallele im Gregorianischen Choral
Feria VII	M	95 v.	22	Alleluia		E	Excita		+	Dom. I Adv.	All. Excita
				Laudate pueri	112, 1	E	Idem		+		
			a	Sit nomen domini	112, 2	E	Idem var.		+		
			b	Alleluia		(E)			—		
	V	96 r.	23	Alleluia		G	II		+	(Nat. Dom. II)	All. Dominus regnavit
				Cantate domino	97, 1	G	II+I		+		
			a	Notum fac	97, 2	a	III		+		
			b	Ante conspectum	97, 2	G	I	★	+		
			c	Alleluia		(G)	(II)		/		
	V	96 r.	24	Alleluia		G	II		+	(Nat. Dom. II)	All. Dominus regnavit
			a	Ὅτι οὐρανοὶ διηγοῦνται	18, 2	G	III+III+III +I		+		
			b	Ἡμέρα τῇ ἡμέρᾳ	18, 3	G	III+III+I		+		
				Alleluia		(G)	(II)		/		
Dom. oct.	M	96 v.	25	Alleluia	94, 3	G	s. Beisp. (Var. II)		—		All. Dominus regnavit
			a	(cf. fol. 98. r.: "Ὅτι θεὸς μέγας)		G			—		
				Alleluia		G			—		
	V	97 r.	26	Alleluia		G	II		+	(Nat. Dom. II)	All. Dominus regnavit
			a	Δεῦτε ἀγαλλιασώμεθα	94, 1	G	III+III+I		+		
			b	Προσθέσωμεν τὸ πρόσωπον	94, 2	G	III+III+I		+		
				Alleluia		(G)	(II)		—		
	V	97 r.	27	Alleluia	94, 3	G	s. Beisp. (Var. II)		+		Alleluia Quoniam magnus Deus
			a	Ὅτι θεὸς μέγας κύριος							
				Alleluia							
	V	97 v.	28	Alleluia		G	II		+	(Nat. Dom. II)	All. Dominus regnavit
			a	Omnes gentes plaudite	46, 2	G	III+III+I		+		
			b	Quoniam Deus summus	46, 3	G	III+III+I		+		
			c	Ascendit deus in iubilatione	46, 6	G	III+I		+		
				Alleluia		(G)	(II)		—		
Dom. II p.P. 9	M	98 r.	29	Alleluia		G	Ostende (Diffusa est)		+	Ostende: Dom. II Adv. Diffusa: De virgine usw	All. Dominus regnavit
			a	Quoniam confirmata est	116, 2	G	idem		+		
			b	Ὅτι θεὸς μέγας κύριος	94, 3	G			—		
				Alleluia		(G)			—		

[65]

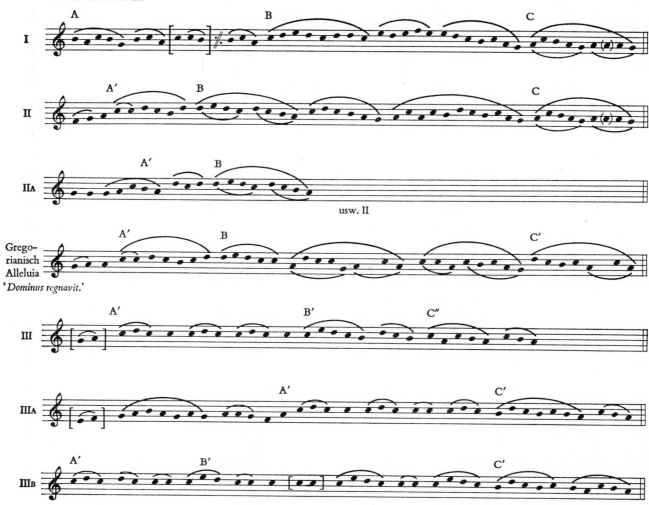

I.

Ankündigen (Annuntiationes)

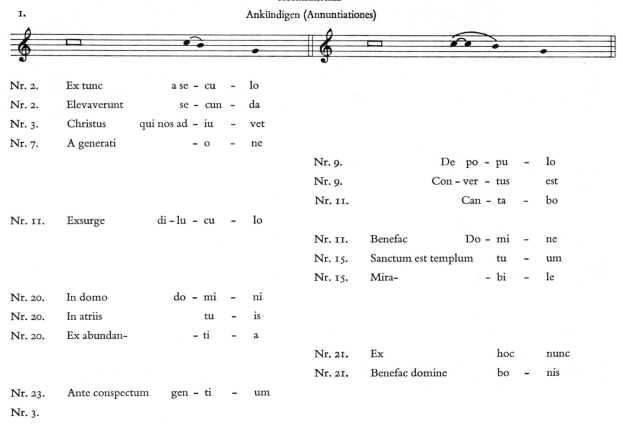

Nr. 2.	Ex tunc	a se – cu – lo
Nr. 2.	Elevaverunt	se – cun – da
Nr. 3.	Christus	qui nos ad – iu – vet
Nr. 7.	A generati	– o – ne

Nr. 9.		De po – pu – lo
Nr. 9.		Con – ver – tus est
Nr. 11.		Can – ta – bo

Nr. 11. Exsurge di – lu – cu – lo

Nr. 11.	Benefac	Do – mi – ne
Nr. 15.	Sanctum est templum	tu – um
Nr. 15.	Mira–	– bi – le

Nr. 20.	In domo	do – mi – ni
Nr. 20.	In atriis	tu – is
Nr. 20.	Ex abundan–	– ti – a

Nr. 21.	Ex	hoc nunc
Nr. 21.	Benefac domine	bo – nis

Nr. 23. Ante conspectum gen – ti – um

Nr. 3.

Alleluia secunda dic Do – mne

Ad. Nr. 3. Ankündigung zur Alleluia – secunda (Pascha Nostra)

1. Primus scholae cum parafonistis infantibus Alleluia (d.h. Alleluia prima): siehe Melodie II.
2. Et respondent parafonistae [viriles]. Wiederholung des Alleluia prima.
3. Sequitur subdiaconus cum infantibus Alleluia. Dominus regnavit et reliqua:

2.

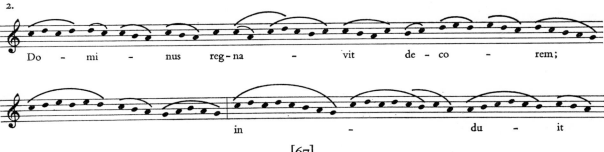

Do – mi – nus reg – na – vit de – co – rem;

in – du – it

in - du - it   Do — mi - nus for — ti - tu — di -

nem   et prae - cin — xit se vir -

tu — tem.

4. Et semper respondent parafonistae [viriles]. Wiederholung des Alleluia prima.
5. Et [parafonistae viriles] adnuntiant verba infantibus. Die Ankündigung:

Pa - ra - ta se - des

6. Versus 'Parata sedes tua Deus' (*parafonistae infantes*):

Pa - ra — ta se — des vi - a De   us.

7. Ankündigung des Folgeverses von den *parafonistae viriles*:

Ex tunc a se-cu — lo

8. (Versus 'Ex tunc a seculo' durch *parafonistae infantes*):

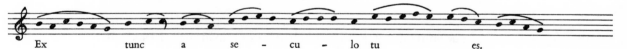

Ex   tunc   a   se - cu - lo tu   es.

9. Iterum Versus 'Elevaverunt flumina Domine'. Ankündigung:

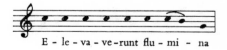

E - le - va - ve-runt flu - mi - na

[68]

10. Idem von den *parafonistae infantes*:

E — le-va-ve — runt flu-mi-na Do — mi — ne.

11. Idem Versus 'Elevaverunt flumina voces suas'. Ankündigung:

E - le - va - ve-runt se - cu - nda

12. Parafonistae infantes:

E — le - va - ve — runt flu - mi - na vo — ces

su — as.

13. Post hos versus salutat primus scolae archidiaconum, et, illo annuente ...
(Salutatio wie im Hs. 5319 zu dem Alleluia 'Pascha nostrum'):

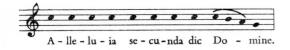

A - lle - lu - ia se - cu-nda dic Do — mine.

14. Incipit Alleluia cum melodiis cum infantibus (*Alleluia secunda*):

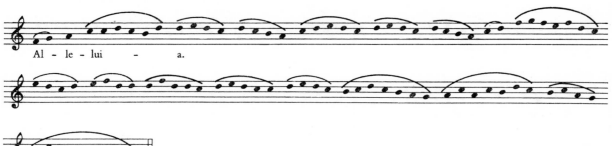

Al - le - lui — a.

15. Qua expleta, respondent parafonistae [Alleluiam] primam.

[69]

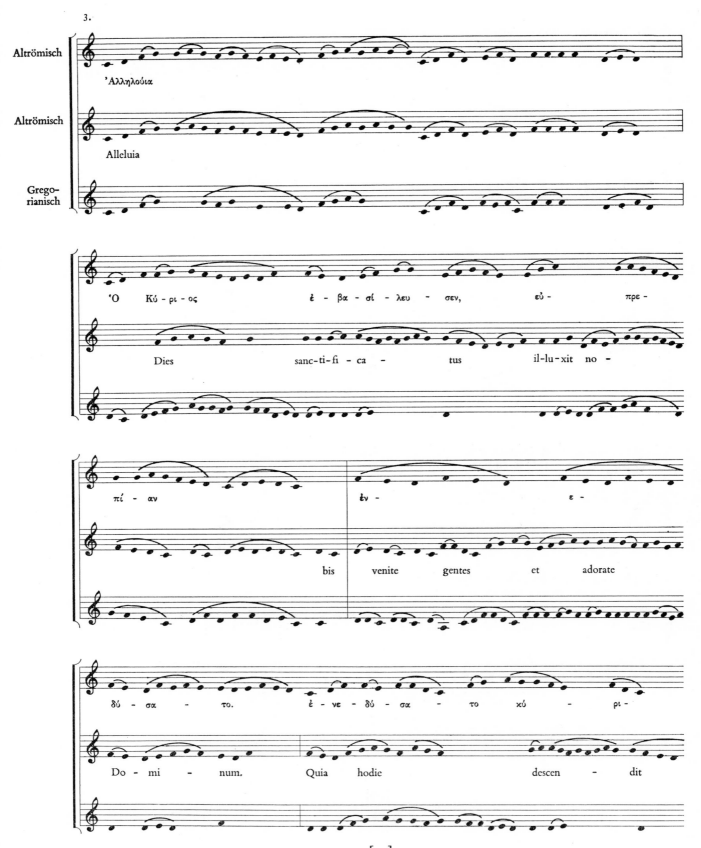

3.

Altrömisch — 'Αλληλούϊα

Altrömisch — Alleluia

Grego- rianisch

'O Κύ - ρι - ος   ἐ - βα - σί - λευ - σεν,   εὐ - πρε -

Dies   sanc-ti-fi - ca -   tus   il-lu-xit no -

πί - αν   ἐν -   ε -

bis   venite   gentes   et   adorate

δύ - σα - το.   ἐ - νε - δύ - σα - το   κύ - ρι-

Do - mi - num.   Quia hodie   descen - dit

ος δύ — να — μιν
lux ma — gna

καὶ πε-ρι-ε-ζώ-σα — το.
su — per terram.

καὶ γὰρ ἐ-στε-ρέ-ω —

σεν τὴν οἰ-χου-με —

νην, ἡ — τις οὐ σα-λευ-θή-σε —

ται

4.

Αλ-λη —————— λού ————— ια ————————

Al - le - lu ———————— ia ——————

[71]

"O - τι θέ - ὸς μέ -

Quo - ni - am De - us   ma -

γας   Κύ   ρι

gnus   Do   mi

ος   καὶ   βασι - λεὺς   μέ   γας

nus   et   rex   ma   gnus

ἐ - πὶ πᾶ   σαν   τὴν

su - per o   mnem

γῆν

ter - ram

5.

Πάσ-χα ἱε-ρὸν ἡμῖν σή-μερον ἀνε-δειχ-νήσ-θη. Πάσ-χα και-νὸν ἅ-γιον. Πάσ-χα μυσ-τι-κόν. Πάσ-χα

παν-σέ-βάσ-μον Πάσχα Χρι-στοῦ τοῦ Λυ-τρω-τοῦ. Πάσ-χα ἄ-μω-μον. Πάσ-χα μέ-γα. Πάσ-χα τῶν πισ-τῶν.

Πάσ-χα τὰς πύ-λας ἡμῖν τοῦ πα-ρα-δεί-σου ἀ-νέ-ω-γε. Πάσ-χα πάν-τας ἀ-να-πλατ-των βρο-τούς.

Καὶ νῦν Πά-παν Χρισ-τέ φύ-λα-ξον.

6

LES CHANTS DE LA *MISSA GRECA* DE SAINT-DENIS

Michel Huglo (Paris)

LE TITRE d'Aréopagite, ajouté à l'auréole de l'évêque et martyr qui évangélisa Lutèce au IIIe siècle,contribua pour une bonne part à la diffusion du culte de saint Denis bien au dela des limites de l'Ile-de-France. Ces titres d'hellénisme conférés au patron de l'abbaye Saint-Denis-en-France eurent d'autres conséquences. Si saint Denis, évêque et martyr, était identifié avec l'Aréopagite converti par Saint Paul (Actes xvii. 34), il devait bientôt se trouver un hagiographe pour le confondre avec l'auteur des œuvres théologiques contenues dans le célèbre manuscrit grec que Louis-le-Pieux avait offert en 827 à l'illustre abbaye.[1] Pourtant, il ne semble pas que ces titres avantageux aient exercé une modification profonde dans le culte rendu par la célèbre abbaye à la mémoire de son patron. Au XIe siècle, saint Denis et ses compagnons sont toujours traités en martyrs, et si leur office[2] fait quelques brèves allusions aux 'glorieuses légendes', les messes du 9 et du 16 octobre empruntent leurs chants au Commun des martyrs.[3]

Au XIIIe siècle, un médecin du nom de Guillaume de Gap, qui devint plus tard moine, puis en 1173 abbé de Saint-Denis, rapporte d'Orient en 1167 quelques manuscrits grecs, parmi lesquels il faut sans doute compter la Vie de Saint Denis par Michel le Syncelle.[4] Guillaume traduit en latin cette biographie. Il est aussi, probablement, à l'origine de la traduction des tropaires byzantins qui célèbrent saint Denis, Aréopagite et Théologien.[5] Est-il aussi l'instigateur de cette 'Messe grecque' du jour octave de saint Denis, qui fut établie entre le XIe et le XIIIe siècle ? Il est permis de le supposer. Cette idée de chanter en grec certaines portions de l'office ou de la messe, faute de

---

[1] Paris, Bibl. Nat., gr. 437: cf. *Bibliothèque Nationale, Byzance et la France médiévale* (Paris, 1958), no. 6. Les ouvrages de l'Aréopagite furent traduits en 832, avec l'aide de moines grecs venus du monastère Saint-Denis de Rome.

[2] Cet office a sans doute Hilduin (+842) pour auteur : il a probablement remplacé un office plus ancien. On le trouve déjà dans l'antiphonaire de Compiègne (*Patrol. lat.* 78, c. 807 ; réed. Hesbert, *Corpus antiphonalium officii*, i) et naturellement dans tous les manuscrits de Saint-Denis ('Antiphonaire du Mont-Renaud', *Paléogr. Music.*, xvi ; B.N. lat. 17296 ; Mazarine 384, fo. 160, liste d'incipit, etc.) et enfin dans des manuscrits souvent très anciens (Antiphonaire d'Hartker ; Leipzig, Rep. i, 93 ; Paris, B.N. lat. 656, fragm. ; lat. 2395, liste d'incipit ; Rouen 211, *etc.*)

[3] Paris, Mazarine 384 (XIe s.) fo. 134 v. ; B.N. lat. 9436 (appelé parfois 'Missel du Sacre', XIe s.) fo. 107 : voir tableau comparatif plus loin, p. 80. Le graduel 'Gloriosus'

est déjà assigné à la fête du 9 octobre par le cantatorium de Monza, du IXe siècle. L'épître, par contre, implique déjà que la 'légende' est admise puisqu'elle raconte la conversion de l'Aréopagite.

[4] Paris, B.N. grec. 933 (Xe siècle).

[5] Paris, B.N. nouv. acq. lat. 1509, p. 152: 'Incipiunt laudes ieromartyris Ariopagitae Dionysii Athenarum archiepiscopi de greco in latinum translatae quas Greci grece decantant...' (jusqu'à la p. 160) : on retrouve dans l'édition romaine des *Ménées*, i (Rome 1888, p. 321) nombre de textes traduits en latin dans ce manuscrit. C'est J. Handschin qui a avancé le nom de l'abbé de Saint-Denis comme traducteur de ces textes (qui n'étaient pas destinés à l'usage liturgique) : 'Sur quelques tropaires grecs traduits en latin.' § IV. 'Textes hymnologiques pour saint Denis', *Annales musicologiques*, ii (1954), p. 48 ss.

pouvoir célébrer toute la liturgie comme à Athènes ou à Byzance, ne devait pas déplaire aux moines de Saint-Denis !

En fait, c'était là moins une innovation qu'une imitation de ce qui se faisait déjà ailleurs dans quelques églises de France. C'est ainsi que, pour mieux honorer saint Nicolas, évêque de Myre, on avait déjà pris l'initiative, au X-XIᵉ siècle, dans une église de France indéterminée, de chanter le tropaire Μύροις παροικήσας,¹ qui figure encore aujourd'hui dans les Ménées.² Dans une autre église un essai avait été tenté dans un sens différent : on avait traduit en grec toutes les pièces de la messe grégorienne du dimanche de Pâques, 'Resurrexi', ainsi que les chants de l'ordinaire.³ À Nevers, au XIᵉ siècle, plusieurs pièces de la messe de la Pentecôte se chantaient en grec.⁴ Il subsiste par ailleurs un certain nombre de versets alleluiatiques occidentaux traduits en grec.⁵ Ces exemples d'adoption d'authentiques pièces byzantines et de rétroversions de pièces latines témoignent de l'engouement admiratif du clergé pour le grec, tant à l'époque carolingienne que dans les siècles suivants. Ces vestiges nous montrent en outre devant quels précédents se trouvaient les moines de Saint-Denis le jour où ils voulurent célébrer en grec l'office de leur saint patron. Deux possibilités s'offraient alors à eux : ou bien utiliser la *Missa greca* qui groupait seulement quatre pièces de l'ordinaire : 'Gloria in excelsis', 'Credo', 'Sanctus' et 'Agnus Dei' en grec;⁶ ou encore traduire en grec les pièces du propre et, pour l'ordinaire, chanter la *Missa greca*.

Depuis le IXᵉ siècle, et jusqu'au XIIᵉ, les pièces de l'ordinaire sont conservées, en grec transcrit en caractères latins, par plusieurs manuscrits occidentaux. Cette *Missa greca* figure entre autres dans un sacramentaire de Saint-Denis, du IXᵉ siècle.⁷ C'est à la Pentecôte que, selon les rubriques de plusieurs manuscrits,⁸ on chantait la *Missa greca*. Rien n'interdit de supposer qu'à Saint-Denis

¹ Ce tropaire, transcrit en lettres latines à la suite d'un des plus anciens témoins de l'office de saint Nicolas (Paris, B.N. lat. 17177, recueil de fragments, fo. 50 v.) est noté en neumes français. Nous avons cherché, en nous basant sur l'ordre liturgique des antiennes et répons de cet office, à déterminer pour quelle église séculière il avait été transcrit (par la suite, il fut adapté à l'usage monastique) : mais aucun des 50 manuscrits du Xᵉ au XIIIᵉ siècle examinés, qui contiennent l'office de St. Nicolas, ne donne une liste de pièces identique à ce fragment (vers le XIIᵉ siècle, l'ordre adopté par la plupart des manuscrits est l'ordre numérique des modes). Quant à la mélodie de ce tropaire, elle doit faire l'objet d'une étude comparative du Professeur O. Strunk, qui a bien voulu nous communiquer auparavant quelques transcriptions.

² Édition romaine, ii (1889), p. 386.

³ Montpelier, Fac. de Médecine H. 306, fo. 138 v. (première moitié du IXᵉ siècle) : pièces du propre et de l'ordinaire, écrites en caractères latins, sans neumes.

⁴ Paris, B.N. lat. 9449, fo. 49 v.–52 : deux pièces du propre et les pièces de l'ordinaire, à l'exception de l'"Agnus Dei', sont traduites en grec, écrit en caractères latins. Dans Paris, B.N. lat. 779, fo. 67 et nouv. acq. lat. 1871, fo. xxii, l'introït de la Pentecôte est traduit en grec et noté.

⁵ E. Wellesz, *Eastern Elements in Western Chant* (*Monum. Mus. Byz.*, Subsidia II), p. 33 ss. ; L. Brou o.s.b., 'Les chants en langue grecque dans les liturgies latines', *Sacris erudiri*, i

(1948), pp. 165–80 ; iv (1952), pp. 226–38. Cet article répond en partie au voeu exprimé par le Docteur Wellesz (*Eastern Elem.*, p. 56) d'une liste de documents liturgiques latins comprenant des pièces en langue grecque. Voir encore E. Jammers, *Die Essener Neumenhandschriften der Landes- und Stadt-Bibliothek Düsseldorf* (Ratingen, 1952), p. 19. Kenneth Levy ajoute à la liste de Brou le verset alléluiatique grec 'Hic est discipulus' (pour le 27 décembre) conservé par Laon, Bibl. munic. 263 (XIIᵉ s.) fo. 105 (cf. *Annales musicologiques*, vi [1958–62], p. 37, n. 2).

⁶ Il n'y a pas lieu de discuter ici l'origine byzantine — ou seulement carolingienne — de la mélodie de ces pièces grecques. Ce problème a été débattu par O. Ursprung, 'Um die Frage der Echtheit der Missa greca', *Musikforschung*, vi, pp. 289–316, qui développe des arguments de critique interne contre l'authenticité. Voir aussi Jammers, op. cit. pp. 19–21. Plus récemment, Levy a défendu l'origine orientale de ces chants en les comparant aux pièces conservées par les manuscrits byzantins ('The Byzantine Sanctus' : *Annales musicologiques*, vi [1958–63], pp. 7–67). Il serait peut-être opportun de se demander si ces pièces grecques ne seraient pas venues d'Orient par l'intermédiaire du répertoire gallican.

⁷ Paris, B.N. lat. 2290 (IXᵉ s.) fo. 7 v. et 8 ; Laon, Bibl. munic. 118 (Xᵉ s.), Sacramentaire-Graduel de Saint-Denis, fo. 156 v. ('Doxa...')

⁸ Levy, art. cit., p. 35.

les pièces grecques aient été affectées à la fête du saint, le 9 octobre, ou au jour octave.[1] Cependant, ce n'est qu'au XIIIe siècle que nous trouvons l'attestation positive de cette affectation de la *Missa greca* à la liturgie de l'octave. Cette messe du 16 octobre comprenait en outre la traduction en grec des pièces de l'ordinaire. Le coutumier de l'abbaye nous fournit dans le détail l'ordonnance de cette curieuse messe. Nous en donnerons le texte établi sur deux manuscrits : M = Paris, Bibl. Mazarine 526, fo. 184,   N = Paris, Bibl. Nat. lat. 976, fo. 137–137[v].

DE OCTABIS BEATI DIONYSII

Ad missam tres cantores. Officium in greco *Zeveta*(1) *a gallia*. Sex(2) *procedentes* ℣. *Zeveta a gallia. Doxa Patri. Kyrie fons bonitatis*(3). Post incipiat sacerdos *Doxa en ipsistis*. Oratio *Protegat nos Domine*(4). Prima epistola legatur(5) in greco alia in latino : *Stans Paulus...*R̃. *Fobite*(6) *ton Kyrion* ℣ *Ide ekzetontes*(7). A III alleluia(8) *Ekekraxan*(9) *dikei*, a IIII(10) sequentia *Gaude prole*(11). Ante evangelium, ant. *O beate Dyonisi*. Post legatur evangelium in greco, aliud(12) in latino *Videns Jesus turbas*.

Si dominica fuerit dicatur *Pisteuo*(13) quod est *Credo* et si dominica non fuerit non dicatur(14). Offertorium *Y ta Cherubim*(15). *Sanctus, agyos, agyos. Agnus, O amnos*(16) *tou Theu* et *Agnus Dei* III.

Communio *Psallate Yri*(17). Postcommunio *Sumpsimus Domine pignus*(18). *Ite missa est* est (19) sicut angelorum.

Variantes (1) *Zeneta* N   (2) Quatuor M   (3) omitt : *bonitatis* M   (4) omitt : *Dne* M, addit : *sepius* N   (5) legetur M   (6) *Phovicite* M   (7) *Ite ezeontes* M   (8) alleluia a IV M   (9) *Ekekrassan* M   (10) omitt. a IIII M   (11) *Superae armoniae* M   (12) alia MN   (13) *Physteuo* M   (14) Dicatur *Phisteuo* quod est *Credo* etiam si dominica non fuerit N   (15) *Kerouvin* M, Pref. *Qui sanctorum addit* M   (16) *agnos* MN   (17) *Ysu* N   (18) omitt : *pignus* M   (19) omitt : est N

Les variantes entre M et N sont minimes. Deux seulement retiennent plus particulièrement l'attention. La première porte sur le choix des séquences : 'Superae armoniae', l'ancienne séquence, dans M[2]; 'Gaude prole Grecia', séquence plus récente, dans N.[3] La seconde variante porte sur la prescription du 'Credo' : M prescrit le 'Credo' si l'octave de saint Denis tombe un dimanche — ce qui était alors la règle habituelle — tandis que N l'impose de toute façon, que l'octave tombe un dimanche ou en semaine. Rien qu'en se basant sur ces deux points de détail, on peut conclure que M est plus ancien que N.[4] Pour le reste, les deux manuscrits coïncident de manière satisfaisante. Les prescriptions qu'ils fixent pour l'octave de saint Denis appellent plusieurs remarques, tant sur les chants de l'ordinaire et du propre que sur les lectures en grec et en latin.

Les chants de l'ordinaire sont identifiés :

le 'Kyrie' : mélodie occidentale, avec le trope 'fons bonitatis'.[5]

le 'Doxa en ipsistis' ou 'Gloria in excelsis', dont la mélodie nous a été heureusement conservée par plusieurs manuscrits des X, XI et XIIe siècles : l'un d'eux vient d'ailleurs de Saint-Denis.[6]

---

[1] L'octave de saint Denis existait bien au XIe siècle (sinon plus tôt) : Paris, Mazarine 384, fo. 135 ; B.N. lat. 9436, fo. 108 v. (voir plus loin le tableau comparatif des pièces pour cette messe de l'octave). Pour illustrer la 'poussée d'hellénisme' dans le culte de saint Denis, rappelons que le nom du saint est écrit en caractères grecs dans le calendrier du sacramentaire B.N. lat. 2290 ; en outre, Jean Scot avait écrit un vers en grec en l'honneur de saint Denis : M.G.H. *Poëtae aevi carolini*, iii, p. 546.

[2] *Repertorium hymnologicum*, no. 19815 ; *Analecta hymnica*, ix, p. 141.

[3] *Repertorium hymnologicum*, no. 6912 ; *Analecta hymnica*, lv, pp. 130–1. On la trouve notée dans le missel de St.-Denis du XIIIe siècle : Paris, B.N. lat. 1107, fo. 381.

[4] D'après Molinier (*Catalogue des manuscrits de la Mazarine*, i, p. 211), le manuscrit M serait un peu postérieur à 1234, tandis que le ms. N est assigné par le *Catalogue général des manuscrits latins* au XIII–XIVe siècle. Ces datations seraient sans doute serrées davantage par une analyse comparative de M et N.

[5] C'est-à-dire la mélodie de la messe II de l'Édition Vaticane. Sur ce Kyrie et son trope, voir *Rassegna gregoriana*, iii, (1904), c. 531–44.

[6] Paris, B.N. lat. 9436, fo. 1 v. On trouvera la liste des manuscrits et la restitution de la mélodie du 'Doxa' dans mon article 'La mélodie grecque du Gloria in excelsis', *Revue grégorienne*, xxix (1950), pp. 30–40.

le 'Pisteuo — quod est Credo' — est connu par plusieurs manuscrits neumatiques — dont le 'Missel du Sacre' de Saint-Denis[1] — mais la mélodie, aux finales ornées, n'a pas encore été déchiffrée.[2]

le 'Trisagion' est également fort répandu en Occident : sa mélodie est connue surtout par les manuscrits aquitains.[3]

enfin l''Agnus Dei', en grec, à peu près aussi répandu que le Trisagion,[4] se trouve également dans le sacramentaire de Saint-Denis (Paris, B.N. lat. 2290, fo. 8), quoique sans neumes.

En résumé, toutes les pièces de l'ordinaire,[5] chantées en grec le jour octave de saint Denis sont attestées par les manuscrits de l'abbaye dès le IXe siècle et par plusieurs manuscrits français notés des Xe et XIe siècles. Donc pas d'innovation liturgique et musicale de ce côté.

Il n'en est pas de même pour les pièces du propre qui apparemment sont toutes — à l'exception de l'offertoire — des pièces du répertoire grégorien traduites en grec. L'identification de l'introït offre quelque difficulté, car l'incipit de la traduction grecque a été déformé. H. Leclercq[6] propose de restituer les mots 'Zevete a gallia' par Δεῦτε ἀγαλλιασώμεθα soit 'Venite exultemus'. Mais il n'existe pas d'introït grégorien commençant ainsi.

Remarquons que, dans le coutumier, introït et verset psalmique ont même commencement, rencontre fortuite qui ne se trouve qu'une seule fois dans le répertoire, à l'introït 'Venite (adoremus)', suivi du Ps. 'Venite (exultemus)'. Mais si ce dernier incipit traduit correctement le texte grec indiqué par le coutumier, on ne saurait en dire autant pour l'antienne d'introït, à moins de supposer que le copiste du coutumier a confondu les deux incipit, celui de l'antienne et celui du psaume. Pourtant, cet essai d'explication n'est pas satisfaisant, car l'introït proposé, 'Venite adoremus', appartient aux Quatre-Temps de septembre, parfois au dimanche dans l'octave de l'Epiphanie,[7] mais il ne semble pas avoir été affecté à une fête du sanctoral. Il reste une dernière objection contre le maintien de 'Venite adoremus' : les sources du XIe siècle indiquent l'introït 'Exclamaverunt' pour le 16 octobre. Celui-ci aurait-il été remplacé par un autre introït au moment où le propre du 16 octobre fut traduit en grec? Aucune solution ne nous paraît pleinement satisfaisante pour résoudre ces objections.

Le 'Gloria Patri' qui se chante après le psaume et avant la reprise de l'antienne est, soit une rétroversion de la petite doxologie occidentale, soit tout simplement la petite doxologie byzantine[8]

---

[1] Paris, B.N. lat. 9436, fo. 1 v.

[2] En effet, la mélodie du 'Pisteuo' que j'ai publiée dans *Revue grégorienne*, xxx (1951), pp. 74–76, d'après Cologne, Stadtarchiv W. 105, ne 'traduit' pas les neumes que les manuscrits français, allemands et helvétiques portent au dessus du texte grec du 'Pisteuo'. La mélodie du manuscrit de Cologne est entièrement syllabique.

[3] Cf. Levy, art. cit., particulièrement p. 10 ss.

[4] Aux manuscrits mentionnés par Levy (art. cit., p. 44), on peut ajouter Bruxelles 21536–40 (Catal. 484) fo. 102 v.; le fragment noté sur un dyptique d'ivoire du Cabinet des Médailles à la B.N. (facsimilé : *La musique des origines à nos jours... sous la direction de* N. Dufourcq [1946], p. 101 ; notice : J. Hourlier, o.s.b. dans *Études grégoriennes*, vi [1963], pp. 149–52). Dans Vienne, Österr. Nat. Bibl. 1888 (Tropaire de St. Alban de Mayence), fo. 2, l''Amnos' se trouve deux fois, avec deux mélodies différentes.

[5] Mentionnons pour mémoire — puisqu'il n'est pas traduit en grec — l''Ite Missa est' : 'est sicut angelorum'. Il faudrait se garder de l'identifier avec l''Ite missa est' de la 'Messe des Anges' de l'Édition Vaticane (messe VIII), qui est relativement 'récente'. La prescription signifie qu'on prend le même 'Ite Missa est' qu'à la messe votive des anges (ou peut-être le même qu'au 29 septembre?).

[6] *Dictionn. d'archéol. chrét. et de liturgie*, vi, col. 1583, n. 1.

[7] L'introït 'Venite adoremus' se trouve à la place de 'In excelso throno' (texte non scripturaire de l'introït du IIIe dim. après l'Epiph.) dans les manuscrits de Lyon, Valence, Cluny, Grenoble, dans les manuscrits cartusiens, *etc.*

[8] La différence entre la doxologie occidentale et la doxologie byzantine réside dans la suppression de l'incise 'sicut erat in principio' du texte grec.

qui circulait en Occident avec les autres pièces de la *Missa greca*. En voici le texte et la mélodie d'après les manuscrits notés :[1]

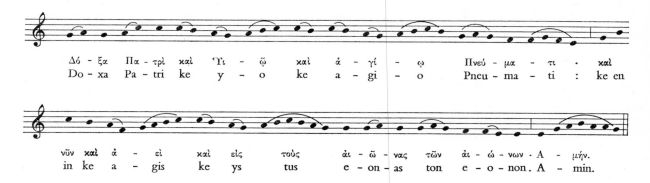

Après l'épître, lue en grec et en latin, on chante une traduction du répons-graduel 'Timete Dominum ℣ Inquirentes', assigné à cette messe de l'octave par tous les manuscrits sandionysiens[2] du XIe au XIIIe siècle. L'alleluia est, lui aussi, une traduction grecque du verset 'Clamaverunt', attesté par les mêmes sources que le graduel.[3] Il est curieux de constater que ce verset alleluiatique grec ne se retrouve pas dans les manuscrits de Saint-Denis : il a été signalé dans le graduel de Saint-Vaast du XIe siècle, où il est précisément assigné à la fête de Saint-Denis au 9 octobre.[4] La séquence et l'antienne *ante evangelium* — tirée de l'office de saint Denis — se chantent en latin. N'étant pas tirées de l'Écriture, ces deux pièces risquaient sans doute de présenter plus d'une difficulté de traduction à un helléniste médiéval : elles furent donc laissées en latin. Nous verrons un peu plus loin que la traduction de la séquence n'arrêtera pas les hellénistes du XVIIe siècle.

L'offertoire est incontestablement la pièce la plus intéressante de cette messe du 16 octobre. Dans l'incipit 'Y ta Cherubim', on reconnaît le *Cheroubicon* ou Hymne des Chérubins, tropaire qui se chante dans la Liturgie byzantine, au cours de la procession de la Grande Entrée, c'est à dire à l'offertoire. Le *Cheroubicon* est conservé en grec, mais transcrit en caractères latins, par un manuscrit de Corvey, du Xe siècle :[5] la pièce est notée. La traduction latine se trouve dans les

[1] D'après Düsseldorf, D. 2, fo. 203 v. ; Paris, B.N. lat. 779 fo. 67 v., lat. 909, fo. 37, lat. 1118, fo. 67, lat. 1119, fo. 45 v., lat. 1121, fo. 24, lat. 1834, fo. 1ᵛ, nouv. acq. lat. 1871, fo. 22ᵛ, (dans ces manuscrits, le 'Doxa Patri' se trouve à la Pentecôte ; dans les mss. 1119 et 1121, le texte est écrit en caractères grecs d'imitation). La restitution de cette pièce garde une certaine incertitude, faute de clé et faute d'une diastématie précise. Cependant, comme le 'doxa' accompagne les tropes d'introït de la Pentecôte, il est probable qu'il est écrit dans le mode de Sol. Le même texte, mais sans notation se relève dans Bruxelles 21536-40 (Cat. 484) fo. 102 v. et dans Laon, Bibl. munic. 118, fo. 16 v. Enfin, dans l'Antiphonaire de Leon (fo. 60, 81, 210), avec une mélodie apparemment différente.

[2] Paris, Mazarine 384, fo. 135; B.N. lat. 9436, fo. 108 v. ;

B.N. lat. 1107, fo. 272 v. (voir tableau comparatif plus loin). Le lat. 10505 est privé d'une bonne partie de son sanctoral par suite d'une lacune matérielle.

[3] Ce verset, qui se trouve bien en effet dans les manuscrits de Saint-Denis n'appartient pas au 'fonds grégorien primitif' : il semble avoir été composé dans le nord de la France au X-XIe siècle. Il a été ajouté dans un manuscrit de Corbie (Paris, B.N. lat. 13024, fo. 119 v.) avec neumes français.

[4] Cambrai, Bibl. munic. 75 (XIe s.) fo. 114 : cf. Brou, art. cit., *Sacris erudiri*, i (1948), p. 174.

[5] Düsseldorf, Landes- und Stadt-Bibl. D.2, fo. 203 v. ; Wellesz, *Eastern Elements*, p. 33; Jammers, op. cit., Tafel 9. Ce manuscrit viendrait de Corvey et se rattache donc d'une certaine manière au groupe Corbie-Saint Denis.

[78]

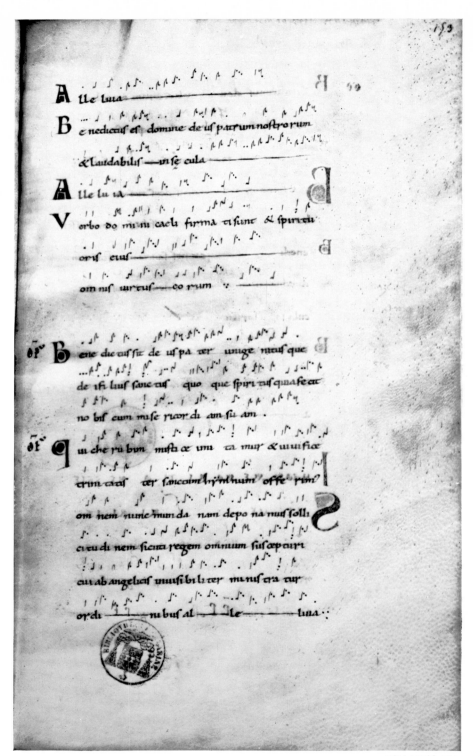

Le *Cheroubicon* en latin (Paris, Bibl. Mazarine 384, fo. 135)

manuscrits de Saint-Denis[1] et dans un manuscrit allemand,[2] d'une part, et d'autre part, dans le processionnal de Saint-Dominique de Sora,[3] en Italie du Sud.

Les divergences textuelles entre ces deux groupes sont assez notables :

SAINT-DENIS (Paris, Mazar. 364, fo. 153)	SORA (Vat. Regin. 334, fo. 78ᵛ)
Qui Cherubim mystice imitamur	Qui Cherubim mystice imitamur
et vivificae Trinitatis ter sanctum	et *vice* Trinitatis ter sanctum
hymnum offerimus,	hymnum *decantamus*,
omnem nunc mundanam	omnem nunc *secure*
deponamus sollicitudinem	deponamus sollicitudinem
sicuti regem omnium	sicuti regem omnium
suscepturi cui ab angelicis	*suscipientes cum*
invisibiliter	inivisibiliter *angelorum*
ministratur ordinibus,	*officio* ministratur,
alleluia	alleluia

Ces variantes suggèrent l'indépendance des traductions opérées à Saint-Denis d'une part et en Italie du Sud d'autre part.[4] Les neumes du texte latin coïncident avec ceux du texte grec de Corvey. Mais ce qui est plus remarquable c'est le fait qu'à Saint-Denis au XIIIᵉ siècle on chantait encore le *Cheroubicon* en grec : malheureusement, aucun manuscrit sandionysien de cette époque[5] n'a conservé la pièce avec sa mélodie : il faut donc nous résigner, jusqu'à plus ample informé, à la perte de cette mélodie[6] transportée de Byzance en Occident : cette perte est d'autant plus regrettable que les manuscrits byzantins — moins anciens que nos témoins occidentaux — nous transmettent une mélodie beaucoup plus ornée[7] qui ne traduit pas les neumes latins, d'une diastématie trop imprécise.

L'identification de la communion 'Psallate Yri' (ou 'Ysu', dans N) est aussi difficile que celle de l'introït. H. Leclercq[8] propose comme modèle 'Cantate Jesu' : mais cette transcription trop

[1] Paris, Collection privée, 'Antiphonaire du Mont-Renaud', reproduit dans *Paléographie Musicale*, xvi : G. Beyssac a remarqué que le *Cheroubicon* devait jadis se trouver en entier, au Capitulum CCXXII, du manuscrit : aujourd'hui, il ne reste que l'incipit 'Qui Cherubim' (fo. 37) avec renvoi (*Revue de Musicologie*, xl [1957], p. 139); Paris, Mazarine 384 (XIᵉ s.) fo. 153, en entier, avec notation neumatique (voir planche ci-joint : on pourra comparer la notation du texte latin à celle du texte grec reproduit par Jammers).

[2] Londres, Brit. Mus. Harl. 3095 (X–XIᵉ s.), fo. 111 v. : cf. Handschin, 'Le Cheroubicon', *Annales musicologiques*, ii (1954), p. 45.

[3] Vatican, Regin. 334, fo. 78 v.–79 : cf. Brou, art. cit. *Sacris erudiri*, iv (1952), pp. 228–9. Le texte du *Cheroubicon* traduit dans l'ouvrage de Claude de Sainctes, *Liturgiae sive Missae sanctorum* (Paris, Morel 1560), p. 38, coïncide avec la traduction du groupe St.-Denis.

[4] On peut faire une observation semblable sur l'antienne 'Sub tuum' : le processionnal de Sora (et d'ailleurs les antiphonaires bénéventains, tel que le ms. V 21 du Chapitre de Bénévent) traduisent 'sub tuis visceribus' là où les autres manuscrits occidentaux donnent 'sub tuum praesidium' : on a dû confondre, en Italie du Sud, σπλάγχνα avec εὐσπλαγχνία.

[5] Paris, B.N. lat. 1107; Rome, Bibl. Casanate 1595 (Missel parisien, en relation avec St.-Denis) ; Londres, National Art Gallery 1346 (Missel de St.-Denis, du XIII–XIVᵉ s.).

[6] Le fait que dans les anciens manuscrits de St.-Denis cités à la note 1, le *Cheroubicon* soit traité en verset d'offertoire de la Messe de la Trinité impliquerait que son mode était le mode de MI. On notera, sur le facsimilé, la répétition du même motif mélodique sur 'imitamur' et sur 'offerimus'.

[7] Sur l'histoire de la mélodie du *Cheroubicon* byzantin, voir Wellesz, *A History of Byzantine Music and Hymnography* (Oxford, 1949), p. 139, 2ᵉ éd. (1961), p. 166 ; Levy, 'A Hymn for Thursday in Holy Week', *Journal of the American Musicol. Soc.*, xvi (1963), p. 165 ss.

[8] *Dict. Archéol. chrét. et de Lit.*, col. 1585, n.3.

matérielle ne correspond à aucune pièce du répertoire grégorien. La déformation du texte grec rend difficile toute conjecture en vue d'identifier la pièce. De toute façon, il est impossible de voir dans cet incipit la traduction des premiers mots de la communion grégorienne 'Posuerunt mortalia', assignée par les sources du XIᵉ au XIIIᵉ siècle pour cette messe du 16 octobre.[1]

Faute de retrouver dans les manuscrits liturgiques de Saint-Denis du XIIIᵉ et du XIVᵉ siècle le texte intégral de ces pièces grecques, il n'est pas facile de les identifier toutes. On ne saurait, en raison même de l'absence de ces pièces dans la tradition liturgique,[2] mettre en doute leur authenticité. Elles se rattachent suffisament à la tradition de Saint-Denis par leur texte latin comme le montre ce tableau-résumé :

Paris, Mazar. 384, fo. 135 Paris, B.N. lat. 9436, fo. 108ᵛ		Coutumier (M & N)	Paris, B.N. lat. 1107 (XIIIᵉ s.), fo. 272ᵛ
Intr.	Exclamaverunt	?	Intret (comme au 9 octobre, fo. 271ᵛ)
Grad.	Timete Dominum	Timete Dom. (grec)	Timete Dominum
Allel.	Clamaverunt (omitt. 9436) Fulgebunt	Clamaverunt (grec)	Justi epulentur
Offert.	Confitebuntur cœli		
	Qui Cherubim (384, fo. 135)	Y ta Cherubim	Mirabilis (comme au 9 octobre, fo. 271ᵛ)
Comm.	Posuerunt	?	Posuerunt

Pour les lectures gréco-latines de la messe du 16 octobre, nous sommes plus heureux que pour les pièces de chant, car nous trouvons la confirmation des prescriptions du coutumier dans deux lectionnaires de Saint-Denis. L'usage sandionysien des lectures en grec et en latin ne saurait évidemment prétendre à une antiquité aussi haute que celui de l'Italie du Sud ou de Rome en matière de lectures bilingues.[3] Mais à Saint-Denis, l'usage peut remonter à s'en tenir aux documents, jusqu'au XIIᵉ siècle, sinon plus haut. Les péricopes grecques du 16 octobre se retrouvent en effet dans deux lectionnaires de Saint-Denis, un grec et un latin : le premier, le ms. grec 375 de la Bibliothèque Nationale de Paris est un lectionnaire byzantin du XIᵉ siècle. Il contient quelques péricopes en caractères grecs ajoutées au XIIᵉ ou au XIIIᵉ siècle sur des pages blanches : nous relevons l'épître (fo. 56) et l'évangile (fo. 154) pour le jour octave de saint Denis.

Dans l'un des plus beaux évangéliaires latins de Saint-Denis, le ms. lat. 9387 de la B.N.,[4] les lectures ont été ajoutées en caractères grecs par une main du XIVᵉ siècle pour les fêtes de Noël, la Dédicace (24 février), Pâques, la Pentecôte et pour la fête de saint Denis (fo. 157ᵛ) ; le texte est surmonté d'une notation qui imite la notation ekphonétique des lectionnaires byzantins.[5] Que le texte de ces lectures ait été copié dans d'authentiques lectionnaires byzantins ou qu'il

---

[1] Voir un peu plus loin le tableau comparatif des manuscrits de St.-Denis.

[2] Il ne reste que deux missels notés de St. Denis (Londres : cf. p. 79, n. 5—Paris, B.N. lat. 1107) ; un troisième manuscrit, un peu plus récent (B.N. lat. 10505) n'a pas le sanctoral d'octobre. Pour tirer argument a silentio il aurait fallu que tous les manuscrits de St. Denis fussent conservés.

[3] F. C. Burkitt, 'Manuscrits bilingues dans la liturgie des églises d'Italie', Miscellanea Amelli (1920), pp. 39–40. A Rome, l'usage des lectures bilingues — conservé dans la messe papale jusqu'à nos jours — remonte à l'époque de transition où l'Église de Rome abandonna le grec comme

langue liturgique pour le latin, c'est-à-dire à la fin du IVᵉ siècle. Signalons enfin que le manuscrit français de Léningrad F v VI 3 contient une épître en grec (Éph. ii 19–22) pour une fête d'Apôtre : A. Staerk, Les manuscrits latins…de St. Pétersbourg, i (1910), p. 42 ; Thibaut, Monuments de la notation ekphonétique (St. Pétersbourg, 1912), p. 24.

[4] Paris, B.N. lat. 9387 (IXᵉ s.), fo. 153–60. Le plat inférieur du ms. est protégé par une plaque ciselée due au même artiste que celui qui exécuta la plaque inférieure du ms. lat. 9436 déjà cité.

[5] A. Gastoué, La Musique française [catalogue], Bibliothèque Nationale (1939), no. 4.

[80]

s'agisse seulement d'une rétroversion du texte liturgique latin en langue grecque, nous trouvons dans ces deux documents confirmation des usages décrits dans le coutumier du XIIIᵉ siècle. Cet usage a duré très longtemps puisqu'il est encore attesté en 1509 par G. Chartelier, conseiller au Parlement de Paris : 'Le samedi IIᵉ jour dudit mois de juin, la Court fut à Monseigneur St.-Denis. La messe fut chantée des benoist martyrs *Intret in conspectu tuo*. Les épîtres et évangiles furent dits en grec et en latin'.[1]

En 1625, Dom Jacques Doublet fait état de ce même usage : 'Es festes solennelles, l'on chante double épistre et double évangile, l'un en latin et l'autre en grec, et ce, en commémoration de l'Apostre de France, sainct Denys l'Aréopagite qui estoit grec de nation... Le jour de l'octave de la feste de sainct Denys, l'on chante toute la messe en grec, mesme le célébrant chante le *Gloria in excelsis* et le *Credo* en grec.'[2] Ces lectures en grec, l'éditeur R. Ballard les imprime en 1658, dans le petit livret intitulé : *Missa in octava sancti Dionysii Areopagitae et sociorum martyrum...*,[3] avec d'ailleurs tout le reste, chants et oraisons, de la messe grecque. Mais cette édition n'est pas un nouveau témoin de l'usage attesté au XIIIᵉ siècle par le coutumier : presque rien de commun entre l'ancien usage et la messe grecque de Ballard. Il suffit de mettre en regard les documents pour s'en convaincre :

COUTUMIER DU XIIIᵉ S.	ÉDITIONS[4] DE 1658 & 1777
INTR. : ?	*Sapientiam* (traduit en grec)
KYRIE : Kyrie (II) *fons bonitatis*	Kyrie IV (de l'Édit. Vaticane)
GLORIA IN EXC. : Mélodie propre	Gloria IV
COLLECTE : *Protegat nos Domine* (en latin)	*Protegat nos Domine* (en grec)
EPITRE : *Stans Paulus...* (en grec et en latin)	*Stans Paulus...* (en grec et en latin)
GRADUEL : *Timete Dominum* (en grec)	*Anima nostra* (en grec)
ALLELUIA : *Clamaverunt* (en grec)	*Justi epulentur* (en grec)
ÉVANGILE : *Videns Jesus turbas* (en grec et en latin)	*Attendite a fermento* (en grec)
CREDO : mélodie spéciale (en grec)	Mélodie du Credo V de l'Ed. Vaticane (en grec)
OFFERTOIRE : 'Cheroubicon'	*Exultabunt sancti* (en grec)
SECRÈTE : ?	*Hostias tibi Dne.* (en latin)
PRÉFACE : *Qui sanctorum* (en latin)	1. Préface commune (en grec)
	2. Préface selon l'us. de Paris (en grec)
SANCTUS : *Agyos...* (mélodie spéciale)	*Agios* (melodié du Sanctus IV de l'Ed. Vaticane) en grec
PATER NOSTER : en latin	
AGNUS DEI : (mélodie spéciale) en grec	(mélodie IV de l'Ed. Vatic.) en grec
COMMUNION : ? (non identifiable) (en grec)	*Dico autem vobis* (en grec)
POSTCOMMUNION : *Sumpsimus Dne.* (en latin)	*Sumpsimus Dne.* (en grec)
ITE MISSA EST : en latin	traduit en grec[5]
BÉNÉDICTION ÉPISCOPALE : ?	traduite en grec[5]

[1] *Mémorial* : le passage en question est cité par Leclercq (art. cit., 1584-5), d'après l'édition de Guilhermoz dans le *Bulletin de la société de l'histoire de Paris et de l'Ile-de-France*, xv (1888), pp. 174-9.

[2] *Histoire de l'abbaye de St.-Denys en France et de ses antiquités* (Paris, 1625), pp. 361 et 366. La curieuse lettre de 'L'Église grecque au vénérable archimandrite de l'abbaye royale...St. Denis-en-France' (Vidieu, *St. Denys* [1889], pp. 416-18) fait également allusion aux lectures bilingues des quatre principales fêtes de l'année. C'est d'après un manuscrit gréco-latin de Mr. Albert Lenoir que Vidieu a publié ce texte. On aimerait connaître le sort de ce manuscrit pour tenter de dater la lettre apocryphe.

[3] Fin du titre : . . . *ad usum regalis ecclesiae ejusdem, S. Dionysii in Francia O.S.B. Congregationis Sancti Mauri*. La messe sera rééditée en 1777 et 1779 par Lottin, mais avec un titre français. Deux manuscrits sandionysiens du XVIIIᵉ siècle la contiennent également : Mazarine 452, à l'usage

du célébrant, et Mazarine 4465, à l'usage des chantres, qui contient les parties notées. La messe grecque imprimée a été étudiée par A. J. H. Vincent, *Note sur la messe grecque qui se chantait autrefois à l'abbaye royale de St.-Denis, le jour octave de la fête patronale* : Revue archéologique, nouvelle série, t. IX, 1864, pp. 268-81. — H. Omont, *La Messe grecque de Saint-Denis* : Études d'Histoire du Moyen-Âge dédiées à Gabriel Monod I, 1896. — H. Leclercq, art. 'grecque', *Dict. d'Archéologie chrét. et de Liturgie*, t. VI c. 1581-6.

[4] Nous avons utilisé l'édition de 1777 qui est, à quelques additions près, identique à celle de 1658. À la fin des deux éditions de 1777 et 1779, on trouve le texte latin des pièces traduites en grec dans le corps du livret.

[5] Voir Leclercq (dans *Dict. d'Archéol. chr. et de lit.*, vi, 1585) sur la curieuse traduction de cette monition (qui ne figurait pas dans l'édition de 1658) et sur la traduction de la Bénédiction épiscopale.

Si on établit le bilan de cette comparaison, force est de reconnaître que rien ne subsiste de la messe grecque du XIIIᵉ siècle dans le domaine des chants : le lien subsiste seulement dans le domaine des lectures[1] et des oraisons. Comment ces modifications se sont-elles effectuées ? Il faut admettre une certaine période de dégradation : ces chants en grec n'ont pu se conserver indéfiniment. Ils furent sans doute abandonnés entre la fin du XIIIᵉ et le début du XVIᵉ siècle, tandis que les lectures en grec et en latin furent maintenues. Mais qui traduisit en grec les pièces de chant de la 'nouvelle' messe grecque ? Quel helléniste traduisit les oraisons, les monitions, la séquence et le reste ?

Il ne semble pas que toutes ces traductions soient le fait des humanistes du XVIᵉ siècle, dont le rôle consista seulement à retoucher la traduction de la messe traditionnelle.[2] C'est du moins la conclusion qui ressort de l'examen de la préface de la Messe imprimée en 1658 ; elle s'achève sur cette note de la dernière heure : 'Pendant l'impression de cette messe, l'abbaye de Saint-Denis nous a communiqué un manuscrit grec où se trouve *une partie* de la Messe grecque de Saint Denis révisée par le célèbre Guillaume Budé qui a mis à la fin une lettre signée et paraphée de sa main. Il mourut en 1540. *Cette messe est différente de celle qui se chante aujourd'hui.* Mais c'est d'après ce manuscrit que nous rétablissons dans le symbole ces deux mots *et expecto*, etc.'

Ne faut-il pas voir dans les mots — que nous avons soulignés — désignant 'cette messe différente de celle qui se chante aujourd'hui' (en 1658), un témoin de la messe grecque fixée par l'usage du XIIIᵉ siècle, ou du moins une partie de cette messe ?[3] La messe 'qui se chante aujourd'hui' est sans équivoque celle que Ballard a imprimée en 1658. Il semblerait donc que ce sont les Mauristes, entrés en 1633 à Saint-Denis, qui sont à l'origine de cette nouvelle messe. Cette déduction s'appuie sur les procédés utilisés par les religieux de la Congrégation de Saint-Maur en fait de liturgie : en effet, les usages traditionnels des monastères repris par la jeune Congrégation cédaient le plus souvent la place a l'uniformité du *Bréviaire* et du *Missel* mauristes et les anciens offices propres à des compositions nouvelles.[4] Il est donc fort probable que les modifications de la Messe grecque imprimée sont dues aux Mauristes.

Pourtant, en relisant le texte de Dom J. Doublet, écrit avant 1625, on se demande si l'allusion au chant de 'toute la messe en grec' ne viserait pas précisément les textes de la nouvelle messe, imprimée ultérieurement en 1658 : dès lors, la 'nouvelle messe' serait antérieure aux Mauristes... Il faut bien reconnaître que l'expression de Dom J. Doublet est assez ambiguë[5] et qu'elle peut s'appliquer aussi bien à la messe grecque ancienne — ou du moins à ce qui en restait alors — qu'à

[1] Encore faudrait-il comparer les deux textes grecs : il ne semble pas que l'éditeur a été chercher le texte de ses lectures dans les manuscrits mentionnés plus haut : mais ceci serait à vérifier (la péricope évangélique est, de toute façon, différente).

[2] Omont (art. cit.) accordait une place beaucoup plus large aux humanistes dans la composition de cette nouvelle messe : nous la réduisons à un travail de révision linguistique et grammaticale effectué sur les textes de l'ancienne messe.

[3] Ce serait en effet une vue trop rigide de l'esprit de croire que cette messe grecque héritée du XIIIᵉ siècle a subsisté telle quelle, au milieu de toutes les vicissitudes extérieures et de la décadence des monastères au XVIᵉ siècle. Peut-être que seules les lectures ont traversé les siècles jusqu'au XVIIᵉ. Le texte du conseiller Chartelier, rapporté plus haut, ne mentionne effectivement que les

lectures en grec : mais la messe décrite, il est vrai, est celle du 11 juin (Invention de St. Denis) et non la messe du 16 octobre.

[4] À titre d'exemple, nous citerons seulement le cas de la Chaise-Dieu où l'ancien office propre de St. Robert fut remplacé par un nouvel office contenu dans le *Proprium ad usum pontificii et regalis monasterii sancti Roberti de Casa Dei* (Clermont, 1765). L'auteur du nouvel office est Dom Hugues Vaillant qui s'était spécialisé dans la composition de nouveaux Propres.

[5] Les termes de Dom Martène — qui concernent sans aucun doute la Messe imprimée — nous offrent la même apparence d'ambiguité : 'In octava vero sancti Dionysii quidquid a choro in missa precinitur, totum greco sermone canitur' (*De antiq. ecclesiae ritibus*, i [1736], p. 281).

la nouvelle. En effet, l'une et l'autre se chantent entièrement en grec et à l'une comme à l'autre 'le célébrant chante le *Gloria in excelsis* et le *Credo*' en grec. La seule différence porte sur les oraisons la séquence, la préface et le 'Pater' qui constituent en somme l'élément nouveau de la messe imprimée.[1] En définitive, cette messe grecque aurait été agencée entre 1633 et 1658, sans tenir compte des traditions anciennes ou du moins de ce qui pouvait en rester.

Cette coutume liturgique du 16 octobre à Saint-Denis a un aspect quelque peu singulier, il faut bien le reconnaître. Elle a aussi un caractère assez traditionnel, puisque la messe grecque, telle qu'elle fut codifiée au XIIIe siècle, avait recueilli plusieurs pièces dignes d'intérêt, entre autres l'Hymne des Chérubins et les chants de l'ordinaire en grec. Mais la tradition ancienne s'étant peu à peu estompée fut un beau jour 'restaurée' d'une manière assez artificielle et sans lien solide avec le passé. Il est vrai que ce n'est pas de ce côté que s'orientent les recherches des byzantinistes. De plus en plus leur attention se porte sur ces pièces grecques transmises par les anciens manuscrits occidentaux. C'est au Docteur Egon Wellesz que revient le mérite d'avoir, notamment dans *Eastern Elements in Western Chant*, attiré l'attention sur ces vestiges et entrepris de retracer leur histoire.

[1] La 'lettre de l'Église grecque' (Vidieu, p. 416) fait allusion à la 'restauration' du grec pour la préface, l'oraison dominicale et les collectes. En fait, il s'agit plus exactement, en comparaison des usages du XIIIe siècle, d'une innovation que d'une restauration.

ESSAI ANALYTIQUE SUR LA FORMATION DE L'OCTOÉCHOS LATIN

Jacques Chailley (Paris)

LES RECHERCHES sur l'origine des huit modes ecclésiastiques ont beaucoup progressé dans ces dernières années. Nous devons notamment à Eric Werner de suggestifs rapprochements avec les traditions symboliques de nombres dans lesquelles elle s'insère, à l'éminent dédicataire de la présente étude maint témoignage de correspondance entre le répertoire occidental et la tradition byzantine dont les modes tirent leurs noms les plus anciens. Et néanmoins cette origine persiste à demeurer mystérieuse. Nous devons désormais renoncer à l'explication trop simple de l'école de Gevaert, qui en retrouvait l'équivalent implicite dans la musique grecque antique, et aucun jalon sérieux ne se présente entre celle-ci et les traités du XIe siècle occidental qui nous en montrent la doctrine déjà élaborée sous sa forme presque définitive.[1] Peut-être, en cette matière comme en d'autres, faut-il se défier de la tentation de confondre la théorie avec la pratique, et de prendre pour la cause ce qui n'est souvent que systématisation faite après coup. La présente étude se propose d'oublier provisoirement la théorie et d'essayer par la simple analyse musicale de reconstituer approximativement l'enchaînement probable des faits, dans les conditions qui furent sans doute celles des chantres anonymes chargés d'élaborer le répertoire. Nous nous excuserons de devoir parfois faire appel à des notions plus familières à l'ethnomusicologie qu'à l'analyse grégorienne traditionnelle, mais n'est-ce pas dans cette collaboration des disciplines que résident nos meilleures chances d'aborder de vieux problèmes avec des regards neufs ?

Le point de départ de cette étude a été la constatation de deux faits auxquels la théorie traditionnelle n'accorde guère d'attention, et qui, jadis négligés, se voient aujourd'hui presque unanimement reconnus : d'une part le caractère pentatonique de la mélodie la plus ancienne (cf. travaux du P. Delalande ou de Y. Hameline) qui laisse conjecturer une certaine similitude d'évolution avec les mélodies pentatoniques du fond ethnomusicologique ; d'autre part l'importance historique de la psalmodie, et par conséquent de la corde de récitation ou teneur (cf. travaux du P. Claire à Solesmes) qui pourtant ne joue aucun rôle réel dans le classement traditionnel, basé presque uniquement sur les finales (absentes pourtant de nombreuses formules psalmodiques).

---

[1] Malgré les affirmations de Gastoué et l'exégèse très sollicitée de Gombosi, nous persistons, à mesure que nous avançons dans une étude de ce texte difficile qui n'est pas encore achevée, à demeurer sceptique sur le rattachement à l'octoéchos du passage de l'alchimiste Zozime de Panapolis (IVe siècle) cité comme le plus ancien témoignage à son sujet. Il y est bien question de πλαγίοι, mais non des authentes, et cela dans une énumération sans aucun rapport avec les autres données du problème.

Le critère initial du mode semble avoir été non un classement d'après la finale, mais la façon dont se groupent les sons et les formules autour de la corde de récitation. Les usages universels de la cantillation nous enseignent que la tendance la plus courante de celle-ci conduit d'une part à des broderies autour de la teneur, d'autre part à une chute mélodique finale au grave de celle-ci, chute qui va parfois ailleurs jusqu'à devenir un véritable *parlando*. Tout se passe comme si les choses s'étaient passées également ainsi pour le chant grégorien, l'échelle de base étant celle du pentatonique anhémitonique divisant facultativement ses trihémitons incomposés par des *piens*[1] faibles et souvent mobiles dont la hauteur (ton ou demi-ton) se seraient vu fixée par l'attraction. Plus tard, la teneur deviendra dominante, c. à d. perdra sa valeur récitative pour n'être plus que l'axe de la mélodie, ou plus exactement la borne supérieure du noyau mélodique principal. C'est du rapport entre cette borne supérieure et la borne inférieure du même noyau, qui deviendra la finale conclusive, puis la 'tonique', que naîtra le mode proprement dit. Inutile de dire que dans cette perspective, la notion de tétracorde est une fiction au même titre que celle d'hexacorde. La première est un résidu scolaire de la théorie grecque (pour qui elle était une réalité), la seconde un artifice pédagogique destiné à la solmisation (bien postérieur par conséquent) et nullement un principe de structure.

Accessoirement se produiront d'autres phénomènes : les *piens* notamment se solidifieront et se verront renforcés en fonction des attractions qu'ils subissent ; parmi ces attractions, la plus forte sera celle de la dominante si le *pien* en est voisin et reste en liaison mélodique avec elle, ensuite viendra celle de tonique ; l'attraction enfin conduira avec force le *pien* faible à la réduction du triton en quarte juste, à l'intérieur du moins d'une même zone attractive, ce phénomène n'ayant naturellement aucune raison de se manifester entre deux zones différentes.

Le rapport Dominante-Tonique se verra également inversé en rapport Tonique-Dominante en passant de la psalmodie à la mélodie libre. Il n'en détermine pas moins dans les deux cas une zone mélodique principale qui constitue le noyau du mode. Un dépassement occasionnel ne crée pas forcément une nouvelle zone, mais si le dépassement s'amplifie et se maintient, il se crée une nouvelle zone indépendante de la première, dans laquelle les attractions peuvent se trouver modifiées et les *piens* transformés. Tant que l'épaisseur du noyau ne dépasse pas la quarte, unité globale d'émission vocale homogène,[2] rien n'empêche de nouvelles zones de se créer tant au grave qu'à l'aigu. On obtient alors un noyau central flanqué de deux zones latérales. Est-ce coïncidence si la théorie appellera ces types 'plagaux', en glosant *id est a latere*?[3] Mais si le noyau atteint ou dépasse la quinte, l'effort vocal créera une zone aiguë caractérisée qui exclura le développement au grave, réduit à une unique note de dépassement que l'on peut assimiler au proslambanomène du système grec. On observe que celui-ci ne se développera vraiment qu'à un ton sous la tonique, refusant aussi bien le demi-ton que la tierce mineure incomposée du pentatonique. On obtient alors un noyau formant zone grave (+proslambanomène éventuel) surmontée d'une zone aiguë dont la dominante forme charnière. Ce sera le mode 'authente', et tel est bien le sens propre de αὐθέντης : 'qui surmonte, qui domine'. Il est curieux que l'étymologie explique avec une telle

---

[1] On rappelle que ce terme, primitivement chinois, a été généralisé par C. Brailoiu pour l'ensemble des études d'ethnomusicologie. Il nous semble pouvoir être également étendu aux autres branches de la musicologie.

[2] Cf. Paul Collaer, 'État actuel des connaissances...' dans *Les Colloques de Wégimont* (Bruxelles, 1956), p. 46.

[3] *Alia Musica*, dans la version du ms. K, non relevée par Gerbert et mal transcrite par Mühlmann. Voir notre édition critique, récemment parue (Centre de Documentation Universitaire).

clarté une terminologie dont la théorie postérieure donnera une définition tout à fait différente et, au contraire de la précédente, bien difficilement justifiable (authente = maître, plagal = serviteur, associé), comme il est fréquent dans le cas de perte du sens initial suivie d'une recherche artificielle d'explication.

Ces considérations générales achevées, examinons un à un les différents cas qui se présentent dans les conditions ci-dessus. Le résultat de notre analyse ne sera autre que, dans ses grandes lignes, la structure des huit modes de l'octoéchos, y compris des formes réputées excentriques que la théorie tardive à eu peine a intégrer et dont cependant on n'a pu dissimuler l'éxistence.

Rappelons d'abord l'échelle de base pentatonique, numérotée par quintes selon le principe que nous avons préconisé ailleurs:[1]

I.	FA sol la do ré fa	=	T T 3 T 3
II.	DO ré fa sol la do	=	T 3 T T 3
III.	SOL la do ré fa sol	=	T 3 T 3 T
IV.	RE fa sol la do ré	=	3 T T 3 T
V.	LA do ré fa sol la	=	3 T 3 T T

Les deux notes *si* et *mi* y sont des *piens*, notes faibles facultatives dont l'absence n'enlève pas conjonction et dont l'emplacement mobile ne dépend pas du cycle des quintes comme les notes structurelles ci-dessus, mais des circonstances de leur emploi au gré des attractions. C'est le problème bien connu du *si bémol*. Mais celui-ci a-t-il jamais été correctement posé? Voici pourquoi nous nous permettons d'en douter :

Lorsque s'est formé le répertoire grégorien, il n'existait ni notation ni solfège approprié. Le seul critère était intervallique. On ne voit donc pas comment aurait pu se concrétiser la raison invoquée que 'seul le degré *si* pouvait recevoir un bémol', phrase intraduisible dans le langage antérieur au IXe siècle. Mais lorsque, vers cette époque, on commença à désigner les degrés solfégiquement, ce fut d'abord en empruntant à la musique grecque antique sa terminologie tétracordale. Celle-ci provenait-elle d'une tradition scolaire conservée, ou bien d'une étude humanistique des auteurs anciens, notamment Cassiodore et surtout de Boèce? Nous pencherions plutôt pour la seconde hypothèse. Quoi qu'il en soit, ces deux derniers survivants latins de la musique grecque antique furent pris abusivement pour des théoriciens de la seule musique alors vivante, la musique ecclésiastique, si bien que lorsque se créa une notation alphabétique latine, elle se vit assigner la théorie de l'échelle antique pré-établie qui s'en rapprochait le plus, celle du système diatonique grec. Or dans celui-ci, il n'y avait place que pour une seule note mobile, le *si*, amené par métabole tétracordale des disjointes aux conjointes (la paramèse devenant *trite synemmenon*). C'est probablement pour cette seule raison que la théorie, puis le solfège et enfin l'écriture, n'ont jamais dans le cadre du grégorien admis d'autre altération possible que celle du *si* au *si bémol*, alors qu'en fait la structure pentatonique en exigeait deux : le *si* et le *mi* (ou même davantage dans certains cas complexes). D'où, au hasard des nécessités, des transpositions qui n'ont pas peu contribué à brouiller la théorie, et par lesquelles nous devrons soigneusement éviter de nous laisser influencer.

[1] 'Essai sur les structures mélodiques', dans *Revue de Musicologie*, déc. 1959, p. 143. Nous noterons T=ton, s=semiton (ou demi-ton), 3=trihémiton incomposé. Par ailleurs D=dominante, T=tonique. Nous chiffrerons les degrés à partir de I tonique avec le signe+en montant et — en descendant : ainsi, pour *sol*=I, nous aurons *la*=+II, *fa*=—II.

En effet, on ne le répétera jamais trop, jusqu'au IXᵉ siècle environ, le concept médiéval est exclusivement intervallique. Les noms de notes sont inconnus, et nous ne les emploierons que pour faciliter la compréhension : il faudra toujours en faire abstraction pour suivre la démarche du raisonnement. Ceci dit, et bien que le point de départ réel soit la dominante plutôt que la tonique, c'est cette dernière que nous placerons par commodité sur le tableau par quintes ci-dessus en faisant coïncider l'extrémité inférieure du noyau avec la tonique. Ce qui nous donne également l'emplacement de la dominante et répond par conséquent aux données du problème. Par exemple, pour rechercher quel système contient un noyau formé de deux tons entiers, écrits T T, nous rechercherons quel système pentatonique commence par T T, et nous trouverons le pentatonique I dit encore pentatonique Fa — (*fa* étant présumé tonique) — dont la D sera par conséquent Fa + T T = La.

Dans ce système, et bien que le point de départ réel soit la dominante, l'habitude de compter en montant nous mènera à poser pour simplifier Iᵉʳᵉ note = tonique, ce qui n'entraînera pas de perturbation notable, puisque la dominante se trouve par là également définie. Il va de soi que cette notation implique que l'on suppose éventuellement développement symétrique de l'échelle au grave (par exemple notre pentatonique Fa étant défini T T 3 T 3, on retrouvera sous cette séquence d'intervalles un autre groupe virtuel T T 3 T 3, que nous devrons naturellement parcourir à l'envers, puisque nous procédons par agrandissement du noyau). De même à l'aigu, l'échelle est censée se continuer aussi longtemps que nécessaire par recommencement.

Nous chercherons donc ce qui se passe dans toutes les hypothèses intervalliques possibles entre une tonique T et une dominante D, en étudiant successivement la forme du noyau, la position et le rôle de ses *piens* mobiles, puis les zones extérieures adjacentes. Ce qui se passe, c'est la formation de l'octoéchos :

Noyau de demi-ton. Il est exclu par définition, puisque cet intervalle est inconnu de l'échelle.

Noyau de ton entier. Théoriquement possible (pentatoniques I, II, III). Il semble attesté dans le répertoire par diverses pièces archaïques dont la théorie n'a jamais pu rendre compte (Sanctus et Agnus de la messe XVIII par exemple). Sa forme rudimentaire permettant peu de développement, il semble avoir rapidement disparu. C'est à partir du noyau de tierce mineure qu'apparaît réellement la modalité définitive.

Noyau de tierce mineure. La tierce est en principe incomposée et divisible par un *pien* + II. Elle répond aux deux pentatoniques IV (ré) et V (la) :

(a) *Le noyau.* Deux formes possibles, T S ou S T selon la place que prendra le *pien* + II. En raison de sa proximité de la D, l'attirance de celle-ci est la plus forte, de sorte que la forme bécarre prédomine largement, sans exclure une bémolisation occasionnelle sous l'attirance du grave (graduel 'Haec dies').

(b) *Zone supérieure.* Les *piens* sont + VI en pentatonique *ré* ou + V en pentatonique *la*. Or + V ne peut que se bécarriser sous peine de triton avec T : il coïncide donc avec + V de l'autre forme. De son côté, + VI ne peut que se bémoliser, car, placé à l'extrémité de l'échelle, il n'est attiré que vers le grave : il coïncide donc avec + VI de l'autre échelle. Comme pour le noyau, les échelles des deux formes coïncident.

[87]

(c) *Zone inférieure.* Les *piens* sont —III en pent. *ré* et —IV en pent. *la* (les autres sont trop éloignés pour entrer en ligne de compte). Tourné en haut vers le noyau, —III est normalement bécarrisé et cesse donc de coïncider avec —III (*fa*) du pentatonique *la*, à moins que, l'échelle se prolongeant exceptionnellement loin au grave, il ne subisse une attraction inverse et se bémolise accidentellement (répons 'Collegerunt'). En fait, ce degré semble particulièrement faible, et l'on observe presque toujours son absence, de sorte que cette divergence ne fait pas objection à l'unification des deux formes. De son côté, —IV coïncide dans les deux cas : il est en effet bécarrisé en pentatonique *la* pour la même raison que —III dans l'autre forme.

(d) *Structure modale.* L'identité d'échelle amène une fusion des deux formes en un mode unique, ayant pour noyau une tierce mineure soit incomposée soit divisée par un *pien* mobile (donc s t ou t s) avec toutefois large prédominance de la forme t s. À l'aigu, t t s t t, au grave (en descendant) t t s t t. Degrés faibles et mobiles = soit —III, +II et +VI, c. à d. pentatonique IV (*ré*) avec élision habituelle de —III, soit —IV, +II et +V, c. à d. pentatonique V (*la*). Les deux formes pourront parfois être juxtaposées par métabole dans une même pièce (offertoire 'Tollite portas')[1].

(e) *Notation.* Selon la position des *piens*, deux notations se montreront possibles : en *ré* ou en *la*. Les deux se verront également employées, sans qu'il y ait lieu de considérer l'une comme la 'transposition' de l'autre.

Le mode que nous venons d'étudier sera classé comme 2ème mode ou *protus* plagal.

Noyau de tierce majeure. Une seule forme possible du noyau, t t, sans *pien* intérieur. Elle répond au seul pentatonique I (*fa*) :

(a) *Le noyau.* Défini ci-dessus, il ne pose aucun problème.

(b) *Zone supérieure.* Les *piens* sont +IV et +VII, mais ce dernier est rarement atteint. A l'extrémité de l'échelle, il aurait tendance à se bémoliser : le cas ne se présente guère, heureusement, car il ne coïnciderait que difficilement avec la théorie ultérieure. +IV est normalement mobile, avec prédominance de bémolisation, puisqu'il est habituellement tourné vers le noyau grave.

(c) *Zone inférieure.* Les *piens* sont —II, normalement bécarre puisque tourné en haut vers le noyau, mais fréquemment omis ; et —V rarement atteint (tourné vers le haut, sa tendance serait au bécarre).

(d) *Structure modale.* Uniforme : noyau t t ; à l'aigu, normalement s t t, mais possibilité théorique de t s t ou de 3 t ; au grave (en descendant) 3 t ou s t t, exceptionnellement t s t. Structure de pentatonique I.

(e) *Notation.* En *fa* ou en *do*.

C'est le 6ème mode ou *tritus* plagal.

Noyau de quarte. La quarte peut être t 3 ou 3 t. D'où deux modes différents :

(A) *Quarte* t 3. Répond aux deux pentatoniques II (*do*), c. à d. t 3 t t 3, et III (*sol*), c. à d. t 3 t 3 t :

(a) *Le noyau.* Pien mobile +III, tendant plutôt à se bécarriser en raison du voisinage supérieur de la dominante, mais sans exclure la bémolisation s'il est tourné vers la tonique et que celle-ci

---

[1] Le *si* bémol grave du répons 'Subvenite' (classé en 4ème mode) qui tourmente si fort les grégorianistes n'est peut-être qu'une métabole de ce genre, car tout le contexte qui l'entoure est à base de 2ème mode, comme cela est fréquent, nous le verrons bientôt, dans le 4ème mode.

laisse se développer sous elle un −II renforcé qui entraîne éviction du triton ; ce qui peut se produire avec le pentatonique *sol* dont −II est un degré fixe.

(b) *Zone supérieure.* Piens +VI ou +VII selon la forme du pentatonique. En pentatonique *sol*, +VI est *pien mi*. Trop proche du *si* +III, lequel est bécarrisé s'il est en relation avec lui (puisqu' alors tourné vers l'aigu) il a peu de chances de se bémoliser, ce qui amènerait triton. Bécarre, il coïncide avec le *la* +VI du pentatonique *do*. Dans celui-ci, c'est +VII qui est *pien si*. Placé à l'extrême aigu, il a peu de chances d'être tourné ailleurs que vers le centre, donc tendra à se bémoliser, coïncidant avec le *fa* +VII de l'autre forme. Les échelles des deux formes coïncideront.

(c) *Zone inférieure.* Piens −II ou −III selon la forme du pentatonique. −II est le *si* du pentatonique *do*. Voisin inférieur de la tonique, il tendrait à se bécarriser, n'était le triton avec la dominante, dont la crainte est plus forte que l'attraction de tonique. Il se bémolise donc et coïncide avec le *fa* −II de l'autre forme (v. par ex. l'alleluia 'Virga Jesse'). Quant à −III, *mi* du pentatonique *sol*, il est tourné vers le noyau sans contre-indication et se bécarrise donc, coïncidant avec le *la* −III du pentatonique *do*. Ici, encore, les deux échelles coïncideront.

(d) *Structure modale.* Conséquence de ce qui précède : noyau de quarte ᴛ 3 avec +III mobile, donc pouvant devenir soit ᴛ s ᴛ soit ᴛ ᴛ s ; à l'aigu, ᴛ ᴛ s ᴛ ; au grave (en descendant) ᴛ s ᴛ ᴛ. Structure soit de pentatonique III avec pour degrés faibles +III et VI, soit de pentatonique II avec pour degrés faibles +III et VII, −II et VI.

(e) *Notation.* +III étant le seul degré véritablement mobile, on généralisera la notation en *sol*, entièrement satisfaisante.

C'est le 8ème mode ou *tetrardus* plagal.

(B) *Quarte* 3ᴛ. Répond aux deux pentatoniques IV (ré) c. à d. 3 ᴛ ᴛ 3 ᴛ, et V (la) c. à d. 3 ᴛ 3 ᴛ ᴛ.

(a) *Le noyau.* Pien +II, trop éloigné de la dominante pour recevoir son attraction. Il subira donc celle, plus faible, de son voisin la tonique, c. à d. se bémolisera, mais à condition que cette bémolisation n'entraîne triton avec aucune note forte en liaison avec lui.

Or la situation de ce point de vue est différente dans les deux pentatoniques en cause. En pentatonique *ré*, la tonique d'où dépend +II est aussi en liaison avec le *pien* −III, qui, tourné vers le noyau, tend à se bécarriser, et par là, pour éviter triton, à bécarriser +II ; au surplus un bémol amènerait triton avec +V, qui est ici note fixe. D'où tendance à une forme bécarre, soit ᴛ s ᴛ. En pentatonique *la*, la situation est exactement inverse. Le *pien* extérieur qui poussera à rejeter le triton est à l'aigu comme +V, et, voisin supérieur de la dominante, est fortement sollicité de se bémoliser, entraînant aussi la bémolisation de +II. Au grave, c'est avec −III que joue la peur du triton : or −III n'est pas un *pien* mobile comme précédemment, mais une note fixe *fa* qui elle aussi pousse +II à se bémoliser, c. à d. que le noyau tendra à une forme s ᴛ ᴛ différente de celle issue du pentatonique *ré*.

Contrairement aux formes précédemment étudiées, le noyau de quarte 3 ᴛ aura donc pour *pien* non une note mobile variant au gré des attractions, mais un degré de position différente selon qu'il se réfère au pentatonique *ré* ou au pentatonique *la* : bémol dans le premier cas, bécarre dans le second.

(b) *Zone supérieure.* On vient de le voir, les *piens* sont +V ou +VI, mais ils ne sont pas interchangeables : avec *pien* +V, nous sommes en pentatonique V (*la*) qui entraîne habituellement

7   [89]

bémolisation de +II et +V, ce dernier restant toutefois mobile ; avec *pien* +VI, nous sommes en pentatonique IV (*ré*) qui entraîne habituellement bécarrisation de +II et +VI, ce dernier restant toutefois mobile.

(c) *Zone inférieure.* Même situation. En pentatonique IV (*ré*), le *pien* qui est −III est bécarrisé comme +II ; en pentatonique V (*la*), le *pien* qui est −IV est par contre mobile : son attirance vers le noyau tend à le bécarriser, la peur du triton avec +II à le bémoliser.

(d) *Structure modale.* Malgré la similitude originelle des noyaux, les deux formes présentent trop de différences pour pouvoir se confondre. Le pentatonique *ré* aboutit à un noyau T S T prolongé à l'aigu par T T S T, au grave (en descendant) par T S T T, avec pour degrés faibles −III, +II, +VI. Le pentatonique *la* aboutit à un noyau S T T prolongé à l'aigu par S T T, au grave (en descendant) par T T S T ou T T T S, avec pour degrés faibles −IV, +II, +V.

En outre, un conflit se déclare souvent, dans la forme à +II bémolisée, entre la structure pentatonique qui donne à ce +II un rôle de *pien* assez faible, et le renforcement considérable qu'il reçoit de la formule cadencielle du fait de sa proximité au demi-ton de la finale conclusive. Ce conflit amènera souvent des artifices de style, dont l'un des plus fréquents consiste à éviter jusqu'à l'approche de la cadence non pas, comme on eût pu s'y attendre, le *pien* +II lui-même, mais la tonique à laquelle il conduit. D'où de longues insistances sur la tierce mineure −II/+II qui mènent pratiquement à un contexte de 2ème mode jusqu'à l'approche cadencielle. (Ex. introït 'Resurrexi'.)

(e) *Notation.* Une notation conforme à l'étymologie est rarement possible en raison de l'importance des bémolisations du *mi*. C'est pourquoi on a noté habituellement soit en *la* soit en *mi* ; mais il faut bien comprendre que dans aucun de ces cas ce n'est là l'orthographe étymologique : même la notation en *la*, avec *si* bécarre, est bien souvent une transposition du pentatonique en *re*, tandis que la notation en *mi* est habituellement une transposition du pentatonique en *la* (avec *si* bémol).

L'explication que nous proposons fait disparaître, croyons-nous, un certain nombre des anomalies accumulées par la théorie traditionnelle, qui s'est toujours vu particulièrement embarrassée devant ce mode. Le considérant comme un mode de *mi*, caractérisé par son noyau S T T, elle ne pouvait que difficilement y rattacher la forme T S T, qu'elle considérait comme une forme divergente en *la*, et elle avait peine à expliquer qu'à des antiennes d'une forme corresponde si facilement une psalmodie de l'autre. Les deux formes en effet, malgré leurs différences considérables, sont issues d'un noyau identique, et c'est pourquoi elles sont restées confondues en un même mode : le 4ème ou *deuterus* plagal.

Noyau de quinte. Ici, pour les raisons exposées dans l'introduction, nous quittons la structure des plagaux (noyau = zone centrale flanquée de deux zones latérales) — pour aborder celle des authentes (noyau = zone grave surmontée d'une zone aiguë). Au grave ne reste qu'un proslambanomène faible, et seulement s'il est à un ton sous la tonique.

La quinte peut revêtir 3 formes selon que son trihémiton est au grave, au centre ou à l'aigu : 3 T T, T 3 T, ou T T 3.

(A) *Quinte* 3 T T. Répond au pentatonique IV (*ré*) soit 3 T T 3 T.
(a) *Le noyau.* Le *pien* +II est soumis à deux forces contradictoires, mais inégales. L'une (la moindre) est l'attraction de la tonique sa voisine, qui tend à le bémoliser. L'autre (la plus forte)

est la peur du triton avec la dominante, qui tend à le bécarriser. Il eût pu dans ces conditions devenir une note mobile, bémolisable ou non selon qu'elle était tournée vers le grave ou vers l'aigu ; en fait les deux hypothèses se sont nettement différenciées et ont mené à deux modes distincts, dont l'un, celui affecté par le bémol, n'a pu résister longtemps à son triton et s'est bientôt transformé en ne laissant que le souvenir d'un archaïsme.

(b) *Le proslambanomène*. Normal : т sous la tonique.

(c) *La zone aiguë*. Plus développée que dans les plagaux, elle atteint facilement +VIII, et peut devenir à peu près autonome. C'est pourquoi le *pien* +VI, qui dans un plagal serait resté presque uniquement tourné vers le grave, donc aurait tendu à stabiliser sa bémolisation, presque imposée par le voisinage de la dominante, restera ici mobile : bémol ou bécarre selon qu'il regarde vers le grave ou vers l'aigu. Le triton avec +III joue aussi un rôle, sans doute, mais n'en est pas pour autant la seule raison déterminante.

(d) *Structure modale*. C'est celle du pentatonique IV. Noyau 3 т т pouvant devenir т s т т, (et même s т т т, mais en ce cas on se trouvera devant un nouveau mode, que nous étudierons avec le noyau de sixte qui a pris la place de celui-ci). Proslambanomène т. Zone aiguë 3 т ou s т т ou т s т . Degrés faibles —II (proslambanomène), +II et +VI (*piens*).

(e) *Notation* en *ré* tant que +II est bécarrisé, mais sous la forme où il se bémolise, on ne pourra noter qu'en *mi*.

C'est, avec +II bécarrisé, le Ier mode ou *protus* authente. Avec +II bémolisé, nous sommes devant la forme archaïque du 3ème mode, noté en *mi* avec dominante *si* bécarre, qui 'glissera' bientôt au *do* pour donner un noyau de sixte mineure.

(B) *Quinte* т 3 т. Répond aux pentatoniques II (do) soit т 3 т т 3, et III (sol) soit т 3 т 3 т.

(a) *Le noyau*. Pien +III à égale distance de tonique et de dominante ; l'attirance de celle-ci étant la plus forte, la tendance serait plutôt à la bécarrisation ; mais celle-ci est surtout imposée par la peur du triton avec +VI, note réelle en pentatonique *do*, fixée par analogie en pentatonique *sol*, comme nous allons le voir. On renonce donc à la forme bémolisée et on écrit т т s т.

(b) *Le proslambanomène*. Normal : т sous la tonique, en pentatonique sol. En pentatonique *do*, il serait *pien* mobile et tendrait plutôt à se bécarriser, mais on a vu que le proslambanomène ne peut être que т. Il y renonce donc, et les deux formes s'égalisent.

(c) *Zone aiguë*. Pien +VI en type *sol*, +VII en type *do*. En aucun cas un +VI bémolisé avec un +III bécarrisé n'eût pu être noté. Est-ce pour cette raison qu'on ne le rencontre jamais, ou bien est-ce l'écriture qui est défaillante? Quoiqu'il en soit, +VI, qui eût pu en droit devenir mobile est toujours en fait bécarrisé. Il coïncide donc avec +VI non mobile du pentatonique *do*, comme dans celui-ci +VII bémolisé coïncide avec +VII non mobile du pentatonique *sol*. Il semble donc que les deux types se soient fondus en un seul, les notes fortes de l'un renforçant les notes faibles de l'autre.

(d) *Structure modale*. Noyau т 3 т ou т т s т avec proslambanomène. Zone aiguë т s т. Les notes faibles, outre le proslambanomène —II, sont +III et, selon les cas, +VI ou +VII. Naturellement —II cesse d'être faible si, par une extension exceptionnelle de l'échelle au grave, il redevient note réelle du pentatonique (ex. graduel 'Jacta cogitatum').

[91]

(e) *Notation.* Généralisée en *sol*, exceptionnellement en *do*.
C'est le 7ème mode ou *tetrardus* authente.

(C) *Quinte* т т 3. Répond au pentatonique I (fa) soit т т 3 т 3.
(a) *Le noyau. Pien* +IV tiraillé entre l'attirance de son voisin la dominante qui tend à le bécarriser et la peur du triton avec la tonique qui tend à le bémoliser. Il sera donc mobile, bémol ou bécarre selon qu'il se tourne à l'aigu vers la zone d'attirance de +V ou vers celle de I au grave.
(b) *Le proslambanomène.* Ne serait pas ici à un ton, mais à un demi-ton ou à tierce mineure. Il ne se développera pas.
(c) *Zone aiguë. Pien* +VII, dont l'attirance est plutôt vers l'aigu +VIII que vers le grave ; forme bécarrisée, favorisée au reste par l'écriture, qui n'eût pu concilier le bémol avec la faculté de bémolisation reconnue à +IV et exigeant la notation en *fa* (on ne pouvait noter un *mi* bémol).
(d) *Structure modale.* Pentatonisme très marqué, le pentatonique I n'ayant pas eu de concurrent. Noyau т т 3 avec +IV facultatif et mobile, soit т т s т ou т т т s ; on relève de fréquentes élisions de +II bien qu'il soit étymologiquement degré fort. Le phénomène serait trop long à étudier ici. Pas de proslambanomène. Zone aiguë т 3 ou т т s formant un véritable tétracorde structuré ; +VII peut s'y renforcer au point d'amener une véritable métabole pentatonique 3 т т entre +III et +VII (ex. graduel 'Ex Sion', sur le mot 'congregate').
(e) *Notation* généralisée en *fa*, exceptionnellement en *do*.
C'est le 5ème mode ou *tritus* authente, avec parfois des interférences sur le 7ème mode transposé en *do* (ex. antienne monastique 'Me suscepit.')

Noyau de sixte mineure. C'est la distance maximum à laquelle puisse se faire sentir un rapport tonique-dominante. Encore ne s'est-il manifesté que dans un seul cas, par extension du noyau de quinte de 3ème mode gêné par son triton entre la dominante, note la plus forte du mode, et un +II renforcé par sa valeur cadencielle très affirmée, malgré son origine de *pien*.

Il va de soi que l'explication traditionnelle selon laquelle la dominante a glissé de *si* à *do* parce que le *si* ne peut recevoir de dominante ne peut être qu'une explication (?) donnée après coup. Ne serait-ce que parce qu'elle suppose un raisonnement solfégique basé sur une nomenclature qui n'existait pas ?

Bien que noté en *mi* en raison de l'insuffisance du solfège, le 3ème mode n'est pas, nous l'avons vu, un mode de *mi*, mais la forme à +II bémolisé du pentatonique IV (*ré*), d'où primitivement sa structure 3 т т 3 т, avec division du premier trihémiton en s т, alors que le même pentatonique avec division en т s avait donné le Ier mode. L'agressivité de son triton +II /+V (+V étant dominante) a amené le déplacement de cette dominante vers +VI, de sorte que du pentatonique *ré*, le mode 'glisse' à son tour vers un pentatonique V (*la*) 3 т 3 т т que l'on orthographiera (en *mi*) *mi-sol-la-do-ré-mi* et qui est en réalité une transposition de *la-do-ré-fa-sol-la*, avec *si* bémol stabilisé. De même que le *deuterus* plagal juxtaposait souvent une structure de *protus* plagal à sa propre cadence, le *deuterus* authente recherchera curieusement les mêmes juxtapositions, fussent-elles appuyées sur des degrés différents (ex. introït 'Sancti tui', qui commence en pentatonique IV sur *ré* puis métabolise en pentatonique V du 3ème mode définitif, sur *mi*...) Dans ces conditions, il ne peut plus être question de bémoliser le nouveau *pien* +V, ancienne dominante, mais

[92]

seulement de le sauter à l'occasion. Tel sera, sous sa forme définitive, le 3ème mode, *deuterus* authente.

Conclusion. On vient de voir que les huit modes de l'octoéchos étaient le résultat, hors de toute théorie, de la création sous la teneur psalmodique et selon une échelle pentatonique ultérieurement comblée de *piens* mobiles, d'une zone mélodique déterminée d'une part par cette teneur ou dominante, d'autre part par une finale ou tonique. Ils épuisent toutes les combinaisons que présente cette hypothèse, de la tierce mineure à la quinte (plus une annexe historiquement expliquée pour la sixte mineure). On sait pourtant que ce n'est pas du tout ainsi que se présente la théorie traditionnelle. Celle-ci présente l'octoéchos comme une succession de finales préétablies formant un tétracorde *ré-mi-fa-sol*, chacune de ces finales commandant deux modes ; un principal ou authente caractérisé par la division en quinte + quarte de son octave modale ; un secondaire ou plagal caractérisé par la division de cette même octave en quarte + quinte. Or tout est faux dans cette description. Elle ne tient compte ni des dominantes ni des notes mobiles. L'exégèse des termes authente et plagal n'est peut-être qu'un contre-sens à partir d'une acception juste que nous avons évoquée plus haut. La notion d'octave modale et de sa division n'est qu'un contre-sens dont on a pu étudier la genèse en la localisant au milieu du IXe siècle[1] et elle n'a en rien son application musicale dans le répertoire. Les finales enfin ne forment le tétracorde justificatif que par suite d'artifices de transposition dont la seule justification est le décalque abusif de l'échelle diatonique tétracordale de l'ancienne musique grecque — décalque dont il ne semble pas probable que l'on se soit réellement avisé avant le IXe siècle.

Si l'octoéchos s'est formé sans théorie par le lent et inconscient travail des chantres anonymes, se confondant avec la constitution du répertoire lui-même, faut-il conclure que cette théorie aurait été dressée après coup (assez mal) par des raisonneurs humanistes plus sensibles aux diagrammes de Boèce et aux symboles de l'Ogdoade qu'à la perception des structures musicales sur lesquelles ils dissertaient, et faut-il déduire de son analyse que cette théorie n'aurait guère pu prendre naissance avant le IXe siècle ? Nous ne prétendrons pas pouvoir l'affirmer ; mais nous ne sommes pas très éloigné de le penser. Quant à déterminer ce qui, dans cette élaboration, revient aux Latins et aux Byzantins, nous ne nous permettrons pas d'aborder ici un problème de ce genre. Tout au plus pouvons nous souhaiter qu'un Egon Wellesz, après tant de travaux prestigieux sur des sujets avoisinants, nous en livre un jour la solution définitive.

[1] Cf. notre introduction à l'édition de l'*Alia Musica*, qui étudie ce problème, soulevé précisément par ce texte.

AN ENGLISH LIQUESCENT NEUME

John D. Bergsagel (Oxford)

THE NOTATION of plainsong still remains a subject of lively controversy—one to which Egon Wellesz has made important contributions and in which he continues to take an active interest. Whatever else remains uncertain, however, it has for some time apparently been assumed that at least the identification and codification of the neumes is complete and that the problems now lie only with interpretation. Some years ago, however, I noticed that a neume which occurs in a number of English manuscripts was not included in any of the lists of neumes known to me. Since Dr. Wellesz has urged me to publish a note about it, it is appropriate to do so on the present occasion, though it is no more than a footnote to a vast and complex subject.

The simple liquescent neumes *cephalicus* (i.e., the liquescent *clivis*) and *epiphonus* (liquescent *podatus*) are usually represented in English manuscripts by the symbols ∫ and ⟨ respectively. Like all liquescent neumes they are characterized by two features: their association with certain combinations of letters (successive consonants such as *rg*, *nd*, *ng*, or diphthongs such as *au*, *eu* or *ui*), and the indeterminate pitch of the second member of the neume. The conclusion seems obvious that the neume is specially designed to facilitate enunciation by a transition from the first member of the liquescent neume to the pitch of the next symbol by means of the deliberately vague and undefined pitch of the second member. Such a conclusion, which is clearly supported by contemporary commentators such as Guido d'Arezzo,[1] is perfectly consistent with the ideals of early monophonic notation, however unsatisfactory it may be for anyone preparing a modern transcription. Such a lack of precision cannot, however, be so easily tolerated in polyphonic music, and when we find the same symbols being used in the notation of polyphonic pieces in the thirteenth and fourteenth centuries it is usually necessary to interpret their second components as neighbouring passing notes.

The unsuitability of liquescence to polyphonic music was quickly recognized and the use of the symbols for this purpose abandoned. Towards the end of the fifteenth century, however, a symbol using the form of the *cephalicus* reappears in a special so-called 'playnsong' notation for polyphonic music, which is encountered in many English sources until well into the mid-sixteenth century. In such contexts as the Mass by Henry Petyr[2] and John Sheppard's *Playnsong Mass for a Mene*,[3] the symbol ⋀ represents a breve, whereas ■ represents the semibreve. This mensural

[1] 'Liquescunt vero in multis voces more litterarum, ita ut inceptus modus unius ad alteram limpide transiens, nec finiri videatur.'

[2] London, Brit. Mus., Add. 5665.
[3] London, Brit. Mus., Add. 17,802–5.

Antiphonale Sarisburiense (ed. W. H. Frere), p. 498

significance is clearly expressed by Marbeck in *The Booke of Common Praier noted* (1550), where he says: 'The first note is a strene note and is a breve. The second a square note and is a semy breve.' It is evident too that during this same period when plainchant melodies are used as *cantus firmi* the *cephalicus* is often treated in polyphony as a note of double length, not as two notes of different pitch. This fact has led some scholars to the practice of transcribing the plainchant *cephalicus* regularly as a note of double length. The uncertainty of connecting the monophonic with the polyphonic practice is demonstrated by the evidence of Marbeck himself, who apparently did not regard the *cephalicus* as a 'strene' note. The *cephalicus* which appears at the beginning of the antiphon 'Per arma justitiae' is treated not as a note of double length but as a neume of two pitches when he uses it as *cantus firmus* for his big Lenten Mass:[1]

Ex. 1

MARBECK: Mass 'Per arma justitie' (Gloria)

Per ar-ma ju-sti-ti-e

Gra - ti - as   a - gi - mus ti - bi

Uncertainty as to the pitch significance of the final component of a liquescent neume is therefore, one might suppose, axiomatic. It is all the more remarkable to discover in some English manuscripts of the thirteenth to the fifteenth centuries, coexistent with the usual liquescent forms, another liquescent neume ᠌, of which the most immediately noticeable feature is the precise definition of the pitch of the final member. This neume, which has not, so far as I know, been remarked upon hitherto, is, I believe, distinctively English; its occurrence in a manuscript would almost certainly indicate an English provenance, or at least an English scribe. It can be seen near the end of the top line of the first column and the seventh line of the second column of the accompanying plate. That it is a liquescent neume seems unquestionable from its almost invariable association with the usual combinations of letters, as here with the -*rg*- of *virgo* and -*t s*- of *Et sanctum*. It is true that it can be found very occasionally in conjunction with phonetic conditions which one would not expect necessarily to call for liquescence, but these, I think,

---

[1] Oxford, Bodleian, Mus. Sch. e 376–81.

[95]

can be explained as attributable to other factors. For example, in the series of 'Benedicamus domino' melodies in an Exeter Gradual,[1] this neume occurs as the first of one to the syllable *Be-* of *Benedicamus*. I suggest this may be explained as a reproduction of the notation used for the *neuma* in its original context, where it accompanied the word *Flos*, which, followed by *filius*, called for liquescence as a means of passing from *s* to *f*. In another situation[2] the neume accompanies the syllable *se-* of *semine*. This, however, is the conclusion of a sequence-type hymn 'Beate virginis fecundat visceris' in which the line ending with *semine* repeats exactly the melody and notation of the previous line, where the neume appears to provide the liquescence required by the consonants *-rg-* of *virgini*. More difficult to explain on these grounds is an instance on fo. 74 of the same manuscript. Here the neume occurs twice in quick succession:

Ex. 2

est vidi cum in-gen-ti

One can only argue that because of the repetition of the melodic figure the notation of the first occurrence has unnecessarily acquired the liquescent characteristics of the second. This curious passage defeats also an alternative explanation for the use of liquescent neumes which might have been applied to the previous two circumstances. This is to be derived from Freistedt's explanation[3] of the term *semivocalis*, by which liquescent neumes are also known, as referring not to 'half-vowels' but, according to Latin grammarians, to voiced consonants such as *f*, *l*, *m*, *n*, and *s*. It is apparent that while this could explain why a liquescent neume might be used with *Benedicamus* and *semine* it would have no bearing on *vidi cum*.

Nevertheless, a liquescent neume with a precisely defined final component would appear to be a contradiction in terms. In fact, the characteristic feature of this neume is the appearance of the first member, whereas the second is normal. How is such a neume to be interpreted? In the example which follows I illustrate how two passages which involve the use of this neume in some manuscripts are rendered in six sources. The first part of each example occurs in the verse 'Benedicta et venerabilis es virgo' of the respond 'Beata es virgo', the second in the closely following respond 'Beatam me dicent omnes':

Ex. 3

(a) Antiphonale Sarisburiense (ed. Frere), p. 498: see Plate I

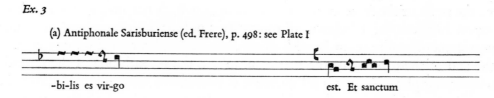

-bi-lis es vir-go   est. Et sanctum

---

[1] Manchester, John Rylands Library, MS. Lat. 24, given as Plate VII in F. Ll. Harrison's *Music in Medieval Britain* (London, 1958), where this neume can be seen on the second line of the second column.

[2] Oxford, Bodleian, Rawl. Lit. d 3, fo. 71.

[3] *Die liqueszierenden Noten des Gregorianischen Chorals* (Freiburg, 1929).

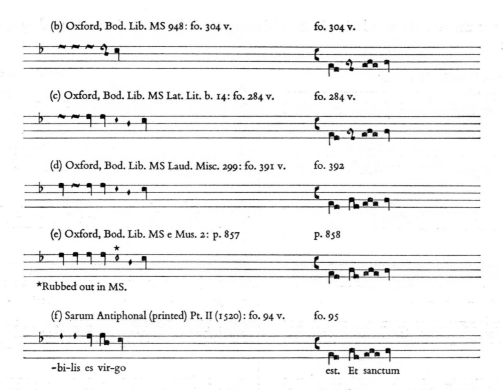

(b) Oxford, Bod. Lib. MS 948: fo. 304 v.   fo. 304 v.

(c) Oxford, Bod. Lib. MS Lat. Lit. b. 14: fo. 284 v.   fo. 284 v.

(d) Oxford, Bod. Lib. MS Laud. Misc. 299: fo. 391 v.   fo. 392

(e) Oxford, Bod. Lib. MS e Mus. 2: p. 857   p. 858

*Rubbed out in MS.

(f) Sarum Antiphonal (printed) Pt. II (1520): fo. 94 v.   fo. 95

-bi-lis es vir-go   est. Et sanctum

From this comparison it is clear that the neume represents a descending interval only, not a rising and falling one, as the curious conformation of its first part might seem to suggest. In other words, it is not a *torculus*, nor the liquescent *torculus*, a *pinnosa*. But if there is agreement as to its starting and finishing points, there is not general agreement as to how best to effect or describe the transition from one to the other. In Ex. 3(c) it will be observed that in the first instance this neume has been replaced by a *climacus* though it has been retained in the second. In 3 (d), similarly, a *climacus* substitutes in the first case but a *clivis* in the second. In 3 (e) the same substitutions are effected, but with this interesting and significant additional fact, that here the middle note of the *climacus* has been partially rubbed out. In the printed source from the beginning of the sixteenth century, 3 (f), the neume is regularly replaced by the *clivis*. It should be noted, too, that when the descending interval represented by this neume is not a third but a fourth, which it very occasionally is seen to be, the *clivis* is the inevitable alternative symbol.

We may again ask if polyphonic usage throws any light on the interpretation of this neume. Unfortunately the evidence is no more consistent than that adduced earlier in connection with the *cephalicus*. The verse 'Benedicta et venerabilis es' of the respond 'Beata es virgo' is used as the *cantus firmus* of both a Magnificat and a Mass by Nicholas Ludford.[1] Of course, one has no way of knowing in what source, hence in what notation, Ludford may have found his *cantus firmus*, but in any case his usage is ambiguous, for, whereas in the Magnificat the notes of the *cantus firmus*

---

[1] Cambridge, Gonville and Caius College, MS. 667. The Magnificat has been published in *Early Tudor Magnificats*, ed. P. Doe (Early English Church Music 4, London, 1964). Both Magnificat and Mass will appear in the forthcoming Vol. II of *The Collected Works of Nicolas Ludford* (American Institute of Musicology, CMM 27), ed. J. D. Bergsagel.

[97]

equivalent to those to the word *virgo* in the plainsong are C B♭ A B♭, in the Mass they are simply C A B♭:

Ex. 4   LUDFORD: Magnificat 'Benedicta'

Mass 'Benedicta' (Gloria)

po - ten - ti - am

Je - su   Chri - ste.

We may conclude that since this unnamed neume appears in some English manuscripts in addition to symbols such as the *clivis* and the *climacus*, which cover the same intervals, and side by side with other signs of liquescence, such as the *cephalicus* and *pinnosa*, it must express some other special subtlety of notation. It is evident that those manuscripts of whose notation it does not form part are not in agreement among themselves concerning the rendering of the words with which the neume is associated in some sources, though it is eventually generally replaced by the *clivis*. Its use is associated with the enunciation of certain difficult letter-combinations, but it is not liquescent in the usual manner of having a specially treated transitional second member. Indeed, it is unique in that its special character is indicated by its first member, and in the way this is connected to the otherwise normal second member. I suggest, therefore, that the neume is one in which the liquescence, that is, the special mode of performance necessary for the treatment of particular phonetic problems, is moved back from the second member of the neume, normally treated as a note of transition, to the first and its transition to the second. The conclusion seems unavoidable that the first note must be specially treated, no doubt slightly prolonged, by the singer and then smoothly joined to the second in such a way that the difficult sound is perfectly formed by the time it is sung to the pitch indicated by the final of the neume. It is, therefore, a liquescent neume of special significance to the English mode of plainsong performance.

In conclusion I should like to call attention to another neume, perhaps the most characteristic in appearance of all neumes in English manuscripts. This is the neume **ς**, which was so much part of English plainsong notation that, despite its inconvenient configuration, it was reproduced in the type of some early Sarum printed books. Its appearance would suggest a derivation from the English *epiphonus* (see above), but it does not seem to be associated with the characteristic phonetic conditions requiring liquescence. Its alternative symbol is almost always the *podatus*, sometimes the *pes stratus* when the upper member extends to the right, but, as in the case of the neume which has been under discussion, it seems quite clear that a special mode of performance is intended by this symbol, in addition to the basic ascending interval of a simple *podatus*. Dom Gregory Suñol has suggested that this neume represents a *podatus* with a median *quilisma*.[1] If the *quilisma* were to be interpreted in the manner advocated by Mocquereau[2] (that is, rendered lightly and the note immediately before the *quilisma* notably lengthened and emphasized), and not in the ornamental interpretation recommended by Gastoué,[3] it is apparent that the effect would be essentially equivalent for an ascending interval to that which we have here suggested for the descending interval of our unique English liquescent neume.

[1] *Introduction à la paléographie musicale grégorienne* (Tournai, 1935), p. 292.

[2] *Le Nombre musical grégorien*, Vol. I (Tournai, 1908), p. 404.

[3] *Cours théorique et pratique de chant grégorien*, 2nd ed., (Paris, 1917), p. 19.

PART TWO

OPERA

A HITHERTO UNPUBLISHED LETTER OF CLAUDIO MONTEVERDI

Albi Rosenthal (Oxford)

MONTEVERDI'S PREOCCUPATION with philosophical speculation and with the theoretical aspects and æsthetic aims of his art is reflected in the prefaces, dedications, and postscripts to his published works. A major treatise, *Seconda Pratica ovvero Perfettione della Moderna Musica*, announced by him in 1605 and still, or again, occupying him in 1633 was apparently never completed. The letters are an even more rewarding source for Monteverdi's ideas than the printed theoretical excursions. J. A. Westrup has observed[1] that 'Monteverdi was at his best—an irresistible best— when he forgot about theories and just wrote music'. It may equally be said that Monteverdi was at his best as a writer on music when he was faced with the immediate and pressing task of composing—when the confrontation with a new text that had to be set to music left no time for invocations of Plato or classical scansion, but forced the composer to apply his dramatic insight and æsthetic judgement to specific situations.

In G. Fr. Malipiero's book on Monteverdi (1929)[2] 119 letters are printed in full under the heading 'Tutte le lettere di Claudio Monteverdi'. Prunières[3] had listed 121 letters, of which he printed 53 in full. There are discrepancies between Prunières and Malipiero: the following letters in Prunières' annotated list of the extant correspondence[4] are not in Malipiero: Pr. 28, to A. Striggio, 28 Nov. 1617; Pr. 36, to the Duca di Bracciano, 13 Dec. 1619; Pr. 37, to the same, 5 Jan. 1620; Pr. 46, to the same, 29 Feb. 1620 (printed in full by Pr. as No. xxviii). Malipiero published the following letters not mentioned by Prunières: M. 11, to A. Striggio, 6 Jan. 1611; M. 20, to the same, 24 Nov. 1615; M. 65, to the same, 21 Oct. 1621. Pr. No. 50, letter of 21 Mar. 1620 is M. 48 dated 20 Mar. 1620; Pr. No. 65, 17 Mar. 1621, is M. No. 62 dated 17 Apr. 1621. There exists no annotated critical edition of the complete letters, and they have not been translated *in toto* into any language, although every study of Monteverdi from Stefano Davari onward has drawn heavily from this all-important source.

A hitherto unpublished letter can now be added to the existing corpus. Formerly in the Alexander Meyer-Cohn[5] and Karl Geigy-Hagenbach[6] Collections of Autographs, it was more recently

---

[1] J. A. Westrup, 'Monteverdi and the Orchestra', *Music & Letters* xxi (1940), p. 244.

[2] G. Fr. Malipiero, *Claudio Monteverdi* (Milan, 1929), pp. 127–297.

[3] H. Prunières, *La Vie et l'œuvre de Cl. Monteverdi* (Paris, 1926; English ed., London, 1926).

[4] Op. cit. pp. 277–86; English ed., pp. 221–30.

[5] Auction Catalogue, J. A. Stargardt, Berlin, 1905, Lot No. 3119.

[6] Auction Catalogue J. A. Stargardt, Marburg, May 1961, Lot No. 896.

shown at the Institut Pédagogique National, Paris, in the exhibition 'La Vie Théatrale au Temps de la Renaissance',[1] and at the Loan Exhibition of Musical Autographs at the Ashmolean Museum, Oxford, in 1964. Its existence was known to E. Vogel in 1887, who was unable to secure a copy of it from the then owner, D. G. Rossi of Rome.[2] It had since vanished from sight and was mentioned neither by H. Prunières nor by Malipiero. The letter is dated from Venice, 18 September 1627, and was written to the Marchese Enzo Bentivoglio (he is not named) who had asked Monteverdi to compose the music for the wedding festivities at Parma at the marriage of Duke Odoardo Farnese to Margherita, daughter of the Grand Duke Cosimo de' Medici. Negotiations had started in August, and on 10 September 1627 Monteverdi had thanked the Marchese Bentivoglio for the text of an *intermedio* received a day earlier. After reading it twice he had become 'dedicated to such a fine work' and at once saw that the *intermedio* called for four different types of 'harmony' which he outlines. Certain passages would cause considerable difficulty. On the same day (10 September) he wrote to Alessandro Striggio about this commission: 'The first *intermedio* is already almost half finished, and it will be easy, because it consists almost entirely of soliloquies'.

The texts to be composed were five *intermedi* written by Ascanio Pio,[3] and the *torneo*, *Mercurio e Marte* by Claudio Achillini.[4] The *intermedi* were to be performed between the acts of Torquato Tasso's *Aminta*. The first concerned the liberation of Ruggiero. The subject of the second was Dido and Aeneas and is referred to in the letter as 'l'intermedio di Didone'. The protagonists of the third, fourth, and fifth were the gods of Olympus, joined in the fifth by the four Continents. The performance took place on 13 December 1628 on a specially constructed stage in the courtyard of S. Pietro Martire. The *torneo*, *Mercurio e Marte* by Achillini was the climax of the festivities at Parma, and with its production on 21 December 1628 the great Teatro Farnese was inaugurated. It was staged with all the mechanical ingenuity and lavish splendour typical of the period.[5] After

[1] Catalogue, ed. by J. Jacquot (1963), No. 371, pp. 194–5.

[2] 'Monteverdi soll sich über den Text und die Musik zu diesem Stücke ausführlich in einem seiner Briefe vom 18. Sept. 1627 geäußert haben. Das Original befand sich im Mai 1887 im Besitze D. G. Rossi's in Rom. Leider kann ich über den Inhalt desselben nichts Näheres mittheilen, da meine Bemühungen um eine Kopie des Briefes erfolglos waren' (E. Vogel, 'Claudio Monteverdi', *Vierteljahrsschrift für Musikwissenschaft* iii [1887], p. 388).

[3] First published at Parma in 1629; reprinted in A. Solerti, *Musica, Ballo e Drammatica alla Corte Medicea dal 1600 al 1637* (Florence, 1905), pp. 428–80.

[4] Reprinted ibid., pp. 481–518. There are two different issues of the first edition of the libretto, both published by Seth & E. Viotti at Parma in 1628. One of these has a plain printed title followed by the text. The other has an engraved title-page with an illustrated border, followed by a dedication and a 'Ristretto del Torneo', and the 'imprimatur'. A reference to the printed *ristretto* (synopsis) of the *intermedi* contained in a letter of A. Giordani to his wife, written five days after he had attended the performance, points to a practice not noticed hitherto: that the quire of the libretto containing the synopsis may have been sold separately at performances. This may explain the bibliographical puzzle why, for instance, extant copies of the libretto of *L'Arianna*, published in 1608, have an unexplained gap between the title and p. [7], the beginning of the text. Giordani writes on 18 Dec. 1628: 'Invio questi ristretti de gl'intermedî acciò si prendano un poco di gusto, fin ch'io potrò poi più distintamente raccontargli: faccia loro aver cura, acciò non si perdano, perchè io n'ho d'altri' (I am sending this synopsis of the *intermedi* so that you can get a taste of them until I can tell you about them in greater detail: take care that it should not get lost, because I have no other). Cf. A. Saviotti, 'Feste e spettacoli nel Seicento', *Giornale storico di Letteratura Italiana* xli (Turin, 1903).

Solerti reprinted the dedication and *ristretto*, but not the *imprimatur*, which is of interest: 'Si protesta che le parole Dio d'Amore, Dea d'Amore, Deità, Divinità, Paradiso, Adorare, Beato & altre simili s'intendono conforme all'uso de' Poeti, & non mai in senso che offenda in parte alcuna imaginabile i sensi e i Dogmi purissimi della Religione Cattolica.' There follow the signatures of the ecclesiastical authorities.

[5] Important new material on these productions is being brought to light by Stuart Reiner: cf. his article 'Preparations in Parma—1618, 1627–28', *The Music Review* xxv (1964), pp. 273–301. Among contemporary accounts cf. specially M. Buttigli, *Descrittione dell'apparato fatto per*

MONTEVERDI

Autograph letter, p. 1

indubio di scriverò il restato in
termedio di Ridone. Ho visto
però che sfuggita gli metri come
parlano, et ho visto la discordia
parimenti. et ho un povero penso
della imitatione, de la detta discordia
et mi pare che sarà un poco difficil
lettera, la ragione è questa che gli
metri douendosi concertare ed armo
nie vocali, circandoperò quelle che
doueranno andare alla imitatione
più possibili di ciascheduno, la concor
dia armonia suo servitio de la dis
cordia, contraria dico a quella che con
uera ali metri, no so al presente im

MONTEVERDI
Autograph letter, p. 2

MONTEVERDI
Autograph letter, p. 3

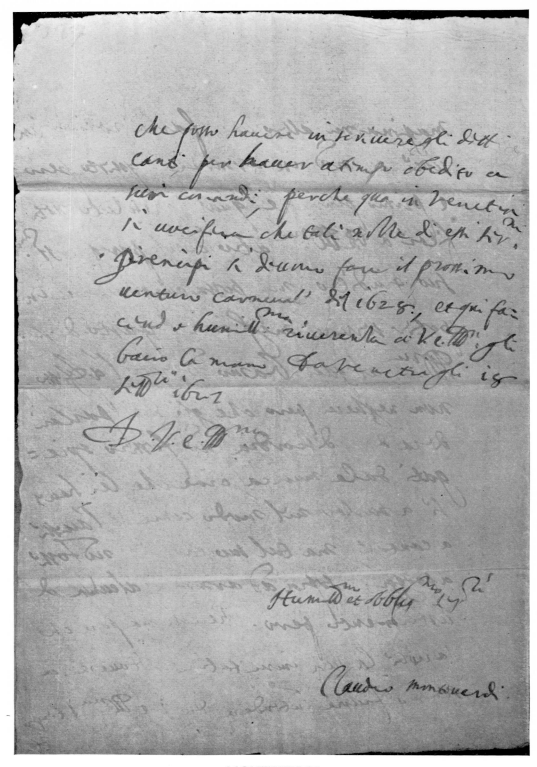

che possi hauere in scriuere gli detti
canti, per hauer a tempo obedito a
suoi comandi; perche qua in Venetia
si uocifera che tali a Me di esi hr̄
prencipi si deuono fare il prossimo
uenturo carneual' di 1628., et qui fa=
cend' a humill.ma riuerenta a V. Ill.ma gli
bacio la mano Da Venetia li 15
settembre 1627

A V. S. Ill.ma

Humil.mo et obblig.mo serv.re

Claudio monteuerdi.

MONTEVERDI
Autograph letter, p. 4

a prologue by Aurora, the months March, June, September, and January sing twelve verses each, and after some verses sung by the Golden Age, Discordia appears on the scene accompanied by two Furies. It is to these Months and Discordia that Monteverdi refers:

Illmo et ecc.mo mio sigr. et padron coll.mo, Sperero senz altro per lo venturo ordinario di sabato mandar a V. E. Ill.ma fatto tutto l'intermedio di Didone credevo mandarlo aver per lo presente, ma se mi è interposto acidente che non mi ha lassiato comporre per duoi giorni; et spero che tal intermedio non dispiacerà a V. E. Illma., poco anco manca al finir il primo. accuso poi la riceuta a V. E. Illma. dal corriere li versi mandatemi per servitio dela Corriera questi per anco non gli ho ben letti per la brevità del tempo hauta et per essere stato intento al scrivere il narato intermedio di Didone. Ho visto però alla sfuggita gli mesi come parlano, et ho visto la discordia parimente. et ho un popoco pensato alla immitatione de la detta discordia et mi pare che sarà un poco difficiletta, la ragione è questa che gli mesi dovendosi concertare con armonie soavi, cercando però quelle che doveranno andare alla immitatione più possibile di ciascheduno, la contraria armonia sarà per servitio de la discordia, contraria dico a quella che converà a li mesi, non so al presente immaginarmi altro che farla recitar in voce et non in armonia, questo però è primo pensiere, qual ho voluto notificare a V. E. Ill.ma afin con il pregatiss.mo suo giudizio mi possa congiovare in poter servire meglio al gusto di V. E. Ill.ma al qual bramo con tutto l'affetto; non negherei però che gli detti parlare de la detta discordia non fossero spiegati dalla musica, cioè che lei havesse a parlar nel modo come se l'avesse a cantare, ma tal suo cantare non fosse appoggiato sopra ad armonia alcuna di ustrimento però; che così mi pare che sarebbe la sua immitatione; Haverei a sommo favore intendere da V. E. Ill.ma il tempo che posso havere in scrivere gli detti canti per haver a tempo obedito a suoi commandi; perchè qua in Venetia si vocifera che tali nozze di essi ser.mi prencipi si devono fare il prossimo venturo carnevale del 1628. et qui facendo humill:ma riverenza a V. E. Ill. gli bacio la mano da Venetia gli 18 sett.re 1627.
Di V. E. Ill.ma

Humill.mo et obblig.mo
Claudio Monteverdi.

[Translation]

I hope without fail to send to your Excellency by the next mail on Saturday the completed *intermedio* of 'Dido'; I meant to have sent it by the present one, but an accident intervened which prevented me from composing for two days; and I hope that this *intermedio* will not displease your Excellency; little also remains to be done to complete the first one. I further acknowledge to your Excellency the receipt by the courier of the verses sent to me through the mail. These I have so far not read thoroughly because of the short time I had, and because I was intent on writing the said *intermedio* of 'Dido'. I have, however, seen at a quick glance how the Months speak, and I have likewise seen Discord; and I have thought a little about the representation of the said Discord, and it seems to me that it will be a little difficult, the reason being that since the Months have to sing together (*concertare*) to soft music[1] (though at the same time one must try to find those which will best imitate each one of them) the contrary music will be used for Discord—contrary, I mean, to the one suitable for the Months; all I can think of at present is to make her declaim (*recitar in voce*) without music; this, however, is my first thought which I wanted to communicate to your Excellency, so that with the help of your most esteemed judgement I may have the pleasure of being able to serve better the taste of your Excellency, to whom I am devoted with all affection; I would not deny, however, that the said speeches of the said Discord would not be illustrated by [the] music, namely, that she [Discord] would have to speak as if she had to sing, but this singing would not be supported by any instruments; for this, it seems to me, would be the way to represent her. It would be the greatest favour to me to hear from your Excellency how much time I may have for writing the said 'songs' (*canti*) so

honorare la . . . *entrata in Parma della . . . Prencipessa Margherita di Toscana* (Parma, 1629; no copy traced in British libraries). Cf. also A. M. Nagler, *Theater Festivals of the Medici 1539–1637* (Yale University Press, 1964), pp. 139–61.

[1] Monteverdi uses the word *armonia* in the wider sense of 'music' or 'musical organization'. Cf. H. F. Redlich, *Claudio Monteverdi* (London, 1952), p. 31, n.

that I may have obeyed your command in time; for here in Venice there is talk that the Wedding of the Most Serene Princes will take place at the coming Carnival of 1628. And here, with most humble reverence to your Excellency, I kiss your hand. From Venice, the 18th September 1627.

Your Excellency's Most humble and obliged
Claudio Monteverdi.

The question of 'imitation' (or representation) was always in Monteverdi's mind as the central issue of artistic expression. The passage concerning the 'representation of Discord' is not altogether clear; it shows Monteverdi trying to find an adequate musical equivalent for the dramatic contrast between the lyrical texts of the Months, which call for gentle music (including instruments), and the sudden challenge of Discord. This was the period between *Il Combattimento di Tancredi e Clorinda* (1624) and the *Madrigali Guerrieri ed Amorosi* (1638) in which the *stile concitato* came to full maturity.

Six weeks later, on 30 October 1627, Monteverdi wrote to the Marchese Bentivoglio:

I find I have finished the first *intermedio*, which is the one of Melissa and Bradamante, but not that of Dido—that will be the second one. I am working on the third, and when that is finished I shall start rehearsing. During the period of the first rehearsals I shall with God's help also finish the fourth. The fifth I have not yet received ... The *torneo* is ready, if not entirely, at least to a large extent.

In a letter to A. Striggio on 9 January 1628 he reports further progress, and on 4 February 1628 he writes:

Here at Parma the music I have composed is being rehearsed ... they say it could be for next May, others believe next September.[1] There will be two splendid *feste*, one an entire play performed with *intermedi* set to music, and there is no *intermedio* that is less than 300 verses long[2] and all of varying moods (*affetti*); ... the other will be a *torneo* ... and there are more than 1000 verses, fine indeed for a *torneo*, but rather remote from music—they have given me a great deal of trouble; now this music of the *torneo* is being rehearsed; and where I was unable to find variations in the ideas (*effetti*) I have tried to bring variety into the music.

Throughout Monteverdi's letters there is a noticeable pattern, linking new tasks of composition with indisposition and with the fear of not having enough time at his disposal. As early as 1604, in his third extant letter, he pleads with the Duke of Mantua, ten days after receiving a new commission, not to burden him ever again with so much work to be completed in so short a time, as this might shorten his life. The next extant letter, written three years later, mentions indisposition in a similar context, and so does the letter of 26 November 1608. There is no doubt that the work at Mantua in that year brought about a state of physical and nervous exhaustion which had a traumatic effect on Monteverdi. On 2 December 1608 he writes to the Counsellor of the Duke of Mantua: 'If I do not rest from wearing myself out with music for the theatre, my life will surely be short.' He describes his headaches, pains, and other symptoms and ascribes their cause partly to 'li studi grandi'. On 6 November 1615 he again refers to the frequent headaches and pains since his 'sufferings when I wrote Arianna'. In February 1617 he writes: 'Do not delay letting me have the text because there is nothing I hate more than being pressed for time.' Ten years later, on 1 May, 1627, he formulates his feelings most poignantly: 'I implore you to have

[1] Cf. Stuart Reiner, op. cit., p. 291 foll. on the details of the various postponements of the wedding and the performances.

[2] Ibid., p. 293.

consideration on two points: (1) that I should have adequate time to write the music, (2) that the text should be by a first-rate author . . . Shortness of time was the reason why I was reduced almost to death when I wrote Arianna. I know things could be done quickly, but speed and good work-manship do not go together.' A revealing testimony is contained in an important letter of the composer Antonio Goretti, recently published by Stuart Reiner:[1]

Signor Claudio composes only in the morning and the evening: during the afternoon he does not wish to do anything at all . . . If it had to be left to him . . . it would take time and plenty of it (and if I were not at his heels so much, he would not have done half of what he has done)[2] . . . He is a man who likes to talk things over in company at great length (and about this, I make it a rule to take the opportunity away from him during working hours).

Even though the music about which he writes is lost, as are all the compositions for the Parma celebrations and so much else, the letter to Bentivoglio confirms the traits of Monteverdi's vivid, complex, indeed modern, personality, and throws light on his methods of composing in the most productive year of his life.

[1] Op. cit., p. 301. Mr. Reiner intends to publish further documents regarding Monteverdi's collaboration with Antonio Goretti at Parma in 1627, which was not known before.

[2] This, of course, refers only to the compositions actually in hand.

IL TAMERLANO DE GIUSEPPE CLEMENTE BONOMI

Dragotin Cvetko (Ljubljana)

PARMI LES compositeurs du passé musical européen dont les biographies n'ont pas encore été l'objet de recherches approfondies ou qui même n'ont pas encore été étudiés et qui dans le monde sont inconnus ou connus seulement en partie, se range aussi Giuseppe Clemente Bonomi,[1] dont l'activité évoluait, en 1732 et très probablement aussi avant et après cette date, à Ljubljana, capitale du Duché de la Carniole qui, à ce temps-là, était une partie du territoire slovène. Il paraît que sa famille fût originaire de ce territoire slovène. Nous sommes amenés à le conclure de la dédicace qui figure dans le livret pour son opéra *Il Tamerlano* et qui était destinée à son seigneur, le vidame carniolais Francesco Antonio Sigisfrido, comte della Torre e Valsassina, où il écrivit, entre autre chose, qu'avec le présent ouvrage, il n'avait que l'intention de commencer à honorer les faibles produits de son génie dans l'illustre duché, c'est-a-dire dans la Carniole, ou à ses ancêtres ne fut pas seulement destiné le berceau, mais où pendant des siècles, ils avaient mené une existence heureuse.[2] Comme la Carniole, territoire limitrophe de l'Italie, était, au cours des âges, colonisée par de nombreuses familles italiennes, il paraît que la famille de Bonomi dont le nom révèle l'origine italienne, se soit, elle aussi, établie sur le territoire slovène où, très probablement elle s'était naturalisée. Il est vrai que nous ne possédons pas encore une documentation qui témoignerait que Bonomi était né, lui aussi, dans le pays natal de ses ancêtres. Toutefois, nous sommes en droit de le supposer. La stylisation du passage cité, comme aussi son activité déployée à Ljubljana, permettent de former cette hypothèse au moins indirectement, bien que le séjour de Bonomi dans cette ville ne soit, d'après la documentation dont nous disposons jusqu'ici, prouvé que pour l'an 1732, lorsqu'au palais du vidame carniolais à Ljubljana fut représenté son opéra *Il Tamerlano*.

Au frontispice du livret de cet opéra qui fut imprimé à Venise en 1732 dans l'imprimerie de Girolamo Savioni : 'In Venezia, MDCCXXXII. Presso Girolamo Savioni. Con licenza de' Superiori', figure le texte suivant :

[1] La littérature lexicographique et encyclopédique existante jusqu'ici ne mentionne pas G. C. Bonomi. Ainsi p. ex. Walther, Eitner, Grove, Riemann, le MGG ne le connaissent pas. Eitner, *Quellenlexikon*, ii, p. 118 ne connaît que Pietro Bonomi (Bonhomius), qui en 1603 fut chanoine à Liège et, à son temps, chantre à la chapelle sixtine de Rome et qui très probablement n'est pas en lien de parenté avec la famille dont fut issu G. C. Bonomi, le compositeur de l'opéra en question et qui, en tant que je sache, n'a été mentionné que dans la littérature musicologique slovène : comp. St. Škerlj, *Italijanske predstave v Ljubljani od XVII.*

do XIX. stoletja — Les Représentations italiennes à Ljubljana du XVIIᵉ au XIXᵉ siècle (Ljubljana, 1936), p. 31; D. Cvetko, *Zgodovina glasbene umetnosti na Slovenskem — Histoire de la musique en Slovénie*, i (Ljubljana, 1958), pp. 260, 261; le même, *Academia Philharmonicorum Labacensis* (Ljubljana, 1962), pp. 174–8, 215.

[2] L'original : '. . . Con il presente però Drama non altro intendo, che cominciare ad onorare i deboli parti del mio ingegno in questo Inclito Ducato/ove i miei Antavi non solo ebbero in sorte di averne la Cuna, ma per più Secoli goderno un felice soggiorno/. . .'

[108]

Il Tamerlano / Tragedia per Musica / Da rappresentarsi in Lubiana / Nel Palazzo del Vice Dominato l'Anno 1732 / Dedicato a Sua Eccellenza il Sig.Francesco Antonio Sigifrido, del Sacro Romano Imperio, Conte della Torre, e Valsassina, libero Barone di Croce, Signore di Plaiburg, Rattmanstorff, Anchen e Plonchenstain, Maggiordomo maggiore Ereditario nel Ducato di Carniolia e della Marca di Slavonia, Maresciallo Maggiore Ereditario nella Contea di Gorizia, Cameriere e Consigliere Intimo di Sua Maestà Cesarea, e Cattolica, e suo Vice-Domo nel Ducato di Carniolia ec.[1]

Le frontispice est suivi par la dédicace, dans laquelle Bonomi chante la louange et la gloire à son seigneur,[2] car ce fut grâce à lui qu'il fut possible de réaliser l'exécution de l'opéra mentionné. À ce qu'il paraît, il jouissait de la renommée de 'mécène des beaux-arts et des sciences sublimes', comme on lit dans le texte de Bonomi.

La dédicace est suivie par l'allocution que Bonomi adresse au lecteur ('Al lettore') et dans laquelle le compositeur raconte l'histoire de Tamerlan et de Bajazet qui 'si legge nell'Istoria Bizantinia Ducae Michaelis Ducae Nepotis'. Il y dit aussi qu'il n'avait pas l'intention d'écrire une histoire, mais de faire représenter une tragédie, en réduisant au décor de théâtre des récits qui historiquement sont probablement authentiques.[3] Ceci prouve que l'auteur du livret fut le compositeur lui-même, qui devait être un homme très instruit et d'une vaste culture, car sans cela, il n'aurait pas réussi à écrire un texte d'un bon style baroque et bien conduit, tel qu'il nous est offert par ce livret d'opéra. À sa manière, la conclusion du texte que Bonomi adresse au lecteur est aussi intéressante et caractéristique. Elle dit : 'Les voix du Destin, des Étoiles, des Divinités etc. doivent être entendues avec la raison du bon chrétien, tel que se confesse celui qui les avait écrites.'[4] Selon toute évidence il voulut, étant abbé (*abbate*), se garantir contre des reproches à cause de l'esprit, dans lequel il avait conçu son livret, dont il avait voulu rendre le contenu le plus fidèlement proche à la matière[5].

[1] L'original se trouve à la Bibliothèque du Séminaire à Ljubljana, Z IV, 1.

[2] À l'exception du passage cité, l'original est le suivant : 'Eccellenza. La naturale inclinazione che fino da miei primi anni portommi sempre alla maggior stima, e venerazione verso i Principi, e Cavalieri di Germania, che in tutti i tempi, ma in questi nostri particolarmente compariscono in numero à norma del Augustissimo CARLO SESTO invitissimo nostro Monarca beneficentissimi MECENATI delle lettere, diventa ora ECCELLENZA, in ne un doveroso, indispensabile tributo, in che mi si offre l'onore di poter da vicino venerare, ed ammirare quelle molte, e rare qualità, e virtù, che in sommo grado l'adornano, ed avevano ben prima d'adesso per fama esatto da me tutto il maggior sentimento di Ossequio. Voi pero ECCELLENZA non contento dello splendore dei Vostri Illustri generosi Antenati, che per lungo serie di Secoli hannosi sempre, e nelle Civili, e nelle Militari incombenze distinto, ed innalzato a quelle onorevolissime cariche, che ora per successione Ereditaria si rendono nella vostra riguardevolissima Famiglia decoroso, e ricchissimo Partimonio, volete anche col dichiararvi MECENATE delle belle Arti, e dell'Ottime scienze rendervi, e famoso, e noto per tutt'i Secoli nelle memoria de' Letterati, che certamente più dell'altre di qualunque sorte si siano, vagliono eternare il Nome. Non intendo pero io qui di riferire, e le gloriose gesta di Vostri PROGENITORI, e quelle d Voi medesimo, perchè in vece di una breve Dedicatoria sarei insensibilmente costretto a formare una vera, e ben lunga meravigliosa Storia; Ma ne riservo un tale attestato del mio ossequio ad altra più opportuna occasione . . . col pregiatissimo Nome dell 'ECCELLENZA VOSTRA al di cui venerato Patrocinio trarrà egli dalla stessa sua debolezza coraggio, ed ardire per accender se medesimo, ed alzarsi dal suo Ordinario, bassissimo volo. Che però ECCELLENZA non siavvi discaro riguardare con l'innata Vostra solita benignità, ed agradimento questa umile mia offerta, sicchè maggiormente incorragito possa con maggiori dimostrazioni dirmi, e gloriarmi, quale con più profondo rispetto mi protesto . . . .'.

[3] A cet endroit, l'original entier dit : 'Ciò non ostante io, che non imprendo di scrivere una Storia, ma di far rappresentare una Tragedia, ho preso dalle sopraccenate favole, ridotte al decoro del Teatro, e alla possibile probabilità, il motivo per un'azione, la quale hà per fine la morte di Bajazet.'

[4] L'original : 'Le voci Fato, Stelle, Numi ec. si devono intendere con la mente di buon Cristiano, quale si protesta chi le ha scritte'.

[5] Comp. l'original, ibid.

Le livret et, par conséquent, l'opéra, a trois actes : le premier embrasse six scènes, tandis que le deuxième et le troisième acte, l'acte final, comportent chacun quatorze scènes. Les lieux où se passe l'action sont décrits avec une grande précision, et de même les indications dramaturgiques. La conception du livret dans son ensemble prouve que Bonomi possédait une connaissance solide de la structure de livrets d'opéra baroques et qu'il avait beaucoup de sens pour la création de contrastes intérieurs dans le contenu d'un genre de composition comme le fut *l'opera seria*, auquel sans doute appartenait 'la tragedia per musica', *Il Tamerlano.*

Les personnages de cet opéra sont : Tamerlano, 'Imperatore di Tartari' ; Bajazet, 'Imperatore di Turchi prigioniero del Tamerlano' ; Asteria, 'Figlia di Bajazet amante di Andronico' ; Irene, 'Principessa di Trabisonda promessa Sposa di Tamerlano' ; Andronico, 'Prencipe Greco confederato del Tamerlano, ed Amante d'Asteria' ; et les deux serviteurs Tamur et Zelbo qui ne parlent pas ('Servi che non parlano'). Des personnages donc qui sont conformes aux exigences du contenu et de la matière et qui pourvoyaient à l'animation de toute l'action scénique.

Comme il résulte du texte qui suit les paroles de l'auteur adressées au lecteur, l'auteur de la musique de cet opéra fut Bonomi.[1] Malheureusement, elle n'est pas connue, elle est perdue, ou bien, elle n'a pas encore été découverte. Toutefois, il est hors de doute qu'elle fut en style baroque, voire orientée vers le haut baroque ou le baroque avancé. Divers facteurs en témoignent. D'abord, le livret de Bonomi, conçu et écrit dans un style baroque marqué qui exigeait une mise en musique adéquate et qui, bien qu'indirectement, parle en faveur de la thèse que son auteur ait reçu aussi sa formation musicale et son orientation de style quelque part en Italie. Comme dans son livret d'opéra, dans la musique de Bonomi le style de son art devait être orienté vers le baroque. En faveur de la thèse sur l'orientation baroque de l'opéra de Bonomi parle ensuite la situation musicale de la ville de Ljubljana de cette époque : d'un côté, l'activité dans le domaine de l'interprétation musicale de l'Academia Philharmonicorum, fondée en 1701 ; de l'autre côté, l'activité créatrice des compositeurs qui travaillaient sur le territoire slovène ; ensuite, les représentations au théatre des jésuites de Ljubljana dans les premières dizaines d'années du dix-huitième siècle ; et à la fin et surtout, les visites des compagnies d'opéra italiennes qui avaient lieu aux environs plus ou moins proches de 1732, date de la naissance et de la réalisation scénique de l'opéra de Bonomi. Dans une certaine mesure, le compositeur devait tenir compte de tous ces facteurs, lorsqu'il travaillait à son opéra, pour être au niveau des exigences spirituelles du climat qui régnait à Ljubljana. Car dans tous les cas cités, l'orientation de la création comme celle de l'exécution fut baroque, et cela dans les deux directions : dans celle du haut baroque comme dans celle du baroque avancé. Dans les premières dizaines d'années du dix-huitième siècle, en Slovénie et notamment dans la ville centrale de ce territoire, de même que dans les domaines des beaux-arts et de l'architecture, dans celui de la musique aussi le baroque eut un véritable épanouissement et un niveau très élevé. De ce fait, et même sans une documentation authentique, rien qu'en tenant compte de ces moments cités, il paraît incontestable que la musique de Bonomi pour son opéra *Il Tamerlano* ne pouvait être autre que baroque

[1] Après l'allocution 'Al lettore', l'original dit : 'La Musica è Virtuosa fatica del sempre celebre Signor Abbate D. Giuseppe Clemente de Bonomi attuale Maestro di Capella di Sua Eccellenza il Sig. Francesco Antonio Sigifrido Conte della Torre, e Valsassina &c.', ibid.

et, eu égard à l'époque, plutôt dans le sens et en accord avec la physionomie du baroque avancé que du haut baroque.

De même que Bonomi fut l'auteur du livret et de la musique, il fut aussi celui qui dirigea la réalisation scénique de son opéra au palais du vidame labacien en 1732, car le livret nous apprend qu'il fut 'Maestro di Capella di Sua Eccellenza il Sig. Francesco Antonio Sigifrido Conte della Torre, e Valsassina &c.'. Du livret nous apprenons aussi les noms des interprètes, chanteurs et chanteuses. Les interprètes (*interlocutori*) furent Giuseppe Cabbiati, Carlo Amaini, Rosa Poshin, Marina Cittadini et Paolo Vida, tandis que les noms des deux serviteurs n'y sont pas indiqués. Cabbiati interpréta le rôle de Tamerlano, Amaini celui de Bajazet, la Poshin celui d'Asteria, la Cittadini celui d'Irena et Vida celui d'Andronico. Le livret nous apprend en outre que Cabbiati et Rosa Poshin furent des chanteurs engagés, membres de la chapelle musicale du vidame. Pour Cabbiati, on y lit qu'il fut l'"attuale Virtuoso di Sua Ecc^za il Signor Conte della Torre', et pour Rosa Poshin qu'elle fut l'"attuale Virtuosa di Sua Ecc^za il Conte della Torre'.[1] Puisque ces indications font défaut pour le reste des interprètes (Amaini, Cittadini, Vida), on peut en conclure qu'ils n'étaient pas des membres engagés de la chapelle du vidame et que, pour cette occasion, on les avait empruntés ailleurs, le plus probablement de quelque compagnie d'opéra italienne.

Ce qui en tout cas est une constatation importante, c'est qu'*Il Tamerlano* ne fut pas exécuté par une compagnie d'opéra italienne, bien qu'en partie, ses membres y eussent collaboré, mais par des interprètes résidant à Ljubljana, c'est-à-dire par ceux dont disposait la chapelle du vidame. Autrement dit : dans son palais, le vidame labacien, le comte della Torre e Valsassina, maintenait une chapelle qui, en 1732 au moins, était composée du maître de chapelle, d'un chanteur (Cabbiati) et d'une chanteuse (la Poshin) et, sans doute aussi d'un certain nombre d'instrumentistes. La documentation incomplète ne nous permet pas d'établir leur nombre. S'il n'était pas suffisant, cela n'aurait en aucun cas entravé la mise au point et l'exécution scénique de l'opéra, car à cette époque il y avait à Ljubljana de nombreux instrumentistes que le vidame aurait pu emprunter pour cette occasion : il y en avait dans l'orchestre de l'Academia Philharmonicorum, il y en avait à la chapelle épiscopale, au théâtre des jésuites et aux diverses chapelles des nobles, p. ex. à celle du prince d'Auersperg.[2] Les sources nous apprennent que les uns comme les autres étaient des musiciens doués et versés en toutes sortes d'instruments.[3]

A Ljubljana, dans les palais des aristocrates, on donnait donc des représentations d'opéras aussi avec des interprètes nationaux. Ceci est confirmé pour la réalisation scénique de l'opéra de Bonomi, et ceci est connu aussi pour quelques cas antérieurs à 1732 et qui remontent jusqu'en 1660,[4] lorsqu'à Ljubljana fut représenté, probablement pour la première fois, un opéra italien, une 'Comedia Italiana in Musica', comme nous apprend la source.[5]

Toutefois, il paraît qu'il y eût, entre les exécutants nationaux et ceux appartenant à des compagnies d'opéra italiennes, une certaine collaboration. Ceci valait en premier lieu pour les

---

[1] Comp. l'original.
[2] Comp. l'ouvrage cité de St. Škerlj, et D. Cvetko, *Histoire de la musique en Slovénie*.
[3] Comp. J. G. Thalnitscher, *Annales Vrbis Labacensis*, et le même, *Bibliotheca Labacensis publica collegii Carolini Nobilium*, les deux dans la Bibliothèque du Séminaire à Ljubljana, ms.

[4] Comp. la remarque citée sous p. 108, n. 1.
[5] Comp. L. de Churelichz, *Breve, e succinto Racconto del Viaggio . . . dell'Augustissimo Imperatore Leopoldo* (Vienne, 1661); J. W. Valvasor, *Die Ehre des Herzogthumes Crain* (1689), x, p. 379.

instrumentistes que les compagnies d'opéra italiennes, exception faite pour le maître de chapelle, ne menaient pas avec elles, mais que, selon l'usage de ce temps, elles engageaient dans les villes où elles donnaient leurs représentations. De ce côté, la collaboration mentionnée fut, en principe, certaine. Elle est du reste prouvée aussi pour divers autres cas où il s'agit de représentations de compagnies d'opéra italiennes à Ljubljana. Dans certains cas, il y eut aussi une collaboration pareille entre les chanteurs, surtout quand à l'occasion ils s'agissait de remplacer un chanteur ou une chanteuse de la compagnie d'opéra ambulante tombés malades, ou bien quand dans une ville il y avait peut-être un chanteur qui par sa qualité surpassait les membres de la troupe d'opéra étrangère. Pour l'une ou l'autre de ces deux raisons, Paolo Vida et Marina Cittadini collaborèrent à la représentation de l'opéra ('dramma in musica') *Euristeo* à Ljubljana en 1733 ('Da rappresentarsi in Lubiana del Ducato di Carniola Nel Carnevale'). A côté d'eux se produisirent, dans l'exécution de cet opéra dont l'auteur fut J. A. Hasse, Chiara Orlandi, Maddalena Carrara, Giuseppe Alberti et Barbara Bianchi qui, le 31 janvier, au temps de son séjour à Ljubljana, mourut dans cette ville.[1] Le livret omet de citer qui fut l'organisateur de l'exécution de cet opéra. Il ne semble pas vraisemblable qu'il fût le même que dans le cas de l'opéra *Il Tamerlano*, c'est-à-dire la chapelle musicale du comte della Torre e Valsassina, car dans ce cas-là, ceci serait sans doute indiqué au frontispice du livret comme il le fut pour l'opéra de Bonomi. L'*Euristeo* fut très probablement monté par quelque autre aristocrate labacien avec sa chapelle et des hôtes. Ce qui cependant paraît le plus probable c'est que l'*Euristeo* fût exécuté par quelque compagnie d'opéra italienne. Si c'est juste, et tout parle en faveur de cette supposition, nous avons d'un côté une preuve de plus pour la thèse sur les échanges occasionnels entre les interprètes italiens et ces nationaux qui étaient capables de se produire aussi dans des opéras, et de l'autre côté, pour les représentations de compagnies d'opéra italiennes à Ljubljana en 1733.[2]

Une documentation qui nous apprendrait quoi que ce soit sur le succès de l'exécution de l'opéra de Bonomi n'existe pas. Son auteur qui, en même temps, dirigea sa mise au point, avait sans doute pris tous les soins que sa réalisation scénique fût en accord avec sa conception et son élaboration. Les instrumentistes ne posaient pas de problèmes et les chanteurs, qui tous devaient être de qualité, non plus. Rien que le cas de Vida et de la Cittadini en est une preuve suffisante non seulement à cause de leur engagement fixe à la chapelle musicale du comte, mais aussi à cause de leur collaboration dans la représentation de l'*Euristeo*, une année plus tard, qui n'aurait pas eu lieu s'ils n'avaient pas été des chanteurs de qualité.

Il est bien probable que l'opéra *Il Tamerlano* ne fût pas l'unique fruit de l'activité de Bonomi dans ce domaine de la création, c'est-à-dire, dans le domaine de l'opéra. C'est aussi la stylisation du passage cité de la dédicace qui nous induit à l'admettre et qui, en même temps nous apprend que Bonomi avait écrit cet opéra 'in questo nobile Ducato', c'est-à-dire le plus probablement à Ljubljana. Il est en outre très probable qu'il ait écrit un certain nombre de compositions pour pourvoir aux besoins musicaux de la chapelle du comte della Torre e Valsassina, tâche, qu'en sa qualité de maître de chapelle, il était obligé d'accomplir. De toute façon, jusqu'ici nous ne possédons aucune documentation qui en porte témoignage, et nous ne sommes pas en état d'en dire

---

[1] Voir le livret pour la représentation de l'opéra l'*Euristeo*, se trouvant à la Bibliothèque du Séminaire à Ljubljana, E, no. 45.

[2] Comp. D. Cvetko, dans l'ouvrage cité, *Academia Philharmonicorum Labacensis*, pp. 177, 178.

quoi que ce soit de certain. En tout cas, la stylisation de ce même passage cité confirme qu'il devait être l'auteur de plusieurs autres compositions. À la base de ce qui nous est parvenu, nous nous croyons bien en droit de conclure que Bonomi fut un maître de chapelle de talent, mais aussi un bon librettiste et surtout un compositeur d'opéra. À ce qu'il paraît, il en fut, lui même, conscient, car il se désigne comme 'sempre celebre' et il s'exprime, quant à sa musique pour *Il Tamerlano* qu'elle est une 'virtuosa fatica'. L'une et l'autre de ces stylisations sont issues, selon toute probabilité, de sa plume.[1] Sans doute il ne se serait pas permis de s'exprimer dans ces termes, s'il n'avait pas été sûr que, par sa qualité, son opéra pouvait soutenir la comparaison avec des opéras italiens, soit avec d'autres opéras italiens de son temps dont prenaient connaissance aussi les auditeurs de Ljubljana qui, comme on peut déduire de diverses sources, étaient assez exigeants et dont le goût esthétique assez formé était orienté vers la musique italienne.

La représentation d'*Il Tamerlano* en 1732 marqua sans doute un événement dans la vie musicale de Ljubljana qui, à ce temps-là, était très intense et à laquelle probablement Bonomi avait participé aussi sous divers autres aspects. Ainsi, il ne paraît guère impossible que l'orchestre de l'Academia Philharmonicorum n'ait exécuté aussi des compositions de divers genres de Bonomi qu'il avait écrites et que peut-être il avait été même obligé d'écrire. Il devait sans doute avoir été en rapports très étroits avec l'Academia Philharmonicorum. Appartenant à la noblesse, il était pour ainsi dire prédestiné à être attiré dans cette institution aristocratique que fut l'Académie. D'autre côté, il devait en être proche aussi à cause des rapports que certainement avait avec l'Academia Philharmonicorum son seigneur, le comte della Torre e Valsassina. L'un et l'autre de ces deux facteurs induisent à la supposition qu'à la réalisation scénique de l'opéra aient collaboré comme instrumentistes aussi des membres de l'Academia Philharmonicorum. La représentation était destinée en premier lieu à l'aristocratie, à laquelle l'Academia Philharmonique était directement liée et par sa structure sociale et par le sens de ses Leges. En tant que sa collaboration fut nécessaire à la mise au point de l'opéra de Bonomi au palais du vidame, elle était absolument compréhensible et conforme à la situation qui régnait dans la société de la ville de Ljubljana de ce temps-là.

Il Tamerlano nous induit donc à former diverses suppositions et à tirer diverses conclusions. Parmi celles-ci, admettons aussi la possibilité que par son style, il exerça aussi une certaine influence sur les autres compositeurs contemporains de cette ville et de ce territoire, et le fait que du point de vue de l'interprétation musicale ainsi que de celui de la création musicale originale, il contribua à la consolidation et à la diffusion ultérieure de l'orientation de style baroque en Slovénie, à laquelle l'auteur avait, avec cette œuvre, donné un apport incontestable aussi du point de vue de la qualité. En outre, les paroles de l'auteur dans la dédicace citée mènent à la supposition que la réalisation scénique et la publication du livret ne constituaient que le début dans cette direction qui, plus tard, devait continuer. À la fin, il faut constater et souligner qu'*Il Tamerlano* de Bonomi fut le premier opéra pour lequel il est connu, jusqu'ici, qu'il fut écrit sur le territoire slovène et qu'il y eut aussi sa première mondiale. C'est dans ces faits que réside, dans un sens déterminé, l'importance et la valeur historiques de cet opéra et de son auteur.

[1] Comp. l'original, ibid.

EXPRESSION AND REVISION IN GLUCK'S
ORFEO AND *ALCESTE*

F. W. Sternfeld (Oxford)

BETWEEN OCTOBER 1762, when *Orfeo ed Euridice* was first performed in Vienna, and April 1774, when *Iphigénie en Aulide* finally reached the boards of the Paris Opéra, musical Europe witnessed one of the numerous revolutions in opera which have kept alive this remarkable hybrid genre, in spite of the many oracles announcing its impending demise. Gluck himself, in his writings, and his followers in Vienna and Paris were inclined to stress the dramatic truth of the reform operas, the absence of empty formalism and of fussy intrigues. Yet an element of even greater importance was hardly discussed in the eighteenth century, nor have modern critics dwelt on it at length. This was the time-dimension of Gluck's music: it was this aspect of *Orfeo* that resulted in such an untypical Italian opera in 1762. In a Metastasian libretto not only was the number of arias in proportion to the rest of the opera excessive and a diet based on solo singing inevitably monotonous, but one objection would always remain in spite of superlative scoring and other musical traits capable of removing the marks of tedious sameness. This was the staccato effect which the time-dimension of the conventional 'number' opera of the eighteenth century induced. It became clear that the aria needed relief not only from chorus and pantomime but also from the *scena*, an integrated unit of several diverse numbers. So obvious a formula was not likely to be completely ignored, and one need point only to the mad scene in Handel's *Orlando* and the various *buffo* finales from Logroscino to Piccini; yet the fact remains that these splendid examples were quite exceptional.

It must be granted that the routine of an opera consisting primarily of arias was supported by many practical considerations. Not the least of these was the ease with which one short number might easily be transferred to a new opera. Certainly, the demands of the courts of Europe for a continuous stream of operatic productions is reminiscent of the twentieth century, where a rapid succession of lavish productions—whether in the theatre, the cinema, or on the television screen—is normally expected. In our own time the repetition of certain formulas for success in the world of entertainment is comparable to the practice in the eighteenth century of the insertion of an aria from an older work into a new opera. Indeed, this practice of parody is well known to students of Handel and Gluck. Yet, while the single aria might accommodate the dictates of the pasticcio productions, the *scena* with all its various members would not be capable of such adaptation. Hence, for Gluck to have shaped his reform operas predominantly in new, vast blocks, incapable

[114]

of transfer to other works, betrays a stubbornness and singleness of purpose doubly commendable in a composer not endowed by nature with an abundance of musical inspiration, as compared with Handel or Mozart.

To achieve symmetry and cogency in the large forms Gluck naturally needed his Calzabigi, as did Mozart his Da Ponte. The increase of the time-dimension of the component parts of opera can never be the exclusive result of musical expansion; it must be predicated on a dramatic structure. Da Ponte did not merely provide finales for the various acts of Mozart's operas: he also fashioned the opening scenes of *Le nozze di Figaro* and *Don Giovanni* in a manner which precluded single and isolated arias, to mention but one mechanical feature of these masterly scenes. Similarly, Calzabigi created not only the spacious underworld scenes in *Orfeo* and *Alceste*, but also provided both operas with opening scenes which eclipsed the time-span of Metastasian opera. In the following paragraphs I propose to concentrate upon the composer's contribution. It may be said, in the first place, that *Orfeo*, though remarkable, is not the perfect reform opera. Nor was Gluck above tampering occasionally with certain aspects of his achievement when he revised an opera in the attempt to meet the public half-way. Nevertheless, the speed with which he fashioned a new kind of lyrical drama is amazing. Without the consummation of this venture the glories of his successors would be unthinkable.

Gluck's artistic creed in eschewing the minuscule number and working in larger units is clearly established in the opening complex of the original version of *Orfeo*, 1762.[1] The *sinfonia* in C minor accompanies shepherds and nymphs who perform the funeral rites. This sad introduction (*mesta sinfonia*) sets the tone and key. The chorus which follows (bars 15–61) has often been admired for the expressive timing with which Orfeo, the soloist, interrupts it three times. No *sinfonia* or *ritornello* supervenes; instead, Orfeo's recitative follows immediately. Now the celebrants of the funeral perform another instrumental number, a *ballo*. After these two interruptions the chorus resumes. It is not, of course, a mechanical repetition, for Orfeo does not interrupt the choral singing, and at the end of the chorus the celebrants have another *ballo*. It goes without saying that when he adapted the work for Paris Gluck was forced to make some changes.[2] One of the most obvious alterations was the voice register of the title role: Guadagni, the castrato, had sung in Vienna; in Paris the part was given to the tenor Le Gros. In later sections of the opera this change caused some severe handicaps to the scheme of tonality, though in the opening scene the *tessitura* of Orfeo is of little importance, and the key of C minor remained intact. The only addition to the Vienna version was a short recitative for Orfeo which intervenes between the repetition of the C-minor chorus and the concluding *ballo*.[3]

The opening scene of the original version, which so expressively combines choral and orchestral music with a minimum of solo singing, was entirely acceptable to French taste and remains equally impressive and unified in the Paris revision. The remainder of the act is another matter, since the new arias for Amor and Orfeo, inserted into the French score, tamper with the original design.

[1] This version was published in Paris in 1764 (C. Hopkinson's bibliography, no. 30A); it is hereafter referred to in the reprint by A. Abert and L. Finscher (Cassel & London, 1963), with convenient bar numbers for each scene.

[2] The score was first printed in Paris in 1774, ten years after the first edition (Hopkinson, no. 41A).

[3] In the Peters vocal score, edited by Alfred Dörffel (Hopkinson, no. 41C [*p*]), *c.* 1882, this short recitative no. 5 is inserted between the chorus no. 4 and the final *ballo* no. 6. For further bibliographical information, see n. 1, p. 117 below.

There is little to be said for the intervention of Amor, which was not one of Gluck's happiest devices, even in the original version. In striking contrast, Hades and Elysium in Act II elicited from the composer some of his finest pages. Once more, the opening scene (occupying 292 bars) is dominated by the chorus of the furies and their dances, while the soloist, Orfeo, is allotted less than a third of the total (81 bars). The scene proceeds rather carefully from C minor, in which key the furies deny Orfeo's plea, to the key of F minor, in which they express first their compassion and finally their consent to let a mortal pass through the infernal portals (bars 245–92). The details of this scheme of tonality are worked out in a manner befitting the time-dimension necessary for a contest between the pleading soloist and the harsh *tutti*. The key of C minor, in which the furies sing twice (bars 24-33, 51–90), is framed by a *ballo* (bars 1–20, 91–110), which starts in the relative major (E♭) but concludes in the tonic.[1]

This is followed by Orfeo's first intervention (bars 111–52) in E♭ major. The succeeding chorus hesitates between E♭ minor, which approaches the tonality of the soloist, and F minor. In his second plea (bars 185–208) Orfeo in turn sings in F minor and C minor, entering the tonality of those whom he seeks to persuade. The last three numbers, two further choruses punctuated by yet another plea, are all in F minor. The stage is thus set for the marvellous transformation from minor to major; for the dance of the blessed spirits (scene 2) makes its impact by the key of F major, which is entirely new in this act and which, to gain its effect, must follow immediately upon the *tierce de Picardie* at the end of the F minor of the furies.[2] The major mode is as important an aspect of the *ballo* of the blessed spirits as is the orchestral texture of flute and strings. Together they endow the noble simplicity of the melody with the necessary dramatic overtones.

Here Gluck violated his own master design in the later version by inserting a piece from the earlier ballet *Don Juan*, the pantomime in D minor. Granted that it is a fine piece of music, that it provided the *corps de ballet* with a splendid opportunity, and the Parisian public with a magnificent spectacle, it still remains true that this inserted dance of the furies retards both the dramatic action and the unfolding of the musical architecture, two sides of the same coin. This form of capitulation to the taste of the Parisian public occurs again and again in the history of opera, whether we deal with Gluck's *Orfeo* or *Alceste* or Wagner's *Tannhäuser*. The second act of *Orfeo* contained several ballets when it was originally composed, both in the Hades and the Elysium scenes. The daring injection of purely orchestral music into an essentially Italian framework had been achieved with due regard for balance and tonality. But the addition of yet another ballet in a key other than F minor could only disturb the equilibrium. Nor is any further action by the furies, dancing or otherwise, dramatically called for. The representatives of Hades have expressed, in turn, refusal, compassion, and consent. Their vigorous *tutti*, articulated in block chords (bars 245–87), gives way in the final bars where bass, alto, tenor, and soprano chant singly. As they sing they retreat from the scene, their *diminuendo* becoming, in the end, an indistinct murmur. Once

[1] The repetition of this *ballo*, one of Gluck's characteristic devices, has been questioned by some editors. It occurs in the first printed edition of 1764; in the Rome MS, Santa Cecilia A. 3768, the repetition, having been written into the score, was then cancelled; in the Vienna MS., National-bibliothek 17783, it is omitted; cf. A. Abert's edition, p. 65

and p. 214, bar 90. I regard the first edition as the best authority and am happy to see the repeated bars re-instated by Professor Abert.

[2] Concerning the natural sign in front of the note 'a', see A. Abert's edition, p. 215, bar 288.

furies and monsters have disappeared, Orfeo is ready to pass through the portals of the under-world:

> . . . si allontanono, finisce finalmente in un confuso mormorio.
> Sparite le Furie, sgombrati i Mostri, Orfeo s'avanza nell'inferno.

And the audience is ready for the serenity which Orfeo so movingly describes after the dance of the blessed spirits, 'Che puro ciel, che chiaro sol, che nuova serena luce'. What possible dra-matic meaning could another dance of the furies, in the minor mode, have at this juncture of the plot?

If the addition of the D minor ballet was a major short-coming of the Paris revision, the dis-position of the tonalities preceding it was certainly a hindrance to a lucid grasp of the architecture of both music and drama.[1] As the result of transferring the title role from the range of a castrato to that of a tenor, which necessitated transposing Orfeo's airs, as well as some of the other music, the keys in the Vienna and Paris versions differ considerably:

Act II No.		Vienna	Paris
18	1st *ballo* of furies	E♭ major — C minor	E♭ major — D minor
19	1st chorus of furies	C minor	D minor
20	2nd *ballo* of furies	C minor	D minor
21	2nd chorus of furies	C minor	D minor
21A	1st *ballo* repeated	E♭ major — C minor	—
22	Orfeo's 1st air	E♭ major	B♭ major
23	3rd chorus of furies	E♭ minor — F minor	B♭ minor — C minor
24	Orfeo's 2nd air	F minor — C minor	C minor — G minor
25	4th chorus of furies	F minor	G minor
26	Orfeo's 3rd air	F minor	C minor
27	5th chorus of furies	F minor	F minor
28	Additional *ballo* of furies	—	D minor
29	*Ballo* of blessed spirits	F major	F major

The progression from C minor to F minor, in the Vienna version, is clear enough. Nos. 18–21A inclusive are each sizeable units in C minor. The first *ballo*, nos. 18 and 31A, though it begins in E♭ major, does not settle in that key but modulates and sequences after three bars and concludes with an extended cadence in C minor. Orfeo's plea, no. 22, preserves continuity in that the accompaniment of harp and *pizzicato* strings opens with two bars of C minor before proceeding to E♭ major. The reaction of the furies, no. 23, is to accept Orfeo's tonic, at least for a time: they start in E♭ minor and modulate to the new key of F minor, in which key they finally yield. This new key opens every component until the end of the scene, no. 27, and provides the tonic for the next scene of Elysium, no. 29.

---

[1] In the following remarks I shall be making frequent references to the individual 'numbers' of Gluck's score. For convenience I refer to Dörffel's numbering, which will be found in the following publications:

Orchestral score, Heinze, Leipzig, 1866, Hopkinson 41A (*n*).
    ,,   ,, Peters,   ,,   1878,   ,,   41A (*p*).

Vocal score,	Peters,	Leipzig,	1864, Hopkinson	41C (*m*).
,,	,, Peters,	,,	1882,	,, 41C (*p*).
,,	,, Novello,	London,	1891,	,, 41C (*q*).
,,	,, Schirmer,	New York,	1959,	
,,	,, Ricordi,	Milan,	1962.	

A glance at the scheme of tonalities in the Paris version reveals the heavy price Gluck had to pay in substituting a tenor. The close union of E♭ major and D minor in the opening *ballo* is obviously a *mariage de convenance*, and the modulation to G minor in nos. 24–25 a circuitous route to the F minor of no. 27. So astute a critic as Berlioz, an ardent admirer of Gluck's art, could not accept this aspect of the Paris revision. Berlioz's ingenious solution saved *Orphée* for posterity: the famous contralto, Pauline Viardot-Garcia, equally distinguished for her acting, was given the title role in the revival of 1859. Not only was the result a performance which moved Dickens to tears, but the substitution allowed Berlioz to re-transpose Orfeo's arias and thus salvage the original key-scheme. He naturally respected such of Gluck's revisions as may fairly be said to represent his intentions as a composer and left unmolested such additions as no. 28. But he felt free to ignore the revisions which were an adaptation to the singing personnel in Paris.[1]

There are, of course, individual parts in the opening scene of Act II where Gluck the musician, rather than Gluck the reformer, speaks: the dramatic contrast between unison and harmony in the choruses of the furies (which influenced Beethoven's *Coriolan*); the howling of the hell-hound Cerberus in no. 21, so admired by Berlioz; the enharmonic conversion of C♭ into B♮ in no. 22, remarked upon by Rousseau[2]—these are touches of musical genius rather than elements of reform carried forward into *Alceste*. The revision of 1774 also contains improvements, as well as those features that disturbed the original design. For one thing, the instrumentation shows greater experience in the handling of the wind instruments, and, for another, Orfeo's main plea, no. 22, has been extended in three places; the rise of pitch at the very end produces an impressive climax. By adding these six bars the expressiveness of the aria is considerably enhanced.

These special graces do not, however, affect the basic aspects of the entire scene, which are twofold: the drama created by the alternation between *tutti* and solo; and the unification, largely rhythmic and tonal, that binds the choruses of the furies together. In a composition where the conflict between *tutti* and solo forms but one of a number of component parts, the desired effect need not occupy a large expanse of time. Beethoven, who learned so much from *Orfeo*, has demonstrated in the slow movement of the fourth piano concerto how concisely the dramatic *concertato* may be handled. But the decisive aspect of Gluck's reform hinges on a quality that the Germans call *Großform*, another of those compound nouns which defies translation into idiomatic English. It is the size of Gluck's canvas that is the vital element. *Concertato*, tonality, rhythm, texture, affect not one but ten numbers; the *scena* comprises the first half of an entire act. In this aspect the original version of *Orfeo* remains the clearest expression of Gluck's reform.

The problem of revision affects the second scene of Elysium very little. The only extensive lyric for Orfeo is the famous *recitativo accompagnato* 'Che puro ciel'. Gluck was able to keep this in the same key, C major, at the same time refining the instrumentation. Euridice's new aria, no. 32 in F major, also posed no problems. At the beginning of the scene the *ballo* of the blessed spirits was extended by two further dances, nos. 30 and 31. But these additional ballets, comprising 60 bars, fitted the scheme of tonalities and, in view of Euridice's new aria, did not disturb

[1] The Berlioz version survives in the vocal score, Escudier, Paris, 1859 (Hopkinson, 41C [*i*]); in the orchestral score, edited by Dörffel (Heinze, Leipzig, 1886), quoted above; and, in fact, in all the seven scores listed in the previous footnote.

[2] G. M. Leblond (ed.), *Mémoires...de la révolution opérée dans la musique par...Gluck* (Paris, 1781), pp. 22–24.

the balance between vocal and instrumental music. The design of the second scene, is, in fact, particularly successful, if not adventurous. Its supporting pillars are all in F major: the opening *ballo*, Euridice's new aria, the chorus no. 34, and the repetition of that chorus as no. 37. These two choruses, framing the *ballo* of no. 35 and Orfeo's recitative of no. 36, symmetrically balance the mourning scene at the beginning of the opera. Several facts about this final portion of the scene are relevant here: it does not contain an aria; solo singing is restricted to recitative; the predominant structural feature is the chorus; and the role of the orchestra, particularly in 'Che puro ciel', is of almost Beethovenian importance. All of these non-Italianate features were already in the Vienna version:

No.		Key Vienna	Key Paris
29	First *ballo* of blessed spirits	F major	F major
30	First additional *ballo*	—	D minor
31	Second additional *ballo*	—	C major
32	Additional aria for Euridice	—	F major
33	Orfeo's recitative	C major	C major
34	Chorus of blessed spirits	F major	F major
35	Second *ballo* of blessed spirits	B♭ major	B♭ major
36	Orfeo's recitative	G minor — C major	G minor — C major
37	Repetition of no. 34	F major	F major

The final act of the Vienna version consists of two large scenes: that between Orfeo and Euridice (469 bars) and the final homage to the God of Love (384 bars). The printed Italian score names these the first and third scenes, and interposes between them as a second scene one in which Amor prevents Orfeo from committing suicide and restores wife to husband. This recitative is, in a technical sense, a scene, in that a new singer, in the person of Amor, is added. But it is hardly a *scena* comparable to the other large dramatic units of the opera. It comprises 19 bars of Orfeo wishing to commit suicide and another 35 bars in which Amor, Orfeo, and Euricide partake in the *accompagnato*. Our main concern is with the two large scenes. The Orfeo-scene (nos. 38 to 43) moves from G major to C major; the Amor-third-scene (nos. 45 to 47, plus no. 52, plus a *ballo* omitted in the Paris version) begins and ends in D major. The recitative no. 44 acts as a modulatory bridge between these scenes. The last scene, with its conventional *licenza*, is, by common consent, an anti-climax. But to dismiss it as poor drama with an obviously contrived happy ending, brought about by a *deus ex machina*, is actually unfair to Calzabigi, who carefully concluded both his first and third acts by the intervention of Amor. Through this symmetry the salvation of hero and heroine by the God of Love becomes dramatically less capricious, and the two scenes of Amor function in the opera much like a *ritornello*. Still, the plot of the finale has a hackneyed air and one cannot help wondering whether the composer might not have rescued his librettist by writing music of a sufficient mastery to endow an otherwise obvious and commonplace conclusion with artistic stature (as Mozart did in the final scene of *Don Giovanni*). Because of the need to compensate for these shortcomings, perhaps, Gluck expanded the final scene of the Paris version more than any other in the opera. For all that, the four new additions had been used previously in other

[119]

operas, as the following tabulation shows. In the Vienna version four *balli* intervene between the orchestral *ritornello* for the final chorus and the chorus itself (no. 45). In the Paris version three of these *balli* follow the final chorus (nos. 46, 47, 52), the fourth is omitted altogether. Also in the Vienna version the chorus has the last word; while in the Paris version the opera concludes with an orchestral *chaconne* of over 350 bars:

No. in Berlioz-Dörffel		Key Vienna	Key Paris	Borrowed from
45	Orchestral ritornello for chorus	D major	A major	
46	1st *ballo*	A major	A major	
47	2nd *ballo*	A minor	A minor	
48	1st additional *ballo*	—	C major	*Trionfo di Clelia*
49	2nd additional *ballo*	—	C major	*Trionfo di Clelia*
50	Trio: Amor, Orfeo, Euridice	—	E minor & major	*Paride ed Elena*
51	[repetition of no. 45 above]	—	A major	
52	3rd *ballo*	D major	D major	
—	4th *ballo*	D major	—	
—	Final chorus [follows in Paris on no. 45]	D major	A major & D major	
53	Final additional *ballo*	—	D major	*Iphigénie en Aulide*

It must be admitted that the Paris version contains, in this final scene, a large amount of better music than is in the original version. And Gluck transferred music from one dramatic context to another with considerable skill. In the case of the final *chaconne* this merely involved judgement in regard to mood, melody, and harmony. But the trio from *Paride ed Elena* required adaptation from one set of Italian words ('Ah, lo veggo') to another set of French words ('Tendre amour'). Moreover, Paride had been sung by a male soprano, Millico, whereas the role of Orfeo had to be performed by the tenor Le Gros. Gluck carried out the adjustment of the words with care and, by transposing the trio a semitone down from F minor in *Paride* to E minor in *Orphée*, he was able to reach a key related both to the preceding C major and the following A major. There can be no doubt that countless audiences have listened to this magnificent piece of music and enjoyed its dramatic as well as musical aptness. The opening 39 bars in the minor key seem to mirror perfectly the emotional exhaustion, as it were, of Orfeo and Euridice. The orchestra, with its eloquent four-note figure, speaks of the frustrations of love ('tes chaînes, tes peines') and makes clear that the protagonists have reached the limits of human endurance. One more vicissitude, and even the powerful god Amor, who builds and destroys the fortunes of humans as a boy builds and razes castles of sand, could no longer perform another miracle. This Beethovenian manner, if one may use this anachronistic term, where expression is obtained by means of instrumental rather than vocal music within the framework of a lyrical drama, was one of the lessons bequeathed by Gluck to later opera composers. One may, perhaps, instance the famous monologue from Verdi's *Otello*, 'Dei! mi potevi' (Had it pleased Heaven to try me with affliction), where an equally eloquent four-note figure, also in the violins, is the symbol of the utter exhaustion of Othello's emotions and strength.

The opening scene of the last act proceeds in the same order in the original and in the Paris versions. No new numbers were added in 1774; the two protagonists have one aria each and also sing a duet, but the remainder is all recitative. As in Act I, scene 2, the chorus is entirely silent. Of course, these extensive recitatives (bars 1–99, 193–217, 341–403) had to be considerably changed for Paris because Gluck was too sensitive to ignore the implications of the French language with its different speech rhythms. As in the earlier portions of the opera, several transpositions were made to accommodate the tenor range. Unfortunate as these were, they have been happily eliminated by Berlioz's cutting of the Gordian knot.

Orfeo's plaint, 'Che farò senz' Euridice' or 'J'ai perdu mon Euridice' has been the subject of heated controversy for two centuries. In the eighteenth century it was praised by Rousseau and Heinse for its expressiveness, but criticized by Boyé and the Princess Esterházy for its inappropriate gaiety. Boyé's famous dictum that it would be just as fitting to sing the words 'J'ai trouvé mon Euridice' to the tune[1] is merely a witty French way of articulating the thought of a good many observers then and since. Gluck took account of these criticisms in the preface to *Paride ed Elena* in 1770: '. . . making only a slight change in the manner of expression in my aria *Che farò senz' Euridice* it becomes a puppet-dance [*un saltarello di burattini*]. One note held longer or shorter, a careless increase in the tempo or the voice [*un rinforzo trascurato di tempo, o di voce*] . . . may ruin a whole scene in a work like this.' Indeed, these changes 'in the tempo or the voice', or tempo or dynamics, as one might say today, are cleverly marked in the Italian printed score. The song is a rondo in the major mode (C in Vienna, F below in Paris). The main melody, '*andante espressivo*', consists of eight bars within which there are five dynamic marks (*p, f, p, f, p*), to which a sixth *forte* is added for an echo of two bars. In the first episode the tempo slows down (after 8 bars) to '*un poco lento*'; after a *forte* start, there are five dynamic marks, *p, f, p, f, p*. The same five dynamics recur for the return of the main theme, '*tempo primo*'. The second episode has two tempo indications (*più lento* and *adagio*) and four marks of dynamics (*p, f, p, f*). The final *Tempo primo* states the main theme twice: first in eight bars with dynamic markings as before (*p, f, p, f, p*), then the last four bars receive a modified echo within which four dynamics are employed (*p, f, p, f*). Such detailed, if not fussy, exactitude in specifying the expression in a printed score proves how concerned Gluck was to ensure that not the whim of a star performer but the carefully calculated effects decided upon by the composer should govern the actual performance: 'The presence, therefore, of the composer in the execution of such a species of music is, so to speak, equally necessary as is the presence of the sun in the works of nature' [Preface to *Paride*].

The expressiveness of Orfeo's aria was assured when the composer made the decisions and could command adequate rehearsals. The unusually large number of rehearsals insisted upon by Gluck in Paris, and later by Berlioz when he coached the incomparable Pauline Viardot-Garcia, bore fruit. After quoting Gluck's famous remark about the *saltarello di burattini* Berlioz describes the performance of Mme. Garcia who 'makes of it ['Che farò'] . . . what it is, one of those marvels of expression, which are well-nigh incomprehensible to vulgar singers—and

---

[1] Boyé is usually quoted from *L'Expression musicale mise au rang des chimères* (Paris, 1779), a brochure of 47 pages. No copies are to be found in the British Museum or the Bodleian. In the Catalogue of the Bibliothèque Nationale the book is listed, but no first name given for Boyé, who is frequently confused with Pascal Boyer, one of the authors of the composite *Mémoires* mentioned on p. 118.

which are, alas, too often profaned'. Gluck's revision of the aria in the Paris version of 1774 was left undisturbed by Berlioz, except for the re-transposition to alto pitch. It is one of the instances where the need to revise was taken by the composer as an opportunity for refinement and even bolder expression. As in Orfeo's aria no. 22 in Act II, Gluck raised the pitch at the end of the piece, and by his carefully saving this effect for the concluding bars, it becomes eloquent and poignant, a simple device which was not lost on Beethoven when he fashioned the coda of the slow movement of his fifth symphony:

Ex. 1   (a) *Orfeo* and *Orphée*, **first and second statements**

(b) *Orfeo*, final statement

(c) *Orphée*, final statement

(d) Beethoven, fifth symphony: first, second, and third statements

(e) Beethoven, last statement

[122]

If *Orfeo* were to be described as the curtain-raiser for the triple bill of the Calzabigi operas, the centre-piece, indeed the masterpiece, would be *Alceste*. Gluck himself recognized the superiority of *Alceste* when he wrote, in the preface to *Paride ed Elena*: 'The drama of *Paride* did not require from the composer's fancy those strong passions, those majestic images and those tragic situations which in *Alceste* shook the spectators.' The success of the Vienna version of *Alceste* was impressive. In spite of the absence of both a castrato and the conventional love-plot, there were some sixty performances. The score was printed in Vienna in 1769.

The Paris version of 1776, with French text, is a far-reaching revision of the original work. Du Roullet (1716–86), who fashioned the French libretto, struggled manfully to follow the composer's various suggestions and to achieve a plot that would evolve more rationally. In a few instances du Roullet and Gluck succeeded, as in the transposition of the court scene between Admetus and Alceste, which in the Vienna version follows the underworld scene, but in the Paris version precedes it. In many respects, however, the material proved resistant to refinement and re-shaping. The introduction of the figure of Hercules, notably absent in the Vienna version, did much to diminish the unity and the tragic passions of the drama. Calzabigi, in summarizing the plot, had stressed his deliberate departure from Euripides in eliminating Hercules and leaving Apollo 'to work the miracle out of gratitude'. Strangely enough, it was Gluck himself who suggested that Hercules be re-instated. Unfortunately, in du Roullet's libretto, Hercules is but another device of salvation. In Calzabigi's original version the importance of Apollo's oracle in the opening act was balanced by the divine intervention in the final act, recalling the formal symmetry achieved in *Orfeo* by the treatment of the character of Amor. It was, of course, possible to develop the hints present in Euripides' tragedy by making of Hercules another Dionysus, a symbol of the power of life. Indeed, in operas of the twentieth century based on adaptations of Hugo von Hofmannsthal and Thornton Wilder this has been attempted. But, as treated by du Roullet, we have two fairly sudden and unconvincing acts of salvation instead of one, and this abundance is not an improvement.

Another aspect of the work—the monumental structure of the music—though not wholly sacrificed in the Paris version, became reduced in scope. In the Italian score the architectural blocks which acted as component parts of the total design were, if anything, increased in size as compared with *Orfeo*. To hold these complexes together Gluck relied once more on repetition. But in the French version these structural repetitions are so reduced that the tragic effusions of Alceste are deprived of the monumental background they require. An important example is furnished by the mourning scene in E♭ major in Act I. This act, which includes the recitative and aria, 'Popoli di Tessaglia', as well as the famous oracle, made a particular impression on Mozart. He reset the text of the recitative and aria for Aloysia Weber in 1778; the oracle re-appears in *Idomeneo* in 1781; and the unrelieved tragic note must have impressed the boy of twelve when he heard it in Vienna. His father's comment on 'the sad opera *Alceste* by Gluck' in a letter of 3 February, 1768 would seem to speak for both of them.

The opera has two introductions: an overture which sets the tone in a manner far superior to that of the overture to *Orfeo*, and a prologue by the herald who announces the tragic predicament of the plot. After this, Gluck proceeds again to compose a mourning scene where a chorus opens and closes the entire complex and, indeed, functions as the main structural element. Enclosed within this framework are a *ballo* (the first pantomime) and a limited amount of solo singing, notably Alceste's first aria. In the following tabulation page references are to the first edition (Vienna, 1769; Hopkinson, No. 37 A). For convenience I have allotted consecutive numbers to the units:

No.		Key	Page
1	Herald's recitative		11
2	Opening chorus	E♭ major	13
3	First pantomime	C minor	17
4	Evander's first recitative		18
5	Opening chorus, 2nd time	E♭ major	20
6	Evander's second recitative		21
7	Second chorus	G minor	22
8	Alceste's recitative: 'Popoli di Tessaglia'		24
9	Alceste's aria: 'Io non chiedo'	E♭ major	26
9a	(At end of aria: quotation of second chorus)	G minor	32
10	Opening chorus, 3rd time	E♭ major	34

Comparison with the mourning scene in *Orfeo* shows the principle of repetition carried further. In the earlier work the opening chorus was sung twice, whereas in *Alceste* it appears three times. Indeed, the opening strain occurs even more frequently: three times in no. 2, twice in no. 5, and once in no. 10. This six-fold statement is easily the most memorable musical material of the entire *scena*, expressive of the dominant emotions, grief and anxiety. In the Paris version progress is swifter, for several numbers have been excised.[1] Nos. 4 and 5 have been excised altogether, no. 3 transferred to a later scene (Act I, scene 4, bar 20). Moreover, in no. 2 the opening strain appears only once (scene 1, bars 38–56). With the cut of no. 5, the characteristic motive is heard twice in the Paris version, six times in the Vienna version. The resultant loss in musical and dramatic coherence is noticeable to those familiar with both versions.

In Alceste's aria, 'Io non chiedo' (no. 9), Gluck carried forward the experiment begun in 'Che farò senz' Euridice', namely, to express the distraction of the singer by carefully specifying variations of tempo and dynamics. In fact, to these elements of differentiation he added a third, the time signatures. Within the hundred-odd bars of Alceste's aria there occur six tempi and as many time signatures. The dynamics, too, are carefully indicated. At Alceste's *Allegro* the crucial quatrain:

> Non comprende i mali miei
> Ne il terror che m'empie il petto
> Chi di moglie il vivo affetto
> Chi di madre il cor non hà

is underlined by 18 dynamic markings within six bars; the Paris version manages with only 6 dynamics. This simplification may or may not be the result of greater wisdom on the composer's part in husbanding orchestral resources:

[1] References are to the *Sämtliche Werke*, where *Alceste* has been edited by R. Gerber (Kassel & London, 1957).

Ex. 2 (a) Vienna, p. 27

(b) Paris, ed. Gerber, p. 39

But there are other economies within this aria which are distinct impoverishments, such as the loss of the section (*Andante*, 3/4) where the children interrupt their mother, with a solo for cor anglais. These 16 bars are an important dramatic contrast to Alceste's own singing (*Allegro*, 4/4) which precedes and follows. Gluck obviously bowed here to one of France's most influential critics, Rousseau. Just as Voltaire had chided Shakespeare for his irregularities, so Rousseau took Gluck to task for violating the canons of unity and logic, an unpardonable sin in the Age of Reason. He objected specifically to the passage of the children because of its change of time signature (*mesure*) and to the earlier interruption of unity in regard to tempo as well as rhythm at Alceste's words 'ma il mio duol' (*Adagio*, 3/4), which acts as so effective an introduction to her *Allegro*, 4/4, just quoted. Gluck yielded on both counts, though the degree to which he did so differed. He excised entirely the *Andante* of the children; Alceste's moving phrase, 'ma il mio duol', remained, but the tempo was kept at *moderato* instead of slowing down to *adagio*;[1] the time signature, on the other hand, was marked 3/4 and thus constituted a much censured *changement de mesure*. In view of the influence which these expressive variations of speed and rhythm exercised on later works such as Beethoven's *Fidelio* and the ninth symphony, Rousseau's attack deserves to be reproduced in the original:

L'air *Io non chiedo, eterni Dei*, est, sur-tout dans son commencement, d'un chant exquis, comme sont presque tous ceux du même auteur. Mais où est dans cet air l'unité de dessin, de tableau, de caractère? Ce n'est point là, ce me semble, un air, mais une suite de plusieurs airs. Les enfants y mêlent leur chant à celui de leur mère ;

[1] In the Paris version Alceste begins *moderato* 4/4, and the change to 3/4 is marked *moderato* as well. This, though not impossible, seems unlikely, and one suspects that either the printer failed to reproduce a *lento* on the pause which precedes the 3/4 or that Alceste and her oboe solo should begin *lento* or *adagio*. See R. Gerber's edition, pp. 415–16, bar 88; also facsimile, p. xix.

ce n'est pas ce que je désapprouve : mais on y change fréquemment de mesure, non pour contraster et alterner les deux parties d'un même motif mais pour passer successivement par les chants absolument différents. On ne sauroit montrer dans ce morceau aucun dessin commun qui le lie et le fasse un : cependant c'est ce qui me paroît nécessaire pour constituer véritablement un air. L'auteur, après avoir modulé dans plusieurs tons, se croit néanmoins obligé de finir en *E la fa*, comme il a commencé. Il sent donc bien lui-même que le tout doit être traité sur un même dessin, et former unité. Cependant je ne puis la voir dans les différente membres de cet air, à moins qu'on ne veuille la trouver dans la répétition modifiée de l'allegro *Non comprende i mali miei*, par laquelle finit ce morceau ; ce qui me paroît pas suffisant pour faire liaison entre tous les membres dont il est composé. J'avoue que le premier changement de mesure rend admirablement le sens et la ponctuation des paroles : mais il n'en est pas moins vrai qu'on pouvoit y parvenir aussi sans en changer.[1]

The next large unit comprises the third scene, so labelled in both versions. The question of tonality does not enter into a comparison of the two versions. For one thing, Admetus does not appear in the scene; for another, he was scored for a tenor in both versions, obviating the need for transposition. It would seem that the absence of that need, and the greater knowledge with which Gluck fashioned Alceste's arias, make the later opera, in either version, a more mature and compelling work of art. Alceste's first aria, just discussed, and her famous second aria, 'Divinités du Styx', show a more astute portrayal of character, which thus makes a misunderstanding analogous to 'Che farò senz' Euridice' improbable. In any event, the large complex about to be discussed hinges, as before, on a chorus functioning as a *ritornello* : one may assume that the composer wished to increase the role of choral singing in his opening act.

No.		Page Italian score	Page French score
11	Second pantomime	37	64
12	Priest's first recitative	38	65
13	Third chorus	39	66
14	Priest's second recitative	46	84
15	Third chorus, 2nd time	48	85
16	Priest's third recitative	50	89
17	Second pantomime, repeated	51	89
18	Alceste's third recitative	52	90
19	Third chorus, 3rd time	53	omitted

The omission of no. 19 in the French score is, obviously, the main difference between the two versions. The excision of this chorus, in C minor, affects the shape of the entire complex and, is comparable to the omission of chorus no. 5 in E♭ major in the earlier *scena*. Moreover, the opening strain of nos. 13, 15, and 19 in the Italian score is more vividly presented and, therefore, more easily remembered in that version. It occurs three times in the chorus in no. 13, and these *tutti* entries form a decisive contrast to the *concertino* episodes in which the priest sings. In the corresponding pages of the French score (bars 49, 64, 86) only the first entry is given to the chorus, the two succeeding ones to the priest. With no choral singing after the repetition of the second pantomime the swifter progress of the drama in the Paris version is achieved at the cost of the splendour and monumentality of a *concertato* which depends on choral sonority for its *ritornello* effects.

[1] 'Fragment sur l'Alceste de M. Gluck', *Œuvres complètes*, ed. P. R. Auguis, 27 vols. (Paris, 1825), xv, p. 318.

Two numbers of particular distinction remain to be discussed: Alceste's second aria, 'Ombre, larve' ('Divinités du Styx') and her *accompagnato* in the underworld scene, 'Ma dove sono' ('Grands Dieux! Soutenez mon courage!'). (The relevant pages in the Italian score are 66 and 87; in the French score 123 and 271.) The very words with which Alceste begins, 'Ombre, larve', must have conjured up in the minds of Calzabigi and Gluck, not to mention some members of the audience in Vienna, the second act of *Orfeo*, where the hero pleads, 'Furie, larve, ombre' (no. 22). The literary parallels in the two operas are abundant and challenge one's notice. Where Orfeo asks for pity:

Vi renda almen pietose il mio barbaro dolor

Alceste as decisively refuses to plead:

Non vi chiedo, non voglio pietà.

Of greater relevance perhaps are the musical analogies. The main effect of no. 22 in *Orfeo* is the *concertato* between the protagonist, accompanied by the second orchestra, *piano*, and the *tutti* of the furies, accompanied by the first orchestra, *forte*. Thus the opening address, 'Furie, larve, ombre', interspersed twice by the 'No' of the *tutti*, has the dynamic marks *p, f, p, f, p*.

In *Alceste* the protagonist addresses an imaginary underworld which exists only in her mind at this point of the drama. As a result, the contrasting *forte* is sounded by the orchestra only, nevertheless, the *concertato* is just as eloquent. At bars 10 and 12 the nouns 'ombre' and 'larve' are accompanied by strings, *piano*; at bars 11 and 13 the *forte* chords, on the wood-wind and brass, represent Hades, which in a later act becomes vocal in the chorus of the *numi infernali* (the bar numbers in the French score, edited by R. Gerber, are identical). In *Orfeo*, no. 22 had been preceded by a short orchestral introduction, played by the *concertino* alone; in *Alceste*, the introduction anticipates the aria proper, wood-wind and brass sound the chords at bars 2 and 4, which answer the strings. Gluck is equally specific about the indications of tempo, which calls to mind his method in 'Che farò senz' Euridice'. In the Italian score of *Alceste* the protagonist starts *andante* and remains in this tempo until the *fine* mark indicates the end of the *da capo*. (French score, bars 10–33, with *adagio* at bars 15 to 17.) The subsequent contrasting section is marked *moderato* (French score, *andante un poco*). But when the words 'ombre larve' return to be sung on the dominant, the marking is again *andante*. (The French score has *animé* at bar 44, *lento* at bar 49, *premier mouvement* at bar 52, and *très animé* at bar 63.) At bar 82 the Italian score merely indicates *da capo al fine*; in the French score the *da capo* is written out, bars 92–115, and several nuances introduced. The succession of tempi, for instance, is now *andante, adagio,* and *animé* instead of *andante, adagio, andante*. In comparing this famous aria in both versions, one is aware that the original two-syllable words, 'ombre, larve', fit the music better, and the *concertato* between voice and instrumental answer on the six syllables of 'divinités du Styx' sounds less natural.[1] On the other hand, the careful specifications of variations of tempo and the modified *da capo* of the French version are indications of the greater wisdom Gluck had gathered in the intervening years.

Gluck's ability to depict in music the imaginary landscapes of classical mythology was one of his signal contributions to Italian opera in the eighteenth century. While his predecessors

[1] Berlioz, *À travers chants*, 2nd ed. (Paris, 1872), p. 173.

concentrated on the emotions, the *affetti*, of such scenes, Gluck painted in the background against which action takes place or emotion is expressed—such as the description of Elysium, perhaps the finest example in *Orfeo*. But the *concertato* in Hades was, as yet, more concerned with the grim determination of the furies than with a description of the world they inhabited. In *Alceste*, on the other hand, Gluck met the challenge and endeavoured to show later composers how to create an inferno in music. If the Elysium music left its traces in Beethoven's 'Pastoral' symphony, Gluck's Hades had a profound influence on the Wolf's Glen scene in Weber's *Freischütz*. One detail of this marvellous scene deserves a special mention—the passage in the woodwind singled out by Alfred Einstein for its expressiveness: 'One of the finest traits is the "lonely" entry of the oboe, descending from B to B flat as it paints the dread silence of the night in which brood the spirits of Hades. Gluck had his own system of key relationships in recitative: turns towards flat keys symbolize depression and those toward sharp keys excitement, and he had already handled this most sensitively in *Orfeo*. This oboe passage is, so to say, a concentration and symbol of this system in the smallest possible form.'[1] Students of music search for this passage in vain, for it occurs only in the Italian score (p. 88; corresponding in the French score to Act III, scene 3, bar 37), which is not readily available in a modern reprint. Its eloquence lies in the fact that the progression C—B♮ in the oboe, in the preceding bar, is doubled by the vocal part and accompanied by the string orchestra. The succeeding B♮—B♭ is marked by the composer 'solo' to indicate that the strings are silent. The voice enters on D and does not reach B♭ until the second beat. Thus, in a passage of which the scoring is far in advance of his time and which, in fact, anticipates Berlioz, Gluck allows a single sonority to speak for itself, dispensing with the eloquence of harmony. In the French score the same progression occurs in a middle part of the string orchestra, but by the time the oboe takes the B♭ from the strings its novelty is tarnished:

Ex. 3 (a) Vienna, p. 88

[1] *Gluck*, revised ed. (London, 1964), p. 111.

This discussion of the relative merits of the Vienna and Paris versions of Gluck's two reform operas raises a number of questions on the general problem of translation and adaptation. Does the historical evidence suggest that once an opera has been completed the work does not lend itself to adaptation for a different audience in another city without impairment of the original excellence? That felicitous touches are sometimes added in the process of revision no student of Wagner's *Tannhäuser* or Verdi's *Don Carlo* would deny. But to lump all the changes under the heading of improvement would be unrealistic. There is a unity of style, a homogeneity of harmonic texture, an almost naïve happiness, so to speak, at having created the apt expression, that is so often missing from a later version. In Mozart's work the changes are sometimes truly staggering. How could the composer of *Figaro* excise 'Deh signor, nol contrastate' from the Finale of Act II, or add the banalities of the duet between Leporello and Zerlina to *Don Giovanni*? We know of no single performance in the twentieth century that has perpetuated these 'improvements'. How could Gluck, in *Iphigénie en Aulide*, disturb the symmetry between the intervention of Calchas at the beginning and end of the opera, by adding to the finale the clumsy appearance of Pallas Athene? Does a work of dramatic music, occupying several hours, once its planning is completed, not permit re-planning? These are questions still to be resolved. In the meantime, we salute the daring and the genius of the first versions of Gluck's reform operas, notwithstanding the several and substantial improvements which that deliberate and self-critical composer was able to bestow upon the later versions.

VINCENZO RIGHINIS OPER *ALCIDE AL BIVIO*

Hellmut Federhofer (Mainz)

RIGHINI IST der Nachwelt vor allem als Schöpfer der Krönungsmesse für Kaiser Leopold II. und als berühmter Gesangslehrer lebendig geblieben, als Opernkomponist dagegen vergessen. Das absprechende Urteil des mit ihm fast auf den Tag gleichaltrigen W. A. Mozart vom 29. August 1781: 'Er gewinnt sich viel geld mit scolarisiren — und vergangene fasten war er mit seiner Cantate glücklich, denn er hat sie 2 mal hintereinander gegeben, und allzeit gute ein-nahme gehabt. — der schreibt recht hüpsch. — er ist nicht ungründlich; aber ein grosser dieb. — er giebt seine gestohlne sachen aber so mit überfluß wieder öfentlich Preis, und in so ungeheuerer menge, daß es die leute kaum verdauen können',[1] mag dazu beigetragen haben, daß sich die Musikfor-schung mit seinem Werk bisher kaum beschäftigt hat. Nun darf nicht übersehen werden, daß die meisten noch erhaltenen Werke Righinis aus der Zeit nach 1781, also nach seinem 25. Lebens-jahr stammen, auf die Mozarts Äußerung nicht ohne weiteres bezogen werden kann. Aus früherer Zeit sind an bühnendramatischen Werken nur das den Don-Giovanni-Stoff behandelnde Dramma tragicomico *Il convito di pietra ossia Il dissoluto punito* (1776 Prag), das Dramma giocoso *La vedova scaltra* (1778 Prag) und die Commedia giocosa *La bottega del cafè* (1778 Prag) bekannt.[2] Aus der Zeit nach 1781 liegen dagegen allein über zehn Opern vor, unter ihnen auch die einaktige *azione teatrale*, *Alcide al bivio* nach einem Text von Pietro Metastasio, den erstmals Johann Adolph Hasse für die Feierlichkeiten anläßlich der 1760 stattgefundenen Hochzeit des Erzherzogs und späteren Kaisers Joseph II. mit Isabella von Bourbon komponiert hatte.[3]

Als Righini seinen *Alcide al bivio* schuf, hatte er seine Stellung in Wien als Leiter der opera buffa und Lehrer der Prinzessin Elisabeth von Württemberg bereits aufgegeben und war 1787 als erster Italiener an die Spitze der kurfürstlichen Hofkapelle in Mainz getreten. Seine Anstellung vermittelten vermutlich Ignaz Franz von Beecke, der ihn schon 1775 in Wien kennengelernt hatte,[4] und die Gräfin Maria Anna Hortensia von Hatzfeld, geb. Gräfin Zierotin (eine Schwägerin des Mainzer Hofmusikintendanten Franz Ludwig von Hatzfeld), die 1782 die Titelrolle in

[1] Mozart, *Briefe und Aufzeichnungen*, Gesamtausgabe, hrsg. von der Internationalen Stiftung Mozarteum Salzburg, gesammelt und erl. von W. A. Bauer und O. E. Deutsch, Bd. 3: 1780–1786, Kassel etc. 1963, 153.

[2] R. Eitner, *Biographisch-bibliographisches Quellen-Lexikon*, Bd. 8, 235 ff.; ferner H. Engel, Art. 'V. Righini' in MGG Bd. 11, Spalte 516.

[3] O. Bauer, *Opern und Operetten in Wien, Verzeichnis*

ihrer Erstaufführungen in der Zeit von 1629 bis zur Gegenwart, Graz-Köln 1955, 3.

[4] E. F. Schmid, Art. 'Beecke' in MGG Bd. 1, Spalte 1503. Über Beziehungen Beeckes zu Righini ferner A. Gottron, 'Ignaz von Beecke, der Intendant der Oettingen-Wallersteinischen Hofmusik am Mainzer Kurfürstlichen Hof', in *Mainzer Kalender 1956*, 97 ff.

Righinis *Armida* im Palais Auersperg zu Wien sang.[1] Die Mainzer Hofkapelle war vor ihm von namhaften Komponisten, u.a. von Jan le Febure, Gabriel Plautz, Philipp Friedrich Buchner, Philipp Jacob Baudrexel, Johann Theodor Herold, Joseph Paris Feckler, Johann Zach und Johann Michael Schmid geleitet worden, erlebte aber erst jetzt ihre Blütezeit, der die kriegerischen Ereignisse im Zuge der französischen Revolution und die Besetzung der Stadt durch französische Truppen allerdings schon 1792 ein jähes Ende setzten.[2] Bedeutende Instrumentalkünstler, wie Georg Anton Kreußer, Ernst Schick und der mit den Mozarts bekannte Kastrat Francesco Ceccarelli gehörten der Mainzer Hofmusik an. Unter den Sängerinnen war am berühmtesten Margaretha Luise Hamel, die 1789 Ernst Schick heiratete, während sich die hervorragende Altistin Maria Anna Lehritter ein Jahr vorher mit Righini vermählte.[3] Wenn dieser trotz der günstigen Voraussetzungen seinen *Alcide al bivio* zwar in Mainz, aber für den kurtrierischen Hof in Koblenz schuf, wo das Werk unter seiner Leitung am 6. Mai 1790 zur Aufführung gelangte,[4] so sind die Gründe hierfür ausschließlich im ehrenvollen Auftrag, der vom benachbarten fürstlichen Hof an ihn erging, zu suchen.

Eine von meinem verehrten Kollegen an der Johannes Gutenberg-Universität Mainz, Herrn Prälaten Prof. Dr. Adam Gottron angefertigte und mir freundlicherweise zur Verfügung gestellte Kopie, nach der der Südwestfunk, Landesstudio Rheinland-Pfalz, am 31. Januar 1965 eine nur in den Rezitativen gekürzte Wiedergabe unter Leitung von Emmerich Smola brachte, ermutigte mich umsomehr zu näherer Beschäftigung mit diesem Werk, als es zeitlich und gattungsmäßig in unmittelbarer Nähe zu Mozarts *La clemenza di Tito* steht. Beide Werke zählen zu den letzten Ausläufern höfisch-auftragsgebundener Festopern.

Über die Beziehungen Righinis zum kurtrierischen Hof und die Entstehung des *Alcide al bivio* konnte kürzlich G. Bereths nähere Einzelheiten mitteilen.[5] In einem Schreiben vom 16. November 1788 teilt Righini mit, daß er mit der Auftragsoper begonnen habe, in der er 'duetti terzetti etc.' vermisse, weshalb er bitte, den Dichter Matthia Verazi mit der Anpassung des Textes an die damaligen Opernbedürfnisse zu beauftragen.[6] Der Kurfürst erklärte sich jedoch mit diesem Vorschlag nicht einverstanden und ließ in seinem Antwortschreiben vom 13. Dezember 1788 darauf

[1] A. Gottron, *Mainzer Musikgeschichte von 1500 bis 1800*, Mainz 1959, 166.

[2] K. Schweickert, *Die Musikpflege am Hofe der Kurfürsten von Mainz im 17. und 18. Jahrhundert*, Mainz 1937; A. Gottron (wie Anm. 1), 40 ff.; ders., 'Joseph Paris Feckler in *Archiv für Musikwissenschaft*, Jg. 19/20, 1962/1963, 186 ff. Ferner liegen über die meisten genannten Namen eigene Artikel in MGG vor.

[3] A. Gottron, *Mainzer Musikgeschichte von 1500 bis 1800*, 140 ff.

[4] Das Autograph befindet sich in Bologna, Civico Museo Bibliografico Musicale; vgl. G. Gaspari, *Catalogo della Biblioteca musicale G. B. Martini di Bologna*, Vol. 3, Bologna 1893, 333: 'Alcide al bivio. Poesia del celebre abate Metastasio, musica di Vinzenzo Righini direttore della musica, e maestro di capella all'attuale servizio di S.A.S. l'Elettore di Magonza, composta e prodotta l'anno 1790 li 6 di maggio in Coblenz per ordine di S.A.S. l'Elettore di Treveri.-Partitura ms. e autografa in tre volumi, colle originali parti di canto e di orchestra.' Auch A. Gottron,

Mainzer Musikgeschichte . . ., 166 führt Koblenz an. Danach ist die Angabe 'Mainz' in MGG, Art. 'Righini', Bd. 11, Spalte 516 zu berichtigen. Zwei Kopien aus dem Anfang des 19. Jahrhunderts verwahrt die Bibliothek der Gesellschaft der Musikfreunde in Wien unter den Signaturen IV 7740 (2 Bände, vollständige Partiturabschrift) und IV 7746 (Partiturabschrift von anderer Hand, beginnend mitten in der 11. Szene mit Edonide 'Ah soffri' bis zum Schluß. Vor dem Schlußchor wird außerdem der aus Corale und Fuga bestehende Kantatenschluß überliefert. Eine neuzeitliche Hand bezeichnet auf aufgeklebter Vignette diese Quelle als Band 3; die beiden ersten Bände, mit dem vorangehenden Teil scheinen verloren zu sein). Eine weitere Kopie befindet sich in der Westdeutschen Bibliothek in Marburg.

[5] *Die Musikpflege am kurtrierischen Hof zu Koblenz-Ehrenbreitstein*, Mainz (1964), 253 ff. (=*Beiträge zur mittelrheinischen Musikgeschichte*, Nr. 5.)

[6] Bereths, a.a.O., 256.

hinweisen, daß in Szene 4, 7 und 11 genügend Ensembles zu finden seien. Da diese aber mit Ausnahme eines einzigen Quartetts nur kurze, von Choristen gesungene Soli in Chorszenen bilden, gab sich Righini in seiner Antwort vom 19. Dezember 1788 mit Recht nicht zufrieden[1] und übersandte dem Kurfürsten einen anderen, nicht näher bekannten Operntext zur Begutachtung zwecks Vertonung. Dieser beharrte aber auf seiner Meinung. Er ziehe den *Alcide* 'surtout pour la moral' dem von Righini vorgeschlagenen Text vor, zumal 'nous sommes toutes fait persuadé que vous vous acquitterez au mieux en dépit de la mediocrité de sujet'. Mit dieser Entscheidung musste sich Righini abfinden, was er auch in seinem Schreiben vom 22. Februar 1790 feststellt: 'La Musique, comme vous [=Musikintendant von Thünnefeld] me l'avez ordonné. . .est composée sur le texte, sans que j'y ai changé un mot.'[2]

Der Kurfürst mochte wohl auch unter dem Eindruck der von J. A. Hasse beherrschten Oper in Dresden, woher er kam, gehandelt und aus diesem Grunde an dem einmal ausgewählten Text festgehalten haben. Ob tatsächlich — wie Bereths annimmt[3] — Matthia Verazi zuletzt doch noch mit dem Text sich befaßt hat, erscheint daher mehr als fraglich. Während Caterino Mazzolà Metastasios *La clemenza di Tito* für Mozart so bearbeitete, wie es etwa Righini für seine Vorlage von Verazi gewünscht hatte, verblieb diese ohne alle Einschübe oder Änderungen. Nur eine Kürzung erfolgte, die *Scena ultima* mit der Erscheinung der Göttin Iris entfiel zur Gänze, so daß Righini bereits mit der elften, der vorletzten Szene schließt, was der obige Brief auch ausdrücklich vermerkt.[4] Diese Kürzung mußte den Intentionen des Kurfürsten entsprechen, da bereits der Schlußchor dieser Szene die moralische Sentenz des Stückes ausspricht:

Alme belle, fuggite prudenti
Quel piacer, che produce tormenti:
Alme belle, soffite costanti
Quel tormenti, onde nasce il piacer.

Im übrigen stützt sich die Vertonung Righinis auf den unverkürzten Text Metastasios, dem die antike Fabel von Herakles am Scheideweg zugrundeliegt.[5] Die Personen der Handlung sind: *Alcide* [=Herakles] *giovanetto* [Tenor]; *Fronimo, suo aio, o sia il Senno* [Baß]; *Edonide o sia la dea del piacere* [Koloratursopran]; *Aretéa o sia la Virtù* [Alt]; *Ninfe, Geni ed Amori seguaci di Edonide*; *Eroi, Eroine e Geni seguaci d'Aretéa*. Dagegen entfallen entsprechend der erwähnten Kürzung *Iride, messagiera di Giunone, e di Giove*, sowie die *Geni seguaci d'Iride* und die *Abitatori del tempio della Gloria*. Die Handlung spielt *nella campagne di Tebe* und umfaßt bei Metastasio zwölf, bei Righini nur die ersten elf Szenen.

Alcide sieht vor sich einen Wald mit zwei Straßen: 'Si divide nel prospetto la Selva in due lunghe, ma differentissime strade, essendo la sinistra di esse agevole, fiorita, ed amena, e l'altra all'opposto difficile, disastrosa e selvaggia.'[6] Sie symbolisieren den Weg des heiteren Lebensgenusses und den Weg der Tugend, zwischen denen

---

[1] Bereths, a.a.O., 256.
[2] Ibid., 259.
[3] Ibid., 257.
[4] Ibid., 258.
[5] H. Hunger, *Lexikon der griechischen und römischen Mythologie*, Wien (1953), 132 ff. E. Frenzel, *Stoffe der Weltliteratur*, Stuttgart (1962), 260 ff. Dort sind auch Vertonungen von Texten, die Motive des Herakles-Mythos als Oper, Oratorium oder Kantate behandeln, durch zahlreiche andere Komponisten, unter denen J. S. Bach und G. F. Händel hervorragen, angeführt. Righini fehlt in der Aufzählung.

[6] Die szenischen Angaben sind speziell in diesem Werk sehr ausführlich. Wiedergegeben nach P. Metastasio, *Opere*, T. 12, Venezia 1783, Alcide al Bivio, 1 ff.

Alcide nach dem Willen seines Vaters Zeus selbst zu wählen hat, wie ihm sein väterlicher Freund Fronimo in der ersten Szene mitteilt. In der zweiten Szene bleibt Alcide allein zurück. Die Zweifel, die ihn plagen, gelangen in einem breit angelegten *recitativo accompagnato* zum Ausdruck, das in sein zunächst nur von Bläsern begleitetes Gebet 'Dèi clementi, amici Dèi' mündet. Durch dieses Gebet gestärkt, schickt er sich an, den Weg der Tugend zu beschreiten. Da hört er 'dal fondo della strada opposta risuonare improvvisamente una soave armonia di flauti, e di cetere. Si rivolge a quel lato, e vedendo uscirne Edonide, la quale va avanzandosi lentamente, s'arresta sorpreso ad ammirarla.' Seinen Entschluß auszuführen, hindert die hervortretende Edonide. In der dritten Szene, deren Höhepunkt Edonides Arie 'Non verranno' mit konzertierender Oboe bildet, sucht sie Alcide an sich zu fesseln und führt ihm aus diesem Grunde in der vierten Szene ihr liebliches, von zahlreichen Genien und Nymphen bevölkertes Reich vor, 'seguaci della dea del Piacere, le quali e col canto, e col ballo esprimono non meno il contento dell'allegro stato, in cui si ritrovano, che la varietà delle dilettevoli occupazioni, che le trattengono'.

Die vierte Szene bestreitet der Chor aus dem Reich der Edonide bis zum Erklingen kriegerischer Musik, die ihn verstummen läßt: 'Alla strepitosa armonia de'marziali stromenti, che da lontano improvvisamente si ascoltano, cessa in un tratto, e la danza, ed il canto, ritirandosi alquanto indietro, i Geni, e le Ninfe in attitudine di stupore, e di spavento.' Diese und die vorherige Regieanweisung bezeugen die Einbeziehung des Tanzes in den Chorgesang der vierten Szene, die durch Marschmusik mit der fünften Szene verbunden wird. Aretéa erscheint, in der Alcide seine Mutter zu erkennen glaubt, während das Reich der Edonide, die Alcide vergeblich zur Flucht auffordert, verschwindet, so daß 'si trovano Edonide, ed Alcide nuovamente nel Bivio, in cui dal fondo della strada disastrosa si vede comparire, e maestosamente avanzarsi Aretéa, o sia la Virtù. Alcide l'ammira prima con istupore, indi prorompe con trasporto di gioia'. Die fünfte Szene bringt eine Auseinandersetzung zwischen Edonide und Aretéa, die mit der Flucht der ersteren endet, als Aretéa nach ihrer Arie 'Quell onda' sich anschickt, Alcide nun ihr Reich zu zeigen: '... È' ripieno il luogo d'Eroi, d'Eroine, e di Geni seguaci della Virtù, i quali così nelle attitudini, e ne'sembianti, come con la danza, e col canto, esprimono quella serena tranquillità, che soddisfa, ma non trasporta.' In der sechsten Szene bleiben Alcide und Aretéa allein zurück, während die siebente Szene mit dem Chor der Heroen und Heroinen Aretéas formal der vierten Szene entspricht. Daß auch dieser Chor mit Tanz zu begleiten ist, beweist die Regieanweisung zur fünften Szene ebenso wie jene zur sechsten: 'Alzandosi impetuosamente Alcide dal suo sedile, tace subito il Coro, rimane sospesa la danza degli Eroi, ed Eroine, e sorge parimente Aretéa a fine di trattenerlo.' Alcide hat nun beide Reiche gesehen, Aretéa verläßt ihn, damit er frei entscheiden kann, ihr Reich entschwindet seinen Blicken, so daß er in der achten Szene, die nur seine Arie 'Dove andò'? enthält, unschlüssig allein 'di nuovo nel Bivio' zurückbleibt.

In der neunten Szene tritt Fronimo zu ihm mit dem Rat 'Sì al risolvere, Alcide, è virtù la lentezza, ma è vizio all'eseguir'. Die elfte Szene bringt Höhepunkt und Entscheidung. Alcide bleibt wieder allein zurück: 's'avvede che i due lati della scena sono guerniti di Geni confacenti alle rispettive opposte strade. Sostengono quei della Virtù differenti arnesi scientifici, e militari: quei del Piacere all'incontro vari stromenti della mollezza, e del lusso.' Nach innerem Kampfe entschließt sich Alcide, den Weg der Tugend zu beschreiten, aber die Genien der Edonide versperren den Eingang 'e procurano con vezzi, con preghiere, e con lusinghe d'impedirgliene il passo'. Alcide läßt sich aber weder von ihren Schmeicheleien noch von entgegenzuckenden Blitzen und Ungeheuern, die ihm entgegentreten, entmutigen: 'Si muove Alcide con impeto per rompere l'ostacolo de' Geni che lo trattengono. Quelli si dileguano. La scena improvvisamente si oscura e fra l'interrotto lume de'lampi, e lo strepito delle cadenti saette si riempie tutta di larve, di prodigi, e di mostri.' Er besteht siegreich den Kampf. Am Ende der zehnten Szene 'nel pronunciare Alcide l'ultimo verso impugna la spada, e, scagliandosi risolutamente tra le fiamme, e tra' mostri, penetra nella strada della Virtù. Inoltratovisi di qualche passo, si dilegua in un tratto l'angusta, e tenebrosa antecedente scena, e si trova egli inaspettatamente nel vasto anteriore recinto dell'eminente lucidissimo tempio della Gloria ...'

Die elfte Szene, die bei Righini den Abschluß bildet, vereinigt alle Mitwirkenden. Der Chor begrüßt Alcide als Helden. Auch Edonide erscheint: 'Nell'illustre cammin, che già scegliesti, Edonide compagna'. Sie beugt sich der Göttin der Tugend, durch die allein wahre Freude zu gewinnen sei: 'Virtù mi regga'. Bei Metastasio vereinigen sich Aretéa, Edonide, Alcide und Fronimo zu einem aus zwei vierzeiligen Strophen bestehenden

Schlußquartett. Da Righini mit diesem Text bereits schließt, trennt er die beiden Strophen voneinander und benützt sie zum Aufbau von zwei selbständigen Nummern. Die erste Strophe wird zum Soloquartett gestaltet, während die zweite den von Metastasio hier nicht vorgesehenen Chor miteinbezieht, wodurch Righini in seiner Schlußnummer, die, wie oben erwähnt, die Sentenz des Stückes bereits enthält, einen wirkungsvollen Solo-Tutti Wechsel erzielt.

Im Gegensatz zur Mehrzahl der dramatischen Werke Metastasios, so auch der *Clemenza di Tito*, verzichtet die Handlung auf den sonst üblichen Schematismus von Intrigen und Verwicklungen, die sich zumeist aus dem Schicksal zweier Liebespaare ergeben; die Handlung beschränkt sich vielmehr darauf, das Ethos des Titelhelden hell erstrahlen zu lassen. Diesem Zweck dienen nicht nur alle übrigen Personen, sondern auch Chor und Tanz, deren Einbeziehung das Werk ungewollt den Reformbestrebungen von Christoph Willibald Gluck annähert. Die reichen Regieanweisungen Metastasios, die oben nur auszugsweise mitgeteilt wurden, lassen keinen Zweifel an der beabsichtigten reichen bühnenmäßigen Ausstattung, die Armut an äußerer Handlung ersetzen sollte. Obwohl das Werk im rationalistischen Geist befangen bleibt und alle Disharmonien in kühnem Optimismus und im Vertrauen auf die Vernunft auflöst und überwindet, so daß selbst Edonide zuletzt der Tugend sich beugt, weisen doch manche Motive auf spätere Werke voraus: auf die Feuer- und Wasserprobe (*Zauberflöte*), auf die Erscheinung der Mutter (*Freischütz*) und auf die Venusbergszene (*Tannhäuser*). Der Entfall der letzten Szene verändert den Sinnakzent. Bei Metastasio und Hasse stand die Verherrlichung des Helden Alcide im Mittelpunkt, in dem sich Erzherzog Joseph widergespiegelt sah. Nunmehr tritt der moralisch belehrende Zweck in den Vordergrund, der den geistlichen Kurfürsten zur Wahl dieses Werkes bestimmt hatte. Die Läuterung des Menschen durch Selbstüberwindung schien in der damaligen Zeit gärender Unruhen ein stofflich besonders geeigneter Vorwurf für die Bühne.[1]

Die formale Anlage des Textes zeigt keine Besonderheit. Wechselreden und Monologe, die eine Kette von Rezitativen und Arien ergeben, werden nur durch die beiden Chorszenen, die das Reich der Edonide und der Aretéa bildhaft machen, unterbrochen. Erst zum Schluß folgt ein Quartett, dem sich ein Chor mit solistischen Einschüben anschließt. Andere Ensemblenummern fehlen gänzlich. Righini mußte sie umsomehr vermissen, als er den Erfordernissen der da-capo-Arien mit ihren Zustandsbildern fremd gegenüberstand und daher umsomehr in den erbetenen Duetten, Terzetten eine seiner musikalischen Form entsprechende textliche Grundlage zu finden hoffen durfte. Daß er sich hierin getäuscht sah, aber dennoch mit diesem Werk eine überdurchschnittliche künstlerische Leistung vollbrachte, rückt seine Begabung ins hellste Licht.

Das Werk verlangt dieselbe Besetzung wie Mozarts *La clemenza di Tito*, nämlich doppelte Holz- und Blechbläser (Flöten, Oboen, Klarinetten, Fagotte, Hörner, Trompeten, Pauken) und Streicher. Das Orchester ist sorgfältig behandelt, die Bratsche weitgehend vom Basse gelöst, und die Bläser nehmen selbständig an der thematischen Entwicklung teil. Das Werk eröffnet eine Ouverture, deren dreiteilige Einleitung a (d-moll, Grave) — b (D-Dur) — a in inhaltlicher Beziehung zur Handlung steht. Der a-Teil symbolisiert die Widerstände, die Alcide auf dem Weg zur Tugend erwarten, das glänzende Marschthema in D-Dur, das den Bläsern anvertraut ist,

[1] Vgl. dazu auch Schweickert, a.a.O., 85, der eine charakteristische Äußerung des Mainzer Theaterintendanten Friedrich Karl Freiherrn von Dalberg von 1791 hinsichtlich der Notwendigkeit eines Theaterbetriebes in Mainz mitteilt.

den siegenden Alcide. Zum a-Teil mag ihn wohl die verwandte Ausdruckssphäre der Ouverture von Mozarts *Don Giovanni* angeregt haben, der 1789 in Mainz aufgeführt wurde.[1] Das der Einleitung folgende *Allegro con spirito* lehnt sich an die Sonatenform von Joseph Haydn an. Das zuerst von den Streichern allein und dann vom Tutti vorgetragene Hauptthema bestreitet auch den Seitensatz, in dem es der Oboe anvertraut wird, und erst der Epilog bringt ein Kontrastthema in den Streichern Das Hauptthema ist mit dem Gesang der drei Damen aus Mozarts *Zauberflöte* verwandt; nur die Tonrepetitionen in der Wiederholung des Themas entsprechen weder Mozarts noch Haydns Idiom, sondern entstammen der opera buffa und weisen auf Rossini voraus:[2]

Righini, *Alcide al bivio*, Ouverture:

Mozart, *Zauberflöte*, No. 12, Quintett:

[1] H. Abert, *W. A. Mozart*, T. 2, [Neudr.] Leipzig (1956), 356.

[2] Auf Rossini machen auch Gottron, *Mainzer Musikgeschichte . . .*, 167 und Engel, a.a.O., Spalte 518 aufmerksam.

glücklich   wieder   fort!

Solche Übereinstimmungen bezeugen keine Entlehnung, die zeitlich auch gar nicht möglich war, sondern das Gemeinsame des musikalischen Vokabulars, dessen sich die damalige Zeit noch erfreuen konnte. Bis zum Ende der Exposition verläuft die Ouverture ausgezeichnet. Mängel der Gestaltung und Erfindungsgabe offenbart erst die Durchführung, die sich damit begnügt, den Kopf des Hauptthemas in zahlreichen Wiederholungen und Quintschrittsequenzen abzuwandeln, ohne harmonisch, rhythmisch, metrisch oder in der Instrumentation wesentlich Neues zu bieten. Auch die Rückführung über dem Orgelpunkt der Dominante wird allein von diesem an sich unbedeutenden Motiv bestritten, in dessen Vortrag sich Flöte, Oboe und Klarinette ablösen. Righini mochte wohl gefühlt haben, daß es schon allzusehr beansprucht worden war, da er die Reprise unter Weglassung des Hauptsatzes samt Überleitung sofort mit dem Seitensatz beginnen läßt, aber wiederum (in gewiß nicht vorteilhafter Variierung der Exposition) sich nur auf den Kopf des Hauptthemas beschränkt, das hier gleichfalls auf die Holzbläser verteilt wird. Kadenzbestätigungen und Epilogthema entsprechen mit geändertem harmonischen Verlauf der Exposition.

Schwierigkeit mußte dem Komponisten die Gestaltung der Arien bieten. Sie gehorchen textlich fast ausnahmslos dem barocken Typus der da capo-Arie, der bei Righini natürlich nicht mehr vorkommt, so daß eine Diskrepanz zwischen der Form des Textes und der Musik unvermeidlich war. Eine formale Entsprechung zwischen Text und Musik ergibt sich bezeichnenderweise nur in Ausnahmefällen, die diesem Typus nicht angehören. So spiegelt sich die textliche Form des Dialogs zwischen Edonide und Alcide zu Beginn der dritten Szene auch in der musikalischen Gestaltung wider:

a	x	b	y	a
Edonide	Alcide	Eldonide	Alcide	Edonide
(1. dreizeilige		(2. dreizeilige		(1. dreizeilige
Strophe)	(Rezitativ)	Strophe)	(Rezitativ)	Strophe)

In ähnlicher Weise besteht sonst nur noch Übereinstimmung in den fast durchwegs homophon gestalteten Chorszenen (4, 7 und 11). Wie frei und willkürlich Righini jedoch in anderen Nummern mit dem Text verfährt, mag die Arie Alcides 'Dèi clementi, amici Dèi' in der zweiten Szene belegen. Textlich zeigt sie das übliche Strophenpaar zu je vier Verszeilen, von denen die ersten vier zur Wiederholung bestimmt waren, musikalisch dagegen die der opera buffa entstammende zweiteilige Form mit ruhigem ersten und folgendem raschen zweiten Teil, die auch Mozart in die opera seria übernimmt:

[136]

1. Teil (C-Dur)			2. Teil	
a	b	a	c (c-moll)	d (C-Dur)
1. Strophe (vollständig)	1. Strophe Vers 1, 2	1. Strophe Vers 3, 4	2. Strophe	1. Strophe Vers 1, 3, 4
				2. Strophe (vollständig)

Der erste Teil weist zwar eine knappe da capo-Form auf, begnügt sich aber mit der ersten Strophe allein und verwendet bei Wiederkehr des a-Teiles sofort die dritte Verszeile, so daß sogar das wiederkehrende Hauptthema zu anderem Text erklingt. Im nachfolgenden Allegro kehrt die erste Strophe im zweiten Abschnitt zwar wieder, aber nicht als da capo gestaltet, sondern mit neuen Gedanken und unter Auslassung der zweiten Verszeile. Außerdem wird dann die zweite Strophe nochmals vollständig wiederholt.

Auch an allen übrigen geschlossenen Nummern wird der Widerspruch zwischen textlicher und musikalischer Form offenbar, die verschiedenen Erlebnis- und Gestaltungsweisen ihren Ursprung verdanken. Der Text Metastasios bietet keine Handlung, sondern kommentiert den durch das vorangehende Rezitativ gebotenen Gemütszustand, der Abwandlungen (z.B. in der zweiten Strophe) aber keine prinzipielle Veränderung zuläßt, wenn anders das da capo nicht sinnlos werden soll. Dieser dichterischen Einstellung entsprechen Beibehaltung und Fortspinnung desselben motivischen Materials in der da capo-Arie. Sie war zur Zeit, als Righini seinen *Alcide* schuf, durch knappere Formen, die vorwiegend der opera buffa, der opera comique und dem Singspiel entstammten, sowie der Sonatenform entthront worden, deren Kontrastreichtum und dynamische Bewegtheit sich auch der Arie bemächtigte. Untersucht man daraufhin etwa die Arie Alcides 'Mi sorprende un tanto affetto' in der dritten Szene, so bietet sie das Bild einer Sonatenform, deren Durchführung den Hauptgedanken bei veränderter Modulationsrichtung, aber gleichartiger melodischer Entwicklung abwandelt und deren Reprise sogleich mit dem zweiten Gedanken einsetzt, so daß Durchführung und Reprise zusammen gleich lang wie die Exposition sind. Diese z.B. von C. Ph. E. Bachs Sonaten her vertraute zweiteilige Anlage der 'primitiven' Sonatenform bedient sich der beiden vierzeiligen Strophen wie folgt:

Exposition		Durchführung	Reprise
1. Gedanke (A-Dur)	2. Gedanke (E-Dur)	1. Gedanke (modulierend)	2. Gedanke (mündet in A-Dur)
1. Strophe	2. Strophe	1. Strophe	2. Strophe

Dieselbe musikalische Form unter Voranstellung eines ausgedehnten zweiteiligen Ritornells, das den Hauptgedanken vorwegnimmt, zeigt auch die große Arie der Aretéa 'Quell' onda, che ruina' mit ähnlicher Textverteilung; in der Reprise wird nach der zweiten Strophe lediglich die erste nochmals wiederholt. Mehrfach schaltet Righini zwischen erstem und zweitem Gedanken eine mehr oder weniger ausgedehnte Überleitungs- und Modulationspartie ein, z.B. in der Arie des Fronimo 'Pensa che questo istante', deren aus zwei Strophen zu vier Versen bestehender Text sich ganz unregelmäßig auf die musikalischen Formglieder, wie folgt, verteilt:

		Exposition	
Ritornell (Es-Dur)	1. Gedanke (Es-Dur)	Modulationspartie	2. Gedanke (B-Dur)
	1. Strophe	1. Strophe, Vers 3, 4	2. Strophe, Vers 4, und 3, 4
		2. Strophe, Vers 1-3	2. Strophe (vollständig)

	Durchführung
Ritornell (modulierend)	1. Gedanke, Beginn (modulierend)
	1. Strophe, Vers 1-2
	Reprise
1. Gedanke, Ende (Es-Dur)	2. Gedanke (verkürzt) (Es-Dur)
1. Strophe, Vers 3-4	2. Strophe

Die Mehrzahl der Arien weist diese zweiteilige Anlage in mannigfachen Abwandlungen auf. In der zweiten Arie des Fronimo 'Come rapida si vede' kontrastiert z.B. der zweite Gedanke mit der zweiten Strophe auch tempomäßig (*Andante*) gegen den Hauptgedanken (*Allegro vivace*), die Durchführung ersetzt ein Orgelpunkt auf der Dominante, und an die Stelle des zweiten Gedankens tritt in der Reprise ein marschartiges Thema aus dem Ritornell, das trotz völlig anderen Charakters dennoch auch die zweite Strophe als Textgrundlage benutzt. Selbst dort, wo der erste Teil ausnahmsweise auf der Tonika endet und sich die knappe Form einer da capo-Arie ergibt, wie in Edonides 'Io di mia man la fronte', wird die Form nicht vom Text bestimmt:

	a	b	a (verkürzt)
Ritornell	1. und 2. Strophe	1. und 2. Strophe	2. Strophe, Vers 3-4

Righini rückt stärker von der textlichen Form ab als Mozart in *La clemenza di Tito*. Mozart liebt zwar ebenfalls die aus einem langsamen und raschen Teil bestehende zweiteilige Arie, und hier kommt es auch vor, daß der Text der ersten Strophe im raschen Teil zu anderer Musik wiederkehrt (Arie der Vitellia, no. 2, 'Deh se piacer mi vuoi'). Dagegen begegnet in *La clemenza* die von Righini bevorzugte zweiteilige sonatenförmige Anlage, mit Exposition, Durchführung und Reprise nicht. Andrerseits finden sich zahlreiche da capo-Arien Mozarts, die dem textlichen Formschema vollkommen entsprechen, wie die Arien des Tito, no. 6, 'Del più sublime soglio', no. 8, 'Ah, se fosse intorno al trono', die Arie des Annio, no. 13, 'Torna di Tito a lato', des Publio, no. 16, 'Tardi s'avvede d'un tradimento' und der Servilia, no. 21, 'S'altro che lagrime'. Alle weisen Übereinstimmung von textlicher und musikalischer Form auf:[1]

	a	b	a
	1. Strophe	2. Strophe	1. Strophe

Obgleich sich Righini mehr als Mozart in *La clemenza di Tito* über die Form des Textes hinwegsetzt, paßt er sich doch dem Stil der Metastasianischen Kunst stärker als dieser an, was eine allegorische Handlung, wie *Alcide al bivio*, und ein kürzeres Werk allerdings leichter ermöglichten als ein mehraktiges mit verwickeltem Intrigenspiel. Die Folge der Arien bleibt trotz Fehlens der von Righini gewünschten Ensemblenummern stets abwechslungsreich. Melodische Erfindungsgabe, sorgfältige Orchesterbehandlung, ausgebildete Akkompagnatotechnik und Sinn für dramatische Entwicklung kommen ihm zustatten. Als Melodiker gelingt ihm der Ausdruck des Feierlichen ebenso wie der des Anmutig-Heiteren. Hier wie dort zeigt er sich von der besten Seite und auf der Höhe der Zeit. Einfälle, wie folgende, können auch einem Vergleich mit Mozart standhalten:

[1] Vgl. H. Zingerle, 'Musik- und Textform in Opernarien Mozarts', in *Mozart — Jahrbuch 1953*, Salzburg 1954, 112 ff.

Alcide al bivio, zweite Szene, instrumentales Zwischenspiel:

Ex. 3

Alcide al bivio, dritte Szene, Anfang der Arie der Edonide:

Ex. 4

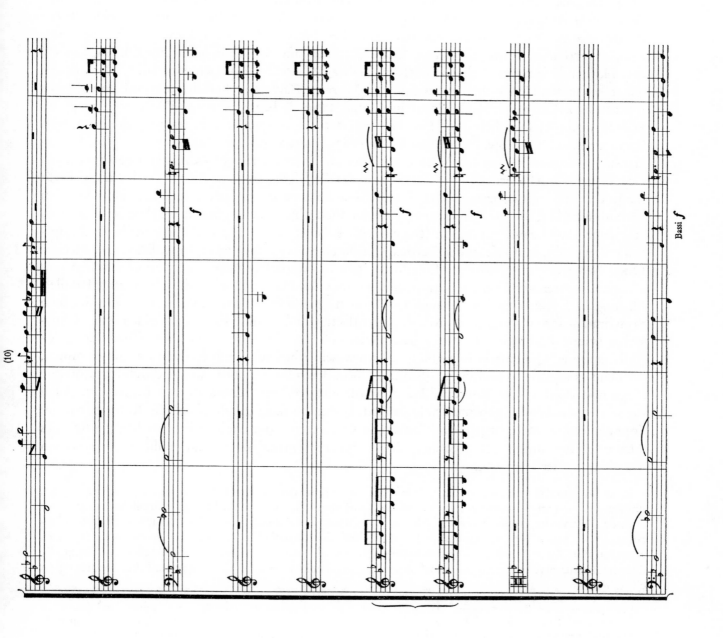

[141]

Dagegen zeigt er sich im Ausdruck des Heroischen noch in der älteren Zeit befangen und schablonenhaft. Weite Dreiklangssprünge, häufige Tonwiederholungen und gleichförmige Rhythmik verhindern die Bildung einer melodischen Linie, an deren Stelle deklamatorisches Pathos tritt, das von ausschweifenden Koloraturen abgelöst wird. Am besten ist ihm in diesem Ausdruckbereich die Arie der Aretéa 'Quell'onda, che ruina' gelungen, an der das Orchester maßgeblich Anteil nimmt. Diesem läßt Righini große Aufmerksamkeit angedeihen. Den vollen Apparat verwendet er nur sehr sparsam. Häufig werden dagegen einzelne Instrumentengruppen mit klangkoloristischen Aufgaben betraut. Das wird schon in der ersten Arie deutlich (Fronimo, 'Pensa che questo istante'), in der zum Streichorchester nur Oboen, Fagotte und Hörner hinzutreten,[1] ebenso auch im Gebet des Alcide 'Dèi clementi, amici Dèi', das in seiner schlichten Größe die Geisteswelt von Mozarts *Zauberflöte* berührt und nur von Bläsern (Flauto solo, Clarinetti in C, Corni in C und Fagotti) begleitet wird. Die Erscheinung der Edonide gibt Gelegenheit zur Einschaltung des in Beispiel 3 mitgeteilten, dreistimmigen Zwischenspieles für Flöte, Fagott und Violoncello, während jene der Aretéa ein im vollen Bläsersatz instrumentierter festlicher Marsch begleitet, der ihrem heroischen Charakter entspricht. Ein Gegenstück zur Marternarie der Constanze in der *Entführung* und zur Arie no. 9 des Sesto 'Parto ma tu ben mio' mit konzertierender Klarinette in *La clemenza* bildet die Arie der Edonide 'Non verrano a turbati i riposi' mit konzertierender Oboe. An den Beginn dieser Arie stellt Righini eine ganze Sonatensatzexposition (Beginn vgl. Beispiel 4), die allerdings innerhalb der Haupttonart verbleibt, und wie in der Tuttiexposition eines Konzertsatzes in ihr schließt; sie bietet der Oboe Gelegenheit zu virtuoser Entfaltung. Mit ihr wetteifert über einem durchsichtigen und abwechslungsreichen Orchestersatz die Singstimme. Als Mangel fällt nur die allzuhäufige Parallelführung in Terzen zwischen ihr und der Oboe in den ausgedehnten Koloraturen — die hier auch vom dramatischen Standpunkt aus voll gerechtfertigt sind — auf. Nur in den beiden ersten Chorsätzen (vierte und siebente Szene) beschränkt sich das Orchester mit Ausnahme der Solosopranepisode 'Quel piacer fra noi si gode' im wesentlichen auf Verdoppelung der Singstimmen, während es im dritten und vierten(Schluß)-Chor, deren homophone Anlage durch imitatorische Züge und rhythmische Kontraste belebt wird, mit größerer Selbständigkeit hervortritt. Auch im satztechnisch solid gebauten Soloquartett, dessen Brillanz durch zahlreiche Koloraturen des Soprans erhöht wird, begegnen selbständige Orchestermotive. Solche beherrschen die Arie des Alcide 'Dove ando' (achte Szene), dessen innere Unruhe sie versinnbildlichen; sie weisen auf die Oper der Romantik voraus.

In der Instrumentaleinleitung zu dieser Arie bewirkt eine Kette pochender Achteltriolen in den beiden Violinen, die sich über einem Bläsermotiv entwickeln, eine wirkungsvolle Steigerung. Eine ganz ähnliche Anlage zeigt auch der Beginn der großen Soloszene Alcides 'In qual mar di dubiezza' (zweite Szene), die denselben Gemütszustand des Helden zum Gegenstand hat und Righini als vortrefflichen Gestalter des *recitativo accompagnato* erkennen läßt. Zweifel und Unsicherheit äußern sich in pochenden, durch Pausen unterbrochenen Achteln, die über einem stufenweise aufsteigenden Baß ihren Ausgangspunkt vom c nehmen und in ähnlicher Steigerung bis c''' führen.

[1] Das gleich einer Devise zweimal gebrachte Motiv über 'Pensa' wird nicht nur durch Fermaten vom eigentlichen Arienbeginn getrennt, sondern erklingt, um die Mahnung eindringlicher zu gestalten, schon am Beginn des Instrumentalritornells in den Hörnern und dann noch mehrmals im Verlauf der Arie in den Bläsern. Am Ende wiederholen es nochmals Singstimme und Hörner.

Righini überwindet durch Bildung größerer Abschnitte mehrfach einen schematischen Wechsel von Rezitativ und Arie, worin ihn die Anlage von Handlung und Text unterstützt. So wird gegen Ende der genannten Szene Alcides Rezitativ durch Wiederholung des in Beispiel 3 mitgeteilten Sätzchens, das Edonide ankündigt, unterbrochen. Ihre liedmäßige Arie 'Ferma Alcide' schließt sich ohne Instrumentaleinleitung unmittelbar an, was vom dramatischen Gesichtspunkt aus ebenso vorteilhaft ist, wie die Unterbrechung ihres Gesanges durch ein Seccorezitativ Alcides. Dadurch findet eine enge Verbindung zwischen der zweiten und dritten Szene statt, die in Edonides Koloraturarie 'Non verranno', mit konzertierender Oboe, eine wirkungsvolle Steigerung findet. Die folgende Chorszene bietet ein dramatisch retardierendes Element. Dasselbe Verhältnis besteht zwischen der dramatisch erregten Arie Aretéas 'Quell'onda' und dem auf sie folgenden Chor, das die Spannung in der kommenden Auseinandersetzung Alcides mit den beiden Mächten erhöht. Ferner ist der Gesamtform förderlich, daß dem dritten Chor 'Vieni Alcide' keine Arie, sondern das dramatisch erregteste *recitativo accompagnato* und dem (zwar nicht vom Dichter intendierten, aber vom Komponisten gestalteten) Schlußchor ein Soloquartett vorangeht.

Die liebevollste Darstellung findet nicht der Held selbst, sondern Edonide. Ihr Ausdrucksbereich reicht — ähnlich jenem der Constanze in Mozarts *Entführung* — von glitzernden Koloraturketten in 'Non verranno', bis zur schlichten liedförmigen Arie 'Io di mia man la fronte'; die ebenso sorgfältige und sparsame Instrumentation verrät eine meisterliche Hand. Am schwächsten dürfte Alcides Arie 'Mi sorprende un tanto affetto' (Maestoso, A-Dur) sein, deren formelhafte und rhythmisch einförmige Melodik mit zahlreichen Tonrepetitionen, Dreiklangsbrechungen, aber auch langatmigen Koloraturen der Situation und dem Text nicht gerecht wird. Auch die Instrumentation kann den Mangel an echtem Pathos nicht verdecken; nur die Hülle der opera seria ist übrig geblieben. Glücklicher erweist sich Righini im Ausdruck des Heroischen, wo er Märsche oder fanfarenartige Motive erfindet und sie an passender Stelle einsetzt, z.B. im zweiten Abschnitt (D-Dur) der Einleitung zur Ouverture, im Auftritt der Aretéa, in den beiden Arien des Fronimo oder im Chor 'Vieni Alcide'. Von ihnen aus führt eine Verbindungslinie zu Spontini und zur Großen Oper.

Der verhältnismäßig lange Zeitraum vom Herbst 1788 bis Anfang 1790, in welchem das Werk entstand, und die Korrespondenz mit dem Kurfürsten von Trier, lassen erkennen, daß Righini mehr Zeit und Mühe für diese Oper aufwendete als Mozart für *La clemenza di Tito*. Righini selbst scheint sein Werk sehr geschätzt zu haben und zeigte sich besorgt um eine gute Wiedergabe 'puisque c'est ma plus grande ambition de la voir applaudir et de S.A.S. Electorale, et de Vous [nämlich dem Intendanten v. Thünnefeld], et de tous les grands connaisseurs qui se trouvent en foule à Votre august Cour.'[1] Die Aufführung am 6. Mai 1790 unter Leitung des Komponisten erfolgte 'mit allgemeinem Beifall' und Wiederholungen fanden am 15. Mai 1790 in Anwesenheit des Herzogs von Sachsen-Teschen und der Erzherzogin Christina, sowie am 26. Juli 1792 vor dem König von Preußen statt,[2] in dessen Dienste er 1793 als Hofkapellmeister treten sollte. Auch außerhalb von Koblenz erntete das Werk Erfolge, so 1804 in Leipzig und Wien. Wohl die Erkenntnis, daß sich die opera seria als Gattung überlebt hatte, bestimmte Righini dazu, das Werk als Kantate aufzuführen und zu diesem Zweck mit einem aus Corale und Fuga bestehenden

[1] Bereths, a.a.O., 255 ff.   [2] Ibid., 238, 261.

neukomponierten Chorsatz zu beschließen.[1] Die Ouverture setzte er, unbekümmert um die Beziehung der Einleitung zur Handlung, auch seinen Opern *Trionfo d'Arianna, Enea nel Lazio* und *Armida* anstelle der ursprünglichen voran.[2]

Righinis Ansehen als Opernkomponist stand um die Wende zum 19. Jahrhundert fest. Seine Oper *Tigrane* wird 1809 als 'berühmt' und die Ouverture als ein 'Lieblingsstück jedes guten Orchesters und gebildeten Auditoriums' bezeichnet.[3] Einer noch ausstehenden Untersuchung von Righinis Opernschaffen soll hier nicht vorgegriffen werden. Aber dem Urteil, das G. Schillings Lexikon 1840 über ihn fällt: 'kein Italiener hat so wie er den gediegenen Ernst und die Harmonie-fülle der Deutschen mit dem Flusse der italienischen Melodie vereinigt; keiner steht Mozart, seinem Vorbild, so nahe wie er'[4] fügt sich sein *Alcide al bivio*. Das Werk rückt ihn geistig in die Nähe des um sieben Jahre jüngeren Simon Mayr,[5] der ebenfalls unter dem Einfluß Haydns und Mozarts steht und eine Verbindung von Ausdruckselementen der italienischen und deutschen Oper anstrebt.

[1] *Allgemeine musikalische Zeitung*, Jg. 6, Leipzig (1803/1804), Spalte 409 ff. und 619 f. Schon in der Konzertsaison 1798/1799 führte er das Werk als Kantate in Hamburg auf; ebenda Jg. 1, Spalte 606.

[2] Engel, a.a.O., Spalte 518; Gottron, *Mainzer Musikgeschichte* . . ., 169.

[3] *Allgemeine musikalische Zeitung*, Jg. 12, Leipzig (1809/1810), Spalte 64.

[4] *Encyclopädie der gesamten musikalischen Wissenschaften oder Universal-Lexikon der Tonkunst*, Bd. 6, Stuttgart 1840, Artikel 'Righini', 5.

[5] L. Schiedermair, *Beiträge zur Geschichte der Oper um die Wende des 18. und 19. Jahrhunderts*, Bd. 1. Leipzig 1907. Righini wird dort nur flüchtig p. 211 f. erwähnt.

WAGNERIAN ELEMENTS IN PRE-WAGNERIAN OPERA

Hans F. Redlich (Manchester)

ON 10 JUNE 1965 exactly a hundred years had passed since the first complete public performance of Richard Wagner's *Tristan und Isolde*. It has remained the greatest individual contribution to opera of that century, and the most consequential musical composition. It is not unlikely that *Tristan* will extend its claim to universal eminence by a further century. No composition of any kind has been written since the deaths of Beethoven and Schubert in 1827–28 that could match the power of this particular work to change the climate of music to a similar extent.

Like J. S. Bach's *St. Matthew Passion*, Mozart's *Don Giovanni* and Beethoven's Choral Symphony it remains not only one of the works which determined and altered the course of musical evolution, but one without whose constant influence the development of music styles within the last century could not even be imagined. The general Wagnerian influence that made itself felt in all departments of music after Wagner's first public successes in the early 1840's reached its zenith only in the first decade of the present century. It was then that the greatest composers of the new century—Richard Strauss, Claude Debussy, and Arnold Schönberg among them—were paying tribute to it in their most revolutionary works. That influence has by now moved into a different stream of world consciousness. It is still indirectly at work in the music of the Second Vienna School and its more recent offshoots. Even in its German homeland (and despite its passing associations with Hitler) Wagner's work is still considered important enough to warrant a complete revaluation of its scenic style at the hands of his grandson Wieland in a resuscitated and re-activated post-war Bayreuth.

The eminence of Wagner, who bestrode his own century like a colossus, and whose posthumous power to mould character, enhance reputations, to make and to break concepts of style, remained unimpaired for so long, is surely to blame for the fact that publications on him have chiefly oscillated between biographical scholarship and official hagiography, neglecting a more reasoned approach to the characteristics of his musical style.[1] Much remains to be done in that direction. It is all the more necessary, since Wagner's genius—despite its breathtaking originality in his mature works—remained curiously eclectic and quite often dependent on outside stimuli, not unlike J. S. Bach, whose indebtedness to the music of older composers, as well as to that of contemporaries, is proverbial. However, while occasional special studies have been devoted to

---

[1] There have been exceptions, of course: T. W. Adorno's stimulating *Versuch über Wagner* (1952), having been preceded by Emil Ludwig's attempt at wholesale debunking in his *Wagner, oder, die Entzauberten* (1913). Paul Bekker's brilliant but incomplete assessment *Richard Wagner* (1924) might also be mentioned here.

describing the formative influence on Wagner of Beethoven's symphonies, of Weber's *Freischütz* and *Euryanthe* and, last but not least, of Liszt's major symphonic and choral works,[1] not much light has yet been shed on pre-Wagnerian composers of less than front rank whose influence, on his own admission, was profound.

Among the latter was Carl Loewe (1796–1869), the master of the romantic *Ballade*, whose Nordic terseness and gloom helped to develop Wagner's peculiar narrative style, especially in parts of the *Ring*,[2] as well as 'der geschickte Lortzing'—Albert Lortzing (1801–51)—whose importance for Wagner as a modest precursor of *Die Meistersinger* in his own *Hans Sachs* (1840) is admitted by Wagner only in a single, condescendingly laudatory, footnote.[3] Among them were also three formidable opera composers of more than local or national reputation, who received praise, tempered by criticism, from Wagner throughout his entire working life. Each of them was responsible for a particular work which remained a special favourite of Wagner's, and to which he either repeatedly referred or about which he remained stubbornly silent for equally weighty reasons.

The operas in which Wagner showed a persistent interest, from his early years as a struggling *Kapellmeister* down to the time of his remote eminence in Bayreuth, are: *La Muette de Portici* by Daniel François Esprit Auber (1828), *Jessonda* by Louis Spohr (1823), and *Hans Heiling* by Heinrich Marschner (1833)—three works of more than passing fame, first launched and well established in the repertory even before Wagner himself had tried his hand at opera.[4]

Of the three, Auber's *La Muette* undoubtedly takes pride of place as the earliest specimen of the sonorous spectacle of *grand opéra*, as the original forerunner of Rossini's more glamorous but less successful *Guillaume Tell* (1829), and, finally, as a work which was revolutionary in itself and also inspired revolution in others. Twice in his life Wagner lavished praise on this work: in his theoretical masterpiece *Oper und Drama* (1851),[5] and twenty years later in his obituary article on Auber, written and published soon after the older composer's death in Paris at the age of nearly ninety on 13 May 1871.[6] Waxing eloquent on the merits of *La Muette*, at the expense of *Guillaume Tell*, Wagner describes in the latter article the tremendous impression created by *La Muette* on the German opera stage around 1830 in contradistinction to the rather tepid reception afforded to Rossini's final masterpiece:

[1] Cf. also the present writer's three analytical studies of *Lohengrin*, *Tristan und Isolde* and *Parsifal*, published in 1948, 1949, and 1951 respectively as part of the series *Covent Garden Operas*, in which some space is devoted to critical arguments on problems of style.

[2] Never mentioned in Wagner's professional writings on music.

[3] Cf. *Richard Wagners gesammelte Schriften und Briefe*: *Gesammelte Schriften*, ed. by Julius Kapp (Leipzig, 1914, in 13 volumes), Vol. I, p. 145.

[4] Quotations from and references to the three operas are from the following scores:

Auber, *La Muette de Portici*, full score, first ed. (Paris, 1828); vocal score, ed. by Natalia Macfarren (Novello, London). Misprints of the latter score have been duly corrected on the basis of the full score.

Spohr, *Jessonda*, vocal score (C. F. Peters Bureau de Musique, Leipzig and Berlin), ed. by Ferdinand Spohr. Since this arrangement was edited by Spohr's son, it has a high degree of authenticity and the full score was not specially consulted.

Marschner, *Hans Heiling*, full score, ed. by Gustav F. Kogel (C. F. Peters, Leipzig). This revised reprint of the full score (dating from the turn of the century) has been collated with the vocal score, edited by the composer himself, and published by Friedrich Hofmeister, Leipzig, some time before 1861.

[5] *Ges. Schriften*, Vol. XI, p. 55 foll. Cf. also Wagner's earlier article 'Halévy und die Königin von Zypern', first published in the Parisian *Gazette Musicale* (1842); cf. *Ges. Schr.*, Band VIII, p. 68 foll.

[6] 'Erinnerungen an Auber' (1871); *Ges. Schr.*, Vol. VIII, p. 125 foll.

Ich berufe mich hierfür auf den Vergleich der Erfolge der 'Stumme von Portici' und des 'Tell' bei uns. Wer das Erscheinen der ersteren Oper auf den deutschen Theatern erlebt hat, weiß von dem ganz erstaunlichen Eindrucke davon zu berichten, während es mit dem 'Tell' nie recht gehen wollte . . . Dagegen überraschte 'Die Stumme' sofort als etwas vollständig Neues: ein Opernsujet von dieser Lebendigkeit war nie da gewesen; das erste wirkliche Drama in fünf Akten, ganz mit den Attributen eines Trauerspiels, und namentlich eben auch dem tragischen Ausgange, versehen . . . Jeder der fünf Akte zeigte ein drastisches Bild von der ungemeinsten Lebhaftigkeit, in welchem Arien und Duetten in dem gewohnten Opernsinne kaum mehr wahrnehmbar waren . . . Es war immer solch ein ganzer Akt, mit all seinem Ensemble, welcher spannte und hinriss. Man fragt sich: wie kam Auber zu solch einem Operntexte? Scribe hat nie vor oder nachher etwas Ähnliches zu stande gebracht . . . wie matt und effektlos fiel schon sogleich der nächste, eben des 'Tell', für Rossini aus! . . . Es muß etwas Besonderes, fast Dämonisches dabei im Spiele gewesen sein. Gewiß ist es, daß nur eben dieser Auber eine solche Musik dazu schreiben konnte, die rechte, einzige Musik, wie sie Rossini mit seiner unbehilflich breiten, altmodisch italienischen Quadratstruktur . . . unmöglich hervorbringen konnte. Denn das Neue in dieser Musik zur 'Stummen' war diese ungewohnte Konzision und drastische Gedrängtheit der Form: die Rezitative wetterten wie Blitze auf uns los; und mitten im Chaos der Wut plötzlich die energischen Ermahnungen zur Besonnenheit oder erneute Aufrufe . . . Man hätte fast wirkliche Musikbilder vor sich zu sehen geglaubt, und der Begriff des Pittoresken in der Musik konnte hier leicht einen fördernden Anhalt finden, wenn er nicht dem bei weitem zutreffenderen der glücklichsten theatralischen Plastik zu weichen gehabt hätte. Der Eindruck dieses Ganzen warf damals bei uns Alles um.

It is interesting to notice that Wagner's praise focuses attention on features of Auber's opera only indirectly related to Wagner's own operatic concepts of style. Reading his apology of 1871 superficially, we should never guess that *La Muette* was in many respects a model for Wagner's own *Lohengrin*. In fact, all enthusiastic references to *La Muette* artfully conceal that close relationship, and the circumstance that it became a determinant work for the evolution of his own dramatic style. This was no isolated instance in Wagner's life, as can be deduced from his strangely ambivalent attitude towards Franz Liszt, some of whose compositions clearly influenced the chromaticism of *Tristan*. To cover up his tracks in the eyes of the public, while privately admitting his indebtedness to another composer of merit, became one of Wagner's habitual reactions. His annoyance with his henchman Richard Pohl for publicly drawing attention to Liszt's influence on the style of the *Tristan* prelude is a case in point. In a letter to Hans von Bülow, dated 13 October 1859—that is, shortly after the completion of the *Tristan* score—he quite openly admits two standards of behaviour in this respect: a private and a public one. Specially, when he says:

So gibt es vieles, was wir unter uns gern uns zugestehen, z.B. daß ich seit meiner Bekanntschaft mit Liszts Kompositionen ein ganz anderer Kerl als Harmoniker geworden bin, als ich vordem war; wenn aber Freund Pohl dieses Geheimnis sogleich *à la tête* einer kurzen Besprechung des Vorspiels von 'Tristan' vor aller Welt ausplaudert, so ist dies einfach mindestens indiskret, und ich kann doch nicht annehmen, daß er zu solcher Indiskretion authorisiert war?[1]

The passage explains Wagner's attitude of artful concealment in the case of *La Muette*. He praises Auber to the heavens for achievements which have but little to do with the Wagnerian *Musikdrama*. In all the pages devoted to *La Muette* he does not mention that because the heroine Fenella is dumb the orchestra has to speak all the more eloquently, and that in consequence Auber

[1] Richard Wagner, *Briefe an Hans von Bülow* (Jena 1916), pp. 125–6.

had to evolve an orchestral style of a strongly descriptive and, indeed, symphonic character, hitherto unknown in opera. It was the style of long orchestral passages in which Fenella had to express her feelings in mime which so strongly influenced Wagner in *Tannhäuser* and *Lohengrin*. The extent to which *La Muette* acted as a model for the style of Wagner's early maturity, especially for the music of *Lohengrin*, becomes apparent in the following quotations, the first of which is taken from one of Fenella's mimed explanations, underlined by an orchestral passage which could have been lifted bodily out of the context of Elsa of Brabant's music in Act I, scene 2, and in the balcony scene in Act II. Elvira asks Fenella what crime she has been guilty of. The mute answer to that is: 'I am innocent; I call Heaven to witness'. Fenella's innocence asserts itself in a woodwind ensemble whose chromatically gliding contrary motion of the inner parts anticipates Elsa's similarly mute pleadings in the second scene of *Lohengrin*, Act I:

Stranger still is the relationship between Auber's music for the bridal procession to the chapel and Wagner's music in *Lohengrin* for exactly the same purpose, namely, for Elsa's bridal procession from the palace to the minster and for the solemnization of her marriage to Lohengrin (Act II, scene 4). A comparison of both scenes reveals that *La Muette* was used as a blueprint by Wagner for the construction of his own musical pageant. The parallels are, indeed, overwhelming. In both cases, the combination of the solemn march with the chorus is preceded by a purely instrumental prelude. In both cases the music endeavours to recreate the sound of a distant organ (which in both operas is not used, but only hinted at—except for a few bars on the organ, off-stage, towards the end of *Lohengrin*, Act II). In both cases the underlying solemn march rhythm is approximately the same:

[148]

In both cases the scoring is similar. To create the gentle sound of a distant organ both composers use only woodwind and horns. In both cases a livelier passage follows, interlaced with a counterpoint in quaver motion. In both cases a restatement of this expository march section brings the melody in the orchestra, while the chorus underpins it harmonically. Of course, Wagner's music is vastly more inspired in melody and harmony than Auber's and more sophisticated in its mixture of orchestral colours, with cor anglais and bass clarinet added to the woodwind. But the structure is in both cases the same, and even Fenella's sudden interruption of the solemn pageant (in a turbulent intrusion by the strings) finds its corresponding parallel in the double interruption of the march, first through Ortrud, later through Telramund, both barring the way across the threshold of the minster.

Here is a juxtaposition of the first bars of the solemn march in both operas:

Auber's wedding march is utilized as a 'reminiscence motif'—as a dramatic flashback, as it were—in Act II for emphasizing the betrayal of Fenella by Alfonso after he had seduced her. When Fenella has confessed to Masaniello, her brother, that she has been betrayed by her seducer, and he swears to avenge her, Ex. 2 reappears as an accompaniment to Fenella's pantomimic explanation that Alfonso had vowed before heaven that he would make her his wife, and that

[149]

she had believed him before yielding to him. This exact reminiscence of Ex. 2 is scored for strings only, thereby underlining the ghostly character of this wisp of memory. However, when Masaniello threatens to compel Alfonso to fulfil his promise to marry her, and Fenella has to inform him of the sad fact that Alfonso has just married another girl, the wedding march reappears very distorted in character—transposed a semitone lower and in the key of B♭ minor. This is most probably the earliest example of the deflection of a *Leitmotiv* for the purpose of dramatic elucidation. It became the model for Wagner's own distortion of Elsa's motif (as presented in *Lohengrin*, I, scene 2, bars 9–12), when in Act III, scene 3 (Breitkopf & Härtel miniature score, p. 731, bars 1–4) she proves unable to meet the King's eye, because she has broken her vow and has asked the forbidden question. Wagner's technique of harmonic distortion is anticipated in the transposition to a lower and a minor key in the following quotation from *La Muette*, Act II (vocal score, p. 143):

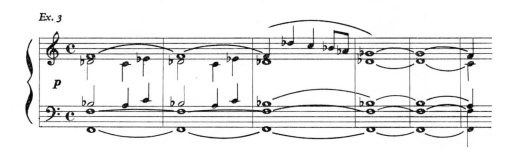

Ex. 3

A similar case of dramatic elucidation through the orchestra, by the deliberate distortion of a melodic reminiscence, occurs towards the end of Auber's opera in the scene of Masaniello's temporary madness. Here (Act V, vocal score, p. 306) Masaniello, out of his mind, quotes the stirring call to revolt which he had intoned earlier in Act III (vocal score, p. 212) in luminous C major, this time a semitone higher, in D♭ major, repeating its original harmonic sequence but with an incongruous diminuendo which pitifully contradicts the flamboyance of its words:

Ex 4 (a) (Act III)

[151]

Here again, a characteristic feature of Wagner's own technique of transformation of themes is boldly anticipated by Auber in his revolutionary masterpiece of 1828.

Spohr's 'Indian' opera *Jessonda* (1822–3) was a similar favourite of Wagner's. He referred to it with affection, whenever he recalled in gratitude Spohr, his old master[1], whose early performances of *The Flying Dutchman* and subsequent active support for *Tannhäuser* in the 1840's seemed doubly remarkable, especially if compared with Spohr's often petulant and downright scathing criticisms of the works of Beethoven's last decade. Wagner singled out this opera for renewed consideration in two late articles, in which he critically assessed the merits of Spohr's peculiar, violin-inspired style of vocal ornamentation, his idiosyncrasies in matters of declamation, and his unique gift for 'consistent melody'[2]. When discussing the tedium that resulted from Spohr's handling of recitative style in *Jessonda*, in particular in the recitative No. 2 (when Nadori refers to his study of the holy Vedas), he pointed out the relief felt by the listener when at long last the orchestra once again intones a consistent melody (No. 3, duet). While Wagner with the help of a music example[3] clearly indicates that he is referring to the scene between Dandau and Nadori which culminates in their duet 'Aus dieses Tempels heil'gen Mauern', he signally fails to inform us of the importance for his own work of Spohr's melody, which he apostrophized thus: 'Freilich hatten die Recitative nicht viel zu sagen und trugen nicht wenig zur Verlangweiligung des Operngenres bei; während z.B. Nadori in Spohrs 'Jessonda' recitativisch sich vernehmen liess: 'Still lag ich an des Sees Fluten . . . und las im Veda . . .' ertwartete man am Ende doch nur ungeduldig den Wiedereintritt des vollen Orchesters, mit bestimmten Tempo und einer festen 'Melodie', sie mochte eben zusammengestellt ('komponiert') sein, wie sie wollte.' For the 'consistent melody' he continues to praise in a whole paragraph has this beginning:

Ex. 5

Aus die - ses Tem-pels heil'-gen Mau-ern,   o Jüng-ling, ruft dich heut' die Pflicht

Every Wagnerian will at once recognize this as the model for Pogner's entry in *Die Meistersinger*, Act I, scene 3, bars 4–7. In a detailed discussion of the whole work, published in January 1875, Wagner again extols its melodic beauties and criticizes its stylistic and structural shortcomings, while totally ignoring the influence it had on his own music to *Tristan*. The importance of *Jessonda* for the latter work was pointed out many years ago by Ernst Bücken,[4] who gave a substantial quotation from *Jessonda*, Act I, finale No. 9, (vocal score, Peters ed., pp. 51–52), the scene in which Nadori, about to pronounce the death sentence on Jessonda, who is to be burnt as a widow, falls in love with her. Bücken's quotation clearly emphasizes the pre-*Tristan* quality of Spohr's chromatically gliding music, culminating in a luminous $\frac{6}{4}$ chord in the key of B♭ (coming surprisingly after a long stretch in swift modulations through sharp keys), which all but

[1] So in his obituary notice of Spohr in *Ges. Schr.* Vol. II, p. 89 foll. (first published 25 November, 1859); as also in his earlier *Eine Mitteilung an meine Freunde* published 1851; *Ges. Schr.* Vol. I, p. 109 foll.

[2] 'Über eine Opernaufführung in Leipzig', published January 1875 in Fritzsch's *Musikalisches Wochenblatt, Ges. Schr.* Vol. XIII, p. 148–58; 'Über das Operndichten und

Komponieren im Besonderen', first published in *Bayreuther Blätter*, 1879; *Ges. Schr.* Vol. XIII, p. 269 foll., p. 272 foll.

[3] *Ges. Schr.* Vol. XIII, p. 272.

[4] *Musik des 19. Jahrhunderts bis zur Moderne (Handbuch der Musikwissenschaft)*, Potsdam 1928, pp. 87–89, and music example No. 86.

anticipates the later notorious abuse of this chord in the works of Richard Strauss and his school. However, this is not the only instance in which Spohr anticipates Wagner's idiom in *Tristan*. The very entry of the orchestra leading up to Jessonda's first recitative, 'O Schwester, stille deine Tränen' (Act I, No. 6), sounds like a passage from *Tristan*, especially if taken out of its context. It culminates in a suspended chord of the ninth which becomes a commonplace in Wagner's *Tristan*, *Ring*, and *Parsifal*, but was a startling newcomer in a score of 1822:

Ex. 6

Also the recitative intoned by Tristan's namesake Tristan d'Acunha in Act II, No. 10, referring to the uneasy relationship between Portuguese and Indians, and punctuated by characteristic *accompagnato* passages with full orchestra and by bellicose interjections from the Portuguese army, became a model for a very similar recitative episode in Wagner's *Lohengrin*, Act I, scene 1, when King Henry the Fowler addresses the Brabantians and describes the prevailing political situation with regard to the Hungarian common foe. While these influences of Spohr's idiom on Wagner are quite obvious, it is not so easy to find a direct echo of the most famous melody in that opera in later Wagner. That melody, a first cousin to the second subject in the 'Adagio ma non troppo' of Mozart's string quintet in G minor, K.516, certainly became the model for its even more famous successor in the finale of the 'Antonia Act' of Offenbach's *Contes d'Hoffmann*:

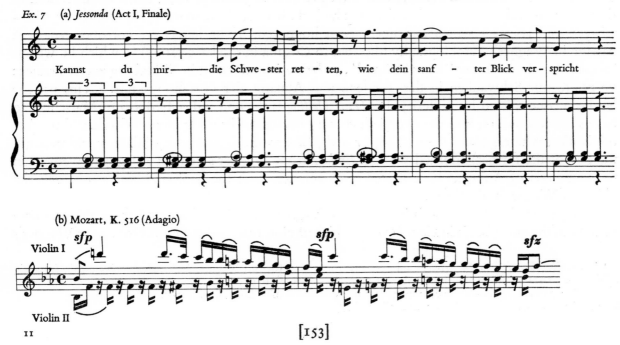

Ex. 7   (a) *Jessonda* (Act I, Finale)

(b) Mozart, K. 516 (Adagio)

Its chromatic undercurrent, specially marked in the foregoing music example, and equally marked in Offenbach's later work of 1880, certainly impinged quite generally on Wagner's chromatic style. The use Spohr makes of this so-called 'Salvation Melody', specially on pp. 97–98 (vocal score, Peters ed.), is in the manner of an *Erinnerungsmotiv* and anticipates Auber's similar technique in *La Muette* as well as Wagner's own early *Leitmotiv* technique.

The case of Marschner's *Hans Heiling* (1833) and its influence on Wagner is less straightforward than the two preceding cases of Auber and Spohr. In his collected writings on music Wagner was always ready to admit Marschner's influence on his own first opera *Die Feen* (1833), and to single out his two earlier operas *Der Vampyr* (Leipzig, 1828) and *Templer und Jüdin* (Leipzig, 1829) for lavish praise, while making good-natured fun of the weaker late score *Adolph von Nassau*, which was first performed in Dresden in 1845 under Wagner's direction. In all his published references to Marschner[1] he seems anxious to ignore *Hans Heiling* and to avoid mentioning its name. In the light of the posthumously published autobiography *Mein Leben* and of the collections of letters, however, it becomes quite clear how great a part in Wagner's life *Hans Heiling* was destined to play. These facts also lead to the conclusion that the silence about *Hans Heiling* in all references to Marschner published during Wagner's life-time was deliberate. To have mentioned *Hans Heiling* in the nineteenth century would have been too revealing, for that opera exercised a profound influence on Wagner's mature style. The work was described in Riemann-Einstein's *Musik-Lexikon* of 1929 as 'dem Problem nach das eigentliche dramatische Vorbild zu Lohengrin'.

How well Wagner knew *Hans Heiling* emerges from his letters to Franz Hauser (*Regisseur* at the Leipzig Opera House in 1834) and to his friend C. Gaillard. In a letter to the former of March 1834 Wagner relates performances of *Vampyr* and *Hans Heiling* during the season 1833–4 at the Municipal Theatre of Würzburg where he was in that year a chorus master. In a letter to the latter, dated Dresden, 5 June, 1845, Wagner expressly refers to the fact that the first performance in Dresden of Marschner's *Hans Heiling* took place on 26 January, 1844, under his direction. In that letter he prides himself on the fact that he had discovered the score in 1843, together with a ten-year-old contract which had never been honoured. These letters are corroborated by a passage in Wagner's autobiography (dictated to Cosima in the later 1860's) in which he writes: 'Seine [Marschners] Oper "Hans Heiling" . . . lernte ich seinerzeit in Würzburg zuerst kennen: sie zeigte mir Schwanken in der Tendenz und Abname der Gestaltungskraft.'[2] This passage has been contradicted by posterity, for *Hans Heiling* is the one and only opera of Marschner to have survived well on into the twentieth century because of its great merits of style and musical originality, whereas *Vampyr* and *Templer und Jüdin*, so much praised by Wagner and even (in the case of the former) adorned with an *Einlage* from Wagner's pen (an Allegro movement in the tenor aria of Aubry),[3] have shared total oblivion with the hapless *Adolph von Nassau*, the object of Wagner's ribald fun.

How penetrating Marschner's influence on Wagner was can be gathered from the *grandioso* melody of the queen's aria in *Hans Heiling*, which obviously served as a model for one of Wagner's

[1] Wagner's references to Marschner and specially to *Adolph von Nassau* in 'Erinnerungen an Auber'; *Ges. Schr.* Vol. VIII, p. 130 foll., and in 'Über das Operndichten und Komponieren'; *Ges. Schr.*, Vol. XIII, p. 262 foll., and 275.

[2] Richard Wagner, *Mein Leben*, Volksausgabe (Munich, 1911), II, p. 100.
[3] *Mein Leben*, I, pp. 101–2.

greatest melodies in *Die Walküre*—the so-called *Todesverkündigung* in Act II, scene 4, first intoned by the brass instruments as Brünnhilde makes her appearance before Siegmund:

Ex. 8 (a) Marschner, *Hans Heiling* (Act II/No. 9)

Sonst bist du ver - fal - len dem rä - chen - den Grim - me ...

(b) Wagner, *Die Walküre* (II/4)

That influence can be studied to an even further degree in Marschner's 'Melodram und Lied' (Act II, no. 12) in which a gruesome atmosphere is conjured up by a division of violas, cellos

Ex. 9

[155]

and double basses and by chromatic sequences of descending scale passages which became the model for Wagner's similarly-conceived chromatic melodies and countermelodies in the overture to *Tannhäuser*, as well as in the symphonic prelude to that opera's Act III (see Ex. 9). The two last quotations make it fairly obvious why Wagner preferred to be silent about Marschner's greatest work, while at the same time mentioning it critically in his autobiography. Together with Carl Loewe's early *Balladen*, it was *Hans Heiling*, especially in the passages quoted, which stimulated Wagner's imagination and proved the starting-point for a development in which he soon outstripped his predecessors.

BIZET'S *LA JOLIE FILLE DE PERTH*

Jack Westrup (Oxford)

THE CARE that has been devoted to producing authentic editions of older music has not always been extended to the works of nineteenth-century composers, perhaps because it was felt that they were able to look after themselves. Composers, however, have no control over what happens after their death. Berlioz was unfortunate in this respect, Bizet equally so.

La Jolie Fille de Perth, to a text by Jules Henri Vernoy de Saint-Georges and Jules Adenis, was first performed at the Théâtre-Lyrique, Paris, on 26 December, 1867. It was given at Weimar in 1883 in a German translation by Julius Hopp, and at Parma, in an Italian version by Angelo Zanardini, in 1885. It was revived in Paris in 1890. In England it was first performed in 1917 under Sir Thomas Beecham. At least three vocal scores were printed. The first (VS 1) appeared in 1868 and may be assumed to correspond fairly closely with what was heard at the first performance. A printed libretto was published in the same year by Michel Lévy. A second vocal score (VS 2) was issued with German and Italian words but without the original French text. Since it was presumably prepared for the foreign performances mentioned above it probably dates from 1883, which is the date assigned to it in the British Museum catalogue. The third vocal score (VS 3), misleadingly described on the cover as 'Opéra Comique', gives the cast of the 1867 performance and also of the revival of 1890, and therefore dates from the latter year: this is the current edition, published, like its predecessors, by Choudens. There is also a lithographed full score (FS), which includes, in a clumsy handwriting, the German text and German stage directions. All these differ from each other in more or less degree, and none of them corresponds to Bizet's autograph score (AS) in the library of the Paris Conservatoire (now at the Bibliothèque Nationale).

It would be tedious to enumerate all the discrepancies. I shall deal first with some of the more important ones and refer later to minor variants. The two casts as printed in the current edition (VS 3) immediately present a problem to anyone who does not know the earlier versions:

Mlle. Devriès	Catherine Glover	. . . .	(Soprano)	Mlle. Cécile Mézeray
– Ducasse	Mab	. . . .	(Soprano)	– Bossy
Mr. Massy	Henri Smith	. . . .	(Ténor)	Mr. Engel
– Barré	Le Duc de Rothsay	. . . .	(Baryton ou Ténor)	– Frédéric Boyer
– Lutz	Ralph	. . . . . .	(Basse ou Baryton)	– Isnardon
– Wartel	Simon Glover	. . . .	(Basse)	– Ferran
– Guyot	Un Seigneur	. . . .	(Ténor)	– Portejoie
	Le Majordome	. . . .	(Basse)	– Belen

The position of M. Guyot in the 1867 cast looks very curious. He comes midway between 'Un Seigneur' and 'Le Majordome' but he cannot have sung both parts, since one is a tenor and the other a bass. Reference to the printed libretto of 1868 shows that 'Un Seigneur' was sung by a M. Boudias, but neither the character nor the singer is listed in vs 1, perhaps because M. Boudias was merely a member of the chorus. There is, however, an additional character in all the sources before vs 3—'Un Ouvrier', who, like 'Le Majordome', is a bass. Both these parts were sung by M. Guyot. In Bizet's autograph there is yet another character: the attendant who comes to summon Catherine to the Duke's palace at the end of Act II (vs 3, pp. 126–7) is not the major-domo but a valet.

The 'Ouvrier' has disappeared entirely from vs 3. In the original he has a short scene with Smith after the latter's serenade in Act II (i.e. between pp. 120 and 121 of vs 3), beginning: 'Qui va là? Ah, c'est vous, maître. Fort bien.' He tries to persuade his master to enjoy the carnival, and they both go into the tavern. Since this scene has been omitted from vs 3 there is no stage direction to say what happens to Smith after his serenade. This is followed immediately by the drunken song sung by Ralph, who at the end 'se laisse tomber sur le banc qui est sous la fenêtre de Smith' (vs 3, p. 125). A little later, when he believes that Catherine has gone off to the Duke's palace, 'il se lève et frappe à la porte de Smith', and Smith, 'sortant vivement de sa maison', sings 'Qui m'appelle' (vs 3, pp. 128–9). But there has been no mention earlier in the act of Smith's house, and it would seem very improbable that he should live within a stone's throw of the Glover family. The stage directions for Act II in the printed libretto refer to two buildings on the stage: (1) Glover's house, with Catherine's window lighted, and (2) the tavern. Since Smith has gone into the tavern with the workman, it is from the tavern in the original version that he rushes in ('sortant vivement de la taverne') when Ralph summons him.

The 'Ouvrier' appears also in Act IV to tell Smith that the signal has been given for the duel with Ralph. Since he has been omitted from vs 3, his part has had to be redistributed between Smith and Catherine. This is how the scene begins in AS, vs 1, vs 2, and FS:

on vous at -tend. Le si-gnal est don-né, cha-cun de nous s'é-ton-ne, De ce com - bat que vous soy-ez ab-

sent !

In vs 3 (p. 226) this has been altered as follows:

Ex. 2

SMITH (qui

Allegro deciso

pp (on entend au loin un appel de clairon) fff

ff

O

The trumpet fanfare, for which there is no authority in the earlier sources, is necessary now, since Smith cannot himself bring the news that they are waiting for the duel: he has to hear the signal in the distance. And since he is a tenor, the vocal line has to be modified.

One of the most curious discrepancies is in Act I, after Mab has taken refuge in Smith's house. She offers to tell his fortune. The libretto runs:

> *Mab.* Je vois dans cette main que Glover et sa fille
> Viennent ici, chez vous, pour souper en famille.
> *Smith.* Elle viendrait ce soir ? Espoir charmant.

Bizet's autograph has the following:

Ex. 3

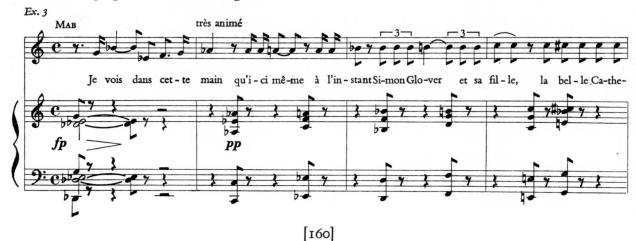

The text here corresponds roughly to the libretto. But in vs 1 the recitative has been interrupted so as to lead into a song for Mab:

The song ends tranquilly and the recitative is then resumed:

In vs 2 and vs 3 Mab's song has disappeared completely. The three opening bars of Ex. 4 are reproduced almost exactly and lead straight into Smith's recitative. Here is the passage as it appears, with French text, in vs 3 (p. 17):

This is one of several places where the cuts and changes which appear in vs 3 (1890) had already been made in vs 2 (1883). What is strange here is that Mab's song is found only in vs 1: it does not occur in the libretto of 1868 nor in Bizet's autograph. A possible explanation is that he had included it in his draft of the scene in piano score and that vs 1 was engraved from this. In the meantime it may have been decided to omit it on the ground that it slowed up the scene unduly, but by that time it was too late to re-engrave the pages of vs 1, which was probably required early for the purpose of solo rehearsals. Some confirmation of this view is to be found in the fact that in the autograph full score Bizet originally wrote the opening words of Ex. 3: 'Je vais dans votre main', but corrected them to 'Je vois dans cette main'. The implication would seem to be that Mab's song was not included when the work was first performed, and since it does not appear in vs 2 and vs 3 it is unlikely to have been included in revivals, whether in France or elsewhere. The fact that it does not appear in the printed libretto is also significant. If it was originally there, there would have been plenty of time to cut it out before the libretto was published in 1868.

The cuts in vs 3 are numerous and sometimes substantial. But in two instances it includes movements (one of them in a truncated form) which do not appear at all in vs 2 or in fs. The first is the opening chorus of Act II—'Bons citoyens, dormez' (vs 3, pp. 71–75). The fact that it is not in fs is extraordinary, since an instrumental version is published as part of the suite which is still popular in the concert hall. Its omission in vs 2 and fs means that the act opens with the brilliant chorus 'Carnaval! A ce joyeux signal'. The original idea, which still has a modest survival in vs 3, was that the noisy celebrations of the carnival should be preceded by a chorus for the watchmen, accompanied by Glover. As they make their rounds in mock dignity they assure peaceful citizens that they have nothing to fear, though the assertion that 'tout est calme et tranquille' is belied by *fortissimo* snorts from the trombones and intermittent noises from outside, ending with 'cris dans la coulisse de très près', which prepare the audience for the outburst of the carnival chorus. The chorus for the watchmen not only emphasizes that we are seeing Perth at night: it is also richly comic. In its original form it was considerably longer than the version in vs 3 and includes a solo for Glover, leading to a reprise of the chorus, where the harmonies of the transition sound rather like an anticipation of the smugglers' chorus in *Carmen* (a passage in the march 'Trompette et tambour' from *Jeux d'enfants* is very similar):

The second movement omitted from VS 2 and FS is the Duke's *cavatina* in Act III (VS 3, pp. 143–5). The current edition has different words from the original and omits (as elsewhere) the chorus parts but retains the music intact. The cut in VS 2 and FS involves altering the end of the Duke's preceding recitative:

> Tenez, depuis hier, messieurs, je suis en quête
> Du minois le plus jeune et le plus séduisant,

which is made to end rather clumsily on F♮ (not on E♭, as in VS 1 and VS 3), sung at the beginning of the first bar of No. 16ter (VS 3, p. 146). Anyone who wishes to perform *La Jolie Fille de Perth* in the current edition is faced by the problem that it is impossible to hire a full score or set of parts containing the *cavatina*. When Beecham revived the work in 1917 he got Eugène Goossens (then aged 24) to provide an orchestration. Although Goossens' version is tasteful enough, this is obviously not an ideal solution; nor is it strictly necessary, since Bizet's own orchestration survives in his autograph.

The awkward transition created by the omission of the *cavatina* in VS 2 and FS is unusual. In general the cuts which have been made, both in VS 2 and VS 3, are skilfully done, even though the reasons for them are not always apparent. There is, however, nothing skilful about the change of key in the Valentine chorus in Act IV (VS 3, pp. 230–8). In the original this is in A♭ major, and is preceded by the dominant seventh in this key at the end of No. 22 (VS 3, p. 229). In VS 2 and VS 3 it has been transposed to A major. There are two possible reasons for this. One is that someone felt that the music would sound more brilliant in the higher key, as indeed it does. The other is that the chorus was popular and was issued separately by the publishers, who may have felt that it would not only be more effective but also easier in A major. Two pieces of evidence point to this conclusion. One is that the pages of this chorus in VS 3 have their own plate numbers, which do not occur anwhere else in the edition; the other is that this is the only movement in the work where the composer's name is printed at the beginning. It might seem curious that, though VS 2 has the A major version, FS still has it in A♭. The reason for this is probably that it was not worth

Ex. 8

[164]

while writing out a transposition for the conductor, who could as easily direct the performance from one key as from the other. What is unmistakably odd is that no one seems to have thought that there was anything awkward about the transition from the dominant seventh in A♭ major to a chorus in A major. The conductor who uses this version has a simple remedy—to alter Bizet's original (see Ex. 8) by inserting an extra diminished seventh:

Ex. 9

It is effective in performance, and the argument that this is not what the composer wrote may be countered by pointing out that a good deal in the current edition is not his work.

This is not the only place where vs 3 reveals evidence of patching by the engravers. An interesting example is the *coloratura* aria 'Vive l'hiver' which Catherine sings in Act I (vs 3, pp. 23–25). This was originally written for Christine Nilsson, but she left the Théâtre-Lyrique in the spring of 1867 and her place was taken by Jane Devriès. The piece, which is in the form of a polonaise, was subjected to criticism at the time, and Bizet himself admitted that such concessions to virtuosity were out of date. Later critics have also found harsh words for it, though it is undeniably effective in performance. In its original form it was longer than it is now and included accompanying parts for Smith, Glover, and Ralph. vs 2 retains the full version but omits the parts for the three men. In vs 3 one whole section of the aria has been cut and the three accompanying parts are still omitted. But by a curious piece of negligence the opening line of the song (vs 3, p. 23) provides staves for Smith, Glover, and Ralph in spite of the fact that their parts, which originally entered in the latter part of the aria, have now disappeared.

Another instance of incautious surgery is Smith's serenade in Act II (vs 3, pp. 116–20). The original version of this (retained in vs 2 and FS) was considerably longer in one respect and shorter in another. The 6/8 section in A minor is interrupted at the point where it changes to C major (vs 3, p. 117, line 1, bar 3). Instead of continuing with a second verse ('Ah! parais, Tu sais si j'admire') Smith begins 'Je t'attends' and then, seeing Catherine's shadow on the window-blind, exclaims 'C'est elle!' Bizet has here re-adjusted the libretto to suit his own interpretation of the

[165]

scene. He followed this section (corresponding to vs 3, p. 177) with a passage of recitative from which he cut out the first four bars, substituting a kind of *cadenza* for solo clarinet, which he used again in Act IV where Smith tries to awaken Catherine from her madness by once more singing the 6/8 portion of his serenade (vs 3, p. 245). This latter portion of the original serenade, beginning with the clarinet solo, is omitted from vs 3, so that the corresponding semiquaver passage in Act II loses its significance. The second half of the serenade, after the brief recitative, is in F major (4/4), beginning 'Viens, ma belle', with words adapted from the text in the printed libretto: like the chorus for the watchmen in Act II this is included in the orchestral suite from the opera. When it becomes apparent that Catherine is not ready to answer, the music gradually dies away on cellos and basses, with horns entering at the change of time:

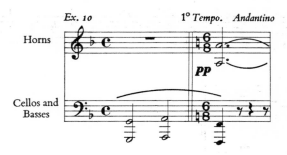

The double bar marks the place where the original version is resumed in vs 3 (top of p. 120). But in this version the F for the cellos and basses is clearly nonsensical, since it no longer refers to anything that has gone before. Even the slur linking it to the previous bar in vs 1 and vs 2 has survived, though it no longer has any meaning. The omission of the second part of the serenade may have been due to the feeling that the scene as a whole was too long; but this does not explain the butchery to which the 6/8 section has been subjected. The real reason is obviously that a concert version of the 6/8 section had become popular, and the publishers, assuming that audiences would want to hear this version in the theatre, substituted it for Bizet's original, regardless of the fact that the whole dramatic impact of the scene would be ruined.

No doubt it was the criticisms of Catherine's *coloratura* aria 'Vive l'hiver' in Act I that persuaded someone to substitute for it the song 'Rêve de la bien-aimée', published by Hartmann in 1868. That Bizet himself was responsible for this substitution seems very unlikely. The song, though pretty enough, is quite out of place in its artificial context, and out of keeping with Catherine's character: it also holds up the action, whereas 'Vive l'hiver' is stimulating enough not to seem an intrusion. It is significant that it does not appear in the German-Italian edition of 1883 (vs 2). In FS it has been written out in a different hand and clumsily pasted over 'Vive l'hiver'. vs 3 makes the best of both worlds by including it in an appendix, together with a necessary modification of the preceding recitative. Who was responsible for the scoring is not clear. The evidence would suggest that the substitution was made at some time after the Weimar performance of 1883.

Bizet himself made comparatively few alterations in his autograph score. Modifications in the orchestration are generally designed to lighten the accompaniment by omitting the wind.

[166]

One or two cuts are made for dramatic reasons. At the point where Mab makes her sudden appearance in Act I and shrieks 'Ah', as Smith is about to attack the Duke with his hammer (vs 3, p. 53), there was originally an extra bar after Smith's 'Malheur'. This would obviously have weakened the force of the interruption and it was deleted. The postlude to Ralph's drinking song in Act II (vs 3, p. 125) originally ended four bars earlier, with Ralph murmuring 'Catherine'. There was also originally a curious passage just before Catherine's ballade 'Écho viens sur l'air embaumé' (vs 3, p. 241, line 3) in Act IV, in which Glover, accompanied by a fanfare-like passage on horns, urges everyone to withdraw. This passage is printed in vs 1 but deleted in AS. The reason is obvious: after Catherine's initial cadenza, accompanied in the original by exclamations of 'C'est elle' from Glover and the chorus, it is distracting to have a mundane interruption before she begins her song. Bizet may have intended some connection between the horns accompanying Glover and the passage for the same instruments (first *ff*, then *ppp*) towards the end of Catherine's song; but any such connection must remain obscure, as indeed must the use of horns in either place.

A number of other cuts are indicated in AS but they do not appear to be Bizet's. They are not, like the passages previously mentioned, deletions but look as if they had been made by the conductor at the first or some later performance: they are indicated in the usual way, by the sign ⊕ at the beginning and end of the passage to be omitted. Some of these cuts have been adopted in vs 2 and vs 3, as well as in FS. One of them concerns the drinking song which Glover sings when he returns to the stage at the end of Act I (vs 3, p. 64). In AS this is considerably longer and is accompanied by brass, punctuated with a figure for the strings. FS cuts this to eight bars, retaining the accompaniment. vs 2 and vs 3 also have the eight-bar version but omit the accompaniment. Glover now begins his song 'dans la coulisse', which clearly makes a heavy accompaniment impossible. Another passage marked to be cut in AS and omitted from vs 2, vs 3 and FS is the first part of the recitative preceding the Bohemian dance (vs 3, p. 93). In the original there is a part here for the chorus, beginning: 'Mais qui vient vers nous ? C'est de la Bohême la piquante reine'.

The most curious, and the most confused, passage occurs in the opening scene of Act III (vs 3, pp. 139–42). In AS, vs 1, vs 2, and FS there are fourteen bars at the beginning which have disappeared from vs 3, which starts at the place marked 'Rideau' in the original. The result of this cut in vs 3 is that the curtain now goes up on the first note, which is clearly ridiculous, if not impossible. In AS, vs 1 and FS the chorus joins in at bar 21 (i.e. bar 7 of vs 3), singing 'Nuit d'amour et de folle ivresse'. In the printed libretto these words do not appear here: the text begins 'Je fais cent pièces d'or', as in vs 3. They do occur, however, later in the act, in a passage omitted from vs 3 (immediately before Récit D on p. 162). In AS the chorus parts are crossed out when they first enter. Someone has written the word 'Bon' against the deletion , but this in turn has been deleted and replaced by a large 'Bon' at the top of the score: in other words, the music is to be played but without voices. This, in fact, is what happens in vs 2, where the chorus parts are lacking. AS also marks a cut in this chorus which is adopted in vs 2, FS, and vs 3. The total result of this is that we are plunged almost too abruptly into the stage orchestra behind the scenes: there is very little left to convey the atmosphere of revelry. As a consequence of this cut the reprise of 'Nuit d'amour' mentioned above (this time in G major) has to be omitted since it would no longer refer to anything that had gone before. Furthermore a reprise of the gaming music in B♭

(at the point corresponding to the double bar in line 2 of vs 3, p. 148) has also disappeared, and the subsequent orchestral passage no longer refers, as it originally did, to the first 14 bars of the act, since these have been omitted.

The alterations in vs 3 are of three kinds: (1) revision of the libretto; (2) omissions designed to quicken up the action; (3) changes which do not seem to have any compelling reason. The original libretto was not distinguished. Glover's

> Un peu de venaison, un superbe pâté,
> Du vieux Wisky d'Écosse, un succulent pudding

is ridiculous enough; but the current version,

> J'apporte, mon garçon, un vrai repas de noce!
> Et pour arroser tout, un vieux Wisky d'Écosse,

can hardly be described as a notable improvement. It is possibly an advantage that the suppression of the 'Ouvrier' in Act IV has delivered us from the truly appalling lines,

> Vraiment il n'est personne qui ne sache aujourd'hui
> Que Ralph pour votre honneur se bat contre Henry Smith,

now replaced by

> *Catherine.* Ah! ma raison chancelle! Un combat avec vous?
> *Smith.* Oui, Ralph pour ton honneur contre moi va se battre;

but the replacement does not give much cause for satisfaction. Often the changes seem merely fussy. The Duke's address to the carnival throng in Act II,

> Moi, grand duc des sauteurs, roi de la cabriole,
> À qui vous devez obéir,

has been altered to

> Moi, j'abdique mon rang, car en cette nuit folle
> Au duc nul ne doit obéir,

perhaps because it was felt that the latter version would be more in the spirit of the Third Republic. Smith's anguished cry,

> O cruelle! infidèle!
> Quoi! ton cœur sans horreur
> S'abandonne et se donne
> À l'amant d'un moment,

has become

> O cruelle! O parjure!
> Qui flétris sans retour
> Une image aussi pure
> En mon cœur plein d'amour!

—which is not more poetical than the original and is certainly a good deal less precise.

It is only fair to say that some of the omissions in the music do serve the purpose of speeding

[168]

up the action. Mab's tumultuous entry in Act I is made more dramatic by shortening. The recitative between Smith and Catherine which originally followed their duet in Act I (i.e. after p. 38 in VS 3) served no useful purpose, and the entry of the Duke is more effective for being abrupt. Again, the cheerful ensemble in B major which followed Glover's invitation to the Duke to be present at Catherine's wedding (VS 3, p. 165) could only be defended as an example of prolonged dramatic irony: it delayed the explosion but offered no satisfaction for the delay. (It is worth noting that the diminished seventh chord which precedes Smith's exclamation 'Qui — moi! votre époux, jamais!' (VS 3, p. 166) is marked *p* in AS, VS 1 and FS, but *ff* in VS 2 and VS 3. The fact that Smith's part is marked '*pp* bas à Catherine' in AS makes it clear that Bizet's intention was rather different from the interpretation implied in VS 2 and VS 3.) But a good many of the omissions in the editions later than VS 1 can be explained only as the result of a desire to prune at all costs. The opera is shorter as a result, but it is not, as a whole, better.

In one respect, in particular, VS 3 is very unreliable, and that is in the provision of stage directions. Those that do occur are generally obvious: those that have been omitted would have helped to explain incidents which are not always clear. When the Duke first enters in Act I (VS 3, p. 38) he is described in the libretto as 'un Étranger enveloppé d'un manteau', which makes it easier to understand why Smith and Catherine do not realize who he is. When Glover returns to the scene (VS 3, p. 64) he exclaims:

> Eh! mais, voici nouvelle compagnie,
> Quoi, vous ici, vous, Monseigneur!

The stage direction in VS 3 reads 'apercevant le Duc de Rothsay', but this is clearly absurd. Glover would not refer to the Duke as 'nouvelle compagnie'. The original stage direction makes everything clear. The first line is sung 'regardant et voyant Mab', and the second 'reconnaissant le duc'. Quite a number of directions are missing from the subsequent pages of this scene. One further place where guidance is lacking may be mentioned. In the duet between Mab and the Duke in Act III Mab removes her mask, after extinguishing the light (VS 3, p. 151): 'Ah! la traitresse', cries the Duke. But a little later in VS 3 (p. 153) we read:

> Le Duc (*désignant la rose de Catherine que Mab porte à son corsage*). Mais que tiens-je là?...

Since they are both in the dark it is difficult to see how the Duke can point to anything. The original stage direction is: 'Rencontrant de sa main la rose'.

The surgery to which the original score was subjected in VS 2 is clearly the work of an expert. Since it was Guiraud who wrote the recitatives for *Carmen*, it seems more than likely that it was he who produced the 1883 version of *La Jolie Fille de Perth*. Certainly it is difficult to think of anyone else with so intimate a knowledge and understanding of Bizet's style. Whether he was also responsible for the further alterations in 1890 is more doubtful, though he was still alive at the time. It is difficult to believe that, having incorporated the music of the duet between the Duke and Mab in the second *L'Arlésienne* suite, he would also have sanctioned its entirely unnecessary insertion as an entr'acte in the opera (VS 3, pp. 132–8). Not only has it been inserted in the vocal score: it has actually been printed from borrowed plates. It bears the puzzling designation 'No. 3', and the page numbers have obviously been altered to agree with the pagination of the rest of the score. This is on all fours with the inclusion in the full score of the Bohemian dance without the voice parts, simply because it was already available as an instrumental piece.

There is clearly an ethical, as well as an æsthetic, question involved here. A composer has every right to revise his own work, and a musician who thoroughly understands a composer's style may be allowed to complete an unfinished work—and may do it successfully. But no one has any right to interfere with any musical work and publish it without the slightest indication that it does not represent what the composer wrote. We are promised a new edition of Berlioz. We need one of Bizet. He was too good a musician to be maltreated by posterity.

THE OPERAS OF SEROV

Gerald Abraham (London)

THAT ALEXANDER NICOLAEVICH SEROV occupies an oddly ambiguous position in the history of Russian opera is not altogether surprising; he occupied an oddly ambiguous position in the Russian musical world in the middle of the nineteenth century. As a critic he had been Wagner's earliest champion in Russia, thereby endearing himself neither to Rubinstein and the 'westernizing' academics on the one hand nor to the nationalist 'young Russian school' on the other; yet in 1863 he made his serious début as a composer with an opera, *Judith*, which seemed to be total denial of his critical principles and of almost everything Wagner stood for. The two works which followed, it, *Rogneda* (1865) and *Hostile Power* (*Vrazhya sila*) (1871), were equally un-Wagnerian. All three remained popular in Russia for many years—Chaliapin sang Eremka in *Hostile Power* in 1916—but none has ever made the slightest impression abroad. The three performances of Act IV of *Judith*, with Chaliapin as Holofernes, which Diaghilev included in his Paris season of June 1909, are the only production of Serov in the West that I have been able to trace. The operas remain unknown to almost all Western musicians, even to those most interested in Russian music. If *Judith* is known to them at all, it is likely to be by the long, sneering account (with numerous musical examples) which Mussorgsky sent to Balakirev some weeks after the first performance rather than by the score itself; but as Andrey Rimsky-Korsakov pointed out in his edition of Mussorgsky letters and documents,[1] Mussorgsky was very conscious of the violently anti-Serovian views of his older friends Stasov and Balakirev; even in this letter Mussorgsky says that *Judith* is the first opera on the Russian stage since Dargomïzhsky's *Rusalka* that one has to take seriously.

Hardly anyone in Petersburg had expected *Judith* to be a success; as Tchaikovsky put it years later, 'we expected a boring, uninspired, pretentious opera'; Serov was forty-three and had so far given no real evidence of creative ability. In 1842, at the age of twenty-two and with no technical training at all, he had set out to rival Verstovsky with an *Askold's Grave*, a project which collapsed when he tried to write his own libretto. Other subjects had appealed to him from time to time— *The Merry Wives of Windsor*, Lazhechnikov's novel *The Pagan* (*Basurman*)—and in 1845 he had actually achieved a little operetta based on a French vaudeville, *La Meunière de Marly*, of which a

---

[1] *M. P. Musorgsky*: *Pisma i dokumentï* (Moscow, 1932), p. 85. Mussorgsky's musical quotations are interesting in that they show the changes made by Serov before his opera was printed, e.g. the Assyrian chorus about 'the coming of the Hebrew beauty' in Act III, where there can be no question of a lapse of memory on Mussorgsky's part.

surviving fragment, some *valse-couplets*,[1] is equally pitiful in both invention and technique. In 1849 he embarked on a *May Night*, with a libretto by Praskovya Mikhaylovna Bakunin (a cousin of the anarchist) based on Gogol's short story, and worked on it until 1853, completing or nearly completing two versions in three acts and a third in two acts. From Serov's correspondence with the Stasov brothers, who were at that time still his closest friends, and with Alexey Bakunin (the anarchist's brother)[2] we know quite a lot about the various numbers. Hanna's prayer from Act III was actually sung, with orchestra, at a charity concert in Petersburg on 29 April/11 May, 1851, when Anton Rubinstein remarked to Dmitry Stasov: 'Je ne m'attendais pas à ça du tout. C'est noblement et aristocratiquement musical.' But Hanna's prayer has not come down to us. The score of one version of *May Night* was burned by the composer; and all that survives of the opera in any form is a 20-bar fragment—probably Levko's serenade, which was the opening number of the third version—which Serov transcribed for piano solo in Lyudmila Shestakova's album in May 1855.[3] It was at the time of the third version of *May Night* that Serov discovered Wagner: not his music but *Oper und Drama* and *Das Kunstwerk der Zukunft*. It was Wagner's views that attracted him; a year or two before, in one of his own earliest critical essays[4] he had proclaimed that 'in *musical* drama what matters first and foremost is *drama*'. When at last, in 1856, he heard some Wagner—it was the *Tannhäuser* overture—he found it 'only curious, interesting, even striking, but in no-wise beautiful, capable of giving pleasure from a "musical point of view"'. It was only in 1858 when he saw *Tannhäuser* on the Dresden stage and *Lohengrin* at Weimar that he became a fanatical admirer of Wagner's music; he heard the *Tristan* prelude at the Leipzig Tonkünstlerfest in 1859; but when he embarked on *Judith* in 1861, after eight years of almost complete silence so far as composition was concerned, Wagner was to him essentially the Wagner of *Tannhäuser* and *Lohengrin*. And *Judith* was originally conceived not as a Wagnerian but, literally, as an Italian opera.

In 1860, after throwing off a *Christmas Song* for female choir, flute, oboe, and clarinet, and a Latin *Pater noster* for chorus and orchestra, Serov again began to dream of operas, and took fire at K. I. Zvantsev's suggestion to base one on Zhukovsky's translation of *Undine*. He got as far as casting it for the artists of the Maryinsky Theatre—as he had done with *May Night*—and then abandoned it for a *Poltava*. But during the winter of 1860–1 Adelaide Ristori was appearing at the Maryinsky as guest-artist in spoken drama—Schiller's *Maria Stuart*, Paolo Giacometti's *Giuditta*, and other tragedies—and, to quote Zvantsev:[5] 'On one occasion, actually 20 December, 1860, during the interval after Holofernes' orgy in the tragedy *Giuditta* . . . I said to Serov: "Well, what about that for an opera finale?" Enraptured by this orgy, he cried out: "Of course! And I will certainly write an opera *Judith*, the more gladly because I've always been attracted by the stories and characters of the Old Testament!"' (Serov was proud of the fact that his maternal grandfather was a Jew; it would be a quibble to object that the Book of Judith is not a canonical

[1] Printed in N. Findeisen, *A. N. Serov: evo zhizn i muzïkalnaya deyatelnost*, 2nd ed. (St. Petersburg, 1904), p. 41. According to V. S. Baskin, *A. N. Serov* (Moscow, 1890), p. 110, the overture was published by Jurgenson but I have not been able to see it.
[2] Findeisen, 'Novïe materialï dlya biografii A. N. Serova. Pisma evo k A. A. Bakuninu (1850–3)', in *Ezhegodnik*

Imperatorskikh Teatrov, iv (1895), supplement 3, p. 110.
[3] Findeisen, 'Otrïvok iz yunosheskoy operï A. N. Serova "Mayskaya noch"', in *Russkaya muzïkalnaya gazeta*, iii (1896), col. 29. Findeisen prints the whole fragment.
[4] 'Spontini i evo muzïka', in *Panteon*, i (1852), p. 1.
[5] Reminiscences of Serov in *Russkaya Starina* (August 1888), reprinted in Findeisen, *A. N. Serov*, p. 88.

book of the Old Testament.) He did not at first contemplate a Russian *Judith* but enlisted the help of an *improvisatore*, a certain Ivan Antonovich Giustiniani, then living in Petersburg, to prepare an Italian libretto, and set about the composition of the last scene (Judith with the severed head and her hymn of triumph), which he proposed to offer to the soprano La Grua, a famous Norma of the day, for her benefit. The 'hymn' was finished in full score by March 1861, but La Grua turned it down and before long Serov decided to turn his work into a Russian opera. In any case, Serov wrote or roughed out a great deal of the music before he had a text. As a Wagnerian, and a skilled man of letters, Serov might have been expected to produce his own Russian libretto; but he doubted his powers and called in Zvantsev, who was at the same time struggling with the translation of *Tannhäuser*,[1] a young friend, D. I. Lobanov, and even a real poet, Maykov. Towards the end of 1861 Serov submitted the full score of his first act to Balakirev, not directly but through Mussorgsky, and received a crushing reply. Balakirev had only glanced at it and, in any case, it was impossible to judge an opera from a single act: 'I can only say that in the orchestra there is a great deal of artistic pretension, but a great deal of it won't come off. The composer handles his masses badly; he is better with light orchestration. Yet one thing I can say: the end is very pretty, beginning with the bar where the basses sing middle C, to which the other voices add chords of *la mineur* (with suspended fifth, G, of a C major chord), and finally to all this the basses—D and A. This is very *pretty*'.[2] It is highly significant that it is this passage at the end of Act I which Mussorgsky allows himself to praise with real enthusiasm in the already mentioned letter to Balakirev after the first performance. 'The very end of the first act is beautiful,' he says. As for the D and A of the basses, 'the fifths in the basses have a peculiar *mystical* sound;—there is a sort of *solemn calm* which *doesn't come to an end*, and this is beautiful; the impression is true and good—this is the best passage in the opera.' As a matter of fact, Serov was very fond of ending a number like this, dying away almost imperceptibly.

The prelude to Act IV, depicting Holofernes' orgy, had a concert performance in February 1862, and in the summer Johann Strauss's orchestra played Holofernes' march and the dance of the odalisques at Pavlovsk. And when the complete opera was duly performed at the Maryinsky, on 16/28 May, 1863, it scored an astounding success—not only with the general public but with the *cognoscenti*, even the Conservatoire staff and the opera personnel. Theophil Tolstoy, who had heralded it with the most malicious advance publicity, was completely conquered and openly recanted. The young Tchaikovsky was 'enraptured' by it and, according to Laroche, he never lost his admiration; he certainly wrote warmly of it in a well-known letter to Nadezhda von Meck (17/29 March, 1878). The one important dissentient voice that of the composer's former friend, now bitter enemy, V. V. Stasov. Stasov attended the performance and the next day wrote a very long, almost hysterical letter to Balakirev,[3] who was far away at Pyatigorsk, demanding to be told why such a work, rubbish which was at the same time 'serious, unsentimental, without love . . . without roulades', should be at once and unanimously hailed as a masterpiece. Mussorgsky had been with him in the theatre 'and seemed to think as I did, but I didn't hear from him

---

[1] He afterwards translated *Lohengrin*.

[2] This letter—with Serov's furious reply, also to Mussorgsky, saying he had expected something better from Balakirev than the pedantry of a *musicus ex professo*—was printed by Theophil Tolstoy in *Russkaya Starina*, ix (February, 1874), pp. 351–2.

[3] *Perepiska M. A. Balakireva s V. V. Stasovïm* (Moscow, 1935), pp. 179–87.

one idea, one word of deep understanding . . . He seems to me a perfect idiot.' Seen in this light, Mussorgsky's own later letter to Balakirev appears as a weak attempt at exculpation. His true reaction to *Judith* was to begin his own *Salammbô* five months later.

Serov lost little time in following up the success of *Judith*. He at once embarked on the composition of an opera named after the favourite wife of Vladimir the Great, Rogneda, and based to some extent on the ballad by Pushkin's friend Rïleev. The historical Vladimir was a monarch whose religious enthusiasm must have been a sore trial to his subjects; he first forced them into idolatry on a massive scale and later obliged them, again *en masse*, to adopt Christianity. In Serov's only slightly historical opera the still pagan Vladimir has abducted Olava (a character who never appears), the bride of a young Christian warrior Ruald, and Rogneda's jealous rage provides the pretext for a close parallel with *Judith*: she determines to murder Vladimir in his sleep. But Vladimir wakes in time. He had already been struck by Ruald's magnanimity in rescuing him from a bear while hunting and now, after sentencing Rogneda to death, he is easily persuaded by a chorus of Christian pilgrims to pardon her. The action of *Judith* has en epic simplicity; it only slightly embroiders the story in the Apocrypha—Holofernes has ambitious dreams of overthrowing his royal master and tempts Judith with the prospect of becoming queen of Babylon. But that of *Rogneda* is a preposterous hotchpotch of spectacular or otherwise theatrically effective scenes. (As Dargomïzhsky remarked, Serov had hunting dogs from the Imperial Kennels on the stage in *Rogneda*, as he had had camels in *Judith*: 'Why shouldn't his operas succeed?') Serov himself confessed in his autobiographical notes[1] that he began with these scenes: 'The music, like that of *Judith*, was composed not to the words of the text, which did not yet exist, but to situations clearly defined in the author's imagination', and the task of providing words to the 'already prepared or half-prepared music' was entrusted to a minor dramatist, D. V. Averkiev.

The parts of Rogneda and Prince Vladimir were conceived for Valentina Bianchi and Sariotti, the original Judith and Holofernes, but Bianchi was now singing Judith in Moscow and the part had to be given to an inexperienced soprano, Yashchenskaya (Broni), who actually sang it at the first performance on 27 October/9 November 1865. But shortly afterwards Serov rewrote the part for a contralto, Darya Leonova, once a pupil of Glinka, many years later the friend of Mussorgsky, though it is described in the published score as for mezzo-soprano. Vladimir was actually sung by the greatest Russian bass of the nineteenth century, Petrov—the original Susanin, Ruslan, Miller (in *Rusalka*), and Varlaam—while Sariotti was the high priest of Perun.

The popular success of *Rogneda* was even greater than that of *Judith*; it enjoyed some seventy performances at the Maryinsky in the first five years—more than any previous Russian opera except *Askold's Grave* (which is also concerned with Vladimir the Great); and it continued to be the most popular of Serov's operas at least until the beginning of the present century. Even Rimsky-Korsakov confessed many years later, in his autobiography, that at the time '*Rogneda* strongly interested me and a great deal in it pleased me, e.g. the witch, the idol-worshipping chorus, the chorus in the audience-hall, the dance of the buffoons, the hunt prelude, the 7/4 chorus and much else—in snatches. I was also pleased by the coarse but colourful and effective orchestration . . . I did not dare to confess all this in the Balakirev circle and even, as one sincerely devoted to their ideas, abused this opera among my acquaintances . . . I remembered a great deal, having heard

[1] Quoted by Findeisen, *A. N. Serov*, p. 113.

[174]

the opera two or three times, and enjoyed playing excerpts from it from memory.' A year or two later his memory was treacherously to offer him the music of the witch scene when he came to write his 'musical picture' *Sadko*,[1] and the triplet figuration of the Act V finale (as he afterwards recognized himself) for the third movement of *Antar*.

After *Rogneda* Serov wanted another Russian subject. He became fascinated by the Ukraine, its Cossack people and its language—as early as 1861 he had become interested in its folk-music—and contemplated a ballet or 'symphonic pantomime' on Gogol's *Christmas Eve*, but nothing came of this except two Ukrainian dances for orchestra, *Grechaniki* (= buckwheat cakes) and a *hopak*, though it is true he returned to it as an opera-subject in the last months of his life. Another Gogol subject, 'a musical illustration to the second chapter of *Taras Bulba*', got no further than an orchestral *Dance of Zaporozhtsy Cossaks*, which was later published by Bessel; it has a characteristic *pp* ending. What he wanted, he told Zvantsev,[2] was 'something, quick-bloody—with slaughter and shooting (in the right place)', but when his final choice in the spring of 1867 fell on Ostrovsky's *Don't live as you'd like to, but live as God commands* (*Ne tak zhivi, kak khochetsya, a tak zhivi, kak Bog velit*), it at first lacked this element of slaughter. It is a typical Ostrovsky play of contemporary life, a thoroughly Russian subject quite in keeping with the 'naturalism', the 'truth to life', fashionable in Russia in the 1860s. A young merchant (Peter), bored by his wife (Dasha) and life in general, is wildly in love with an innkeeper's daughter (Grunya), to whom he represents that he is a bachelor. Grunya discovers the truth, through an overheard conversation, and will have nothing more to do with him. She goes off with another admirer to the *maslyanitsa*, the Shrovetide fair. Eremka, the evil smith of the inn, persuades Peter to go to the fair, too, and when he is drunk suggests that he should murder his wife so as to be able to marry Grunya. Instead. Peter decides to drown himself. But as he is standing by an ice-hole in the Moskva river, the church bells sound for Lent; he pulls himself together and decides to go home and 'not live as he wants to'.

Serov turned to Ostrovsky himself with a request that he would convert his play into a libretto: 'I am convinced that the inner dramatic power calls for warm, truly Russian sounds, quite in character with the matchless *songs* of the Great-Russian people. You yourself—a connoisseur of the songs, know *what* is in them! Remember that even in your play all the characters sing from time to time—at every opportunity they take to song.' Ostrovsky complied and all went well so far as the first three acts were concerned. With the fourth he ran into trouble, for he wished to introduce in the *maslyanitsa* devilish figures, horned and tailed, so that Eremka was made 'a sort of *Freischütz* Caspar: a semi-devil in a peasant's coat'. Serov flatly rejected this idea—though a phrase in the fourth act libretto at least gave him a suitable title for his opera: 'hostile power'—but he was being tempted in another direction. Already Zvantsev had suggested: 'Let your Peter go home and kill his wife like a chicken, and at once over his head booms out the first heavy stroke of the Lenten bells', but Serov had sensibly rejected the idea: 'My hero is no Othello! Peter will go back to drinking as before for some years yet.' Nevertheless, when the first three acts were finished, he changed his mind and decided to end with the murder, 'only not at home behind a screen, but in a tumbledown hut outside the town. Far off, across the snow, one sees the church and hears the bells.' So, for the third time, murder (or attempted murder)

[1] See *Festschrift Friedrich Blume* (Cassel, 1963), p. 17.   [2] Reminiscences, quoted by Findeisen, *A. N. Serov*, pp. 12 foll.

provided the climax of a Serov opera.[1] However Ostrovsky would no more accept this idea for the fifth act than Serov would his devils in the fourth, and in the end the libretto for the last two acts had to be supplied by P. I. Kalashnikov, a well-known hack who had translated *Les Huguenots*, *Le Prophète*, *Traviata*, and Gounod's *Faust*. (The participation of another hand, A. N. Zhokhov, seems to be apocryphal.) Yet Serov did not live to finish the music. He died suddenly, on 20 January/1 February 1871, with Act V only roughed out, and the score had to be completed—the whole act amounts to only twenty-two pages of vocal score—and orchestrated by his young friend N. F. Solovyev, who also had to score the introduction and latter part of Peter's *scena* in Act I. The opera was produced at the Maryinsky within three months (on 19 April/1 May), with Sariotti as Eremka and Petrov singing only two minor parts. The success was very moderate.

Although he had not finished *Hostile Power*, Serov had actually begun yet another opera. It was on his old favourite subject, Gogol's *Christmas Eve*, and no less a poet than Polonsky was to provide the libretto. He already had two completed dances and some sketches from the ballet of 1868, and his widow was able to put together and publish a posthumous suite of four numbers: (1) Oksana, Vakula, and the girls; (2) the Empress's ball—minuet; (3) mazurka; (4) arietta—Oksana's grief in Vakula's absence. The after-history of Polonsky's libretto, *Vakula the Smith*, and of the competition for settings of it—in which Tchaikovsky won the first prize and N. F. Solovyev the second—is well known.

Serov's operas did not, so far as I have been able to discover, survive the Revolution. One can now contemplate them as historically important museum-pieces and consider their music with more detachment than his contemporaries could command. To begin with, we can dismiss the charges of Wagnerism altogether; whatever Serov has in common with Wagner is due to common factors in their musical ancestry: Spontini, Halévy and, above all, Meyerbeer. 'Meyerbeer c'est le favori de mon âme', he said in his youth and, although he came to recognize his favourite's weaknesses, he remained faithful. (Serov makes free use of thematic reminiscence for dramatic purposes, but not more than Weber or Glinka.) *Judith* is a Meyerbeerian grand opera in all but the simplicity of its plot; *Rogneda* lacks that saving condition. *Hostile Power* still retains Meyerbeerian conventions, though the subject and the musical material are totally different; the only opera with which one can compare it is Tchaikovsky's exactly contemporary *Voevoda*, another Ostrovsky subject similarly dressed up in a great deal of folk-melody. Indeed the three operas are musically so different that it is hardly possible to consider them synoptically; they need to be looked at separately. Yet they do reveal a few common traits which one can call 'Serov's style'.

The broad plan of *Judith*, its oriental third and fourth acts framed by the Hebrew 'outside' ones, anticipates that of *Prince Igor* and reminds one that—despite its non-Russian subject—it stands in the line from Glinka and Dargomïzhsky to Mussorgsky and Rimsky-Korsakov. But Serov's orientalism is much less convincing than Glinka's or Borodin's. It is very much a matter of flattened sixths in the major scale and much of it derives from Glinka; Holofernes' march is clearly the child of Chernomor's in *Ruslan* by the march in *Prince Kholmsky*. But the songs and

<hr />

[1] Incredibly, Rosa Newmarch completes the parallel with *Judith* and *Rogneda* by making the woman the murderer: 'The neglected wife discovers her husband's infidelity, and murders him in a jealous frenzy', *The Russian Opera* (London, 1914), p. 158. Since Mrs. Newmarch evidently did not know the score in 1914, we need not take too much notice of her critical remarks in the 1908 edition of *Grove*, which still stand in the fifth edition.

dances of the odalisques and almahs, languorous with cor anglais and harp, or wild and colourfully scored (almost everyone from Wagner downward admitted the effectiveness of Serov's orchestration in general), compare very favourably with the exotic essays of Meyerbeer or Bizet. And Vagoa ('Bagoas the eunuch', but he is a tenor) has a pretty 'Indian song':

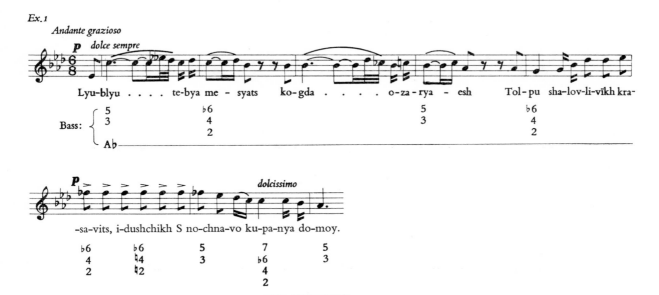

Much more interesting are the points of affinity with Mussorgsky. As I have suggested elsewhere,[1] Mussorgsky may well have been influenced in his choice of *Salammbô* as an opera subject by the parallel with *Judith*, the heroine's penetration of the besiegers' camp to seduce Mâtho and recover the stolen *Zaïmph*, but I would no longer say 'there is no trace of any musical influence': the scene of Salammbô before the image of Tanit would hardly have been written as it is, if Mussorgsky had not had Serov's odalisques in mind. Again: was not the scene of Boris's hallucination probably suggested—dramatically, not musically—by Holofernes'? But the general affinities are also striking. Consider, for instance, Serov's occasional use of curiously angular themes, such as that which accompanies the slow pacing of the elders at the very beginning of Act I:

[1] In my edition of Calvocoressi's *Mussorgsky* (London, 1946), p. 98, n.

[177]

or Avra's melodic line when, near the end of Act II, she pleads with her mistress to give up her plan. A little earlier in the same Act, both Judith's calm:

and the harmony of Avra's outburst of horror:

are not far removed from Mussorgsky's musical world. When Judith, near the end of her prayer, sings of 'the wings of angels' protecting her:

this music too must have planted a general idea in Mussorgsky's mind from which was to come Boris's farewell to his son; indeed the accompaniment figure of Boris's blessing (first flute and

[178]

violas—or harp harmonics and *muted* violas in Rimsky-Korsakov's score)—which we must remember was originally Salammbô's prayer—reflects the figure *X* in Ex. 3. As for bold, empirical but expressive harmony, while there are examples in *Judith*, Serov was to go further in later operas, notably in *Hostile Power*, when Peter learns that Grunya has discovered he already has a wife, and when the murder is done:

Ex. 6

Serov's harmony in general has a good deal in common with Dargomïzhsky's: it is either conventional, in which case it is often clumsy and amateurish, or experimental, in which case the experiment may or may not come off. He does not mind ending a scene with a dissonance: Holofernes' march on its second appearance, where the tonic D is to the end clouded by an unresolved second, followed by a *ppp* A in the bass. This last is typical of the quiet endings already mentioned. They are numerous: the end of Act I (which Mussorgsky, as we have seen, praised even in the letter to Balakirev); the equally quiet end of Act II, where the muttering quaver-figure of the Judith-Avra duet dies away just as the semiquavers of Pimen's cell or the quavers of the idiot scene were to die away in *Boris*; the chorus of worshippers of Perun in Act I of *Rogneda*; the penultimate scene of the fourth act of *Hostile Power*, where as Peter and Eremka leave the stage the overlapping echoes of the folk-songish theme die away in a manner later made familiar by Borodin:

Ex. 7

Yet one more point in *Judith* evidently impressed Mussorgsky: the handling of the chorus. In his own day Serov was accused of treating the chorus, particularly the Jewish choruses, as if the work were an oratorio; there is indeed some rather clumsy, square-cut fugal writing. But he must be given full credit for not using the chorus simply as a musical mass; it is a protagonist even when it is employed monumentally. But it is not always used monumentally; Serov again and again asks for 'not all' the tenors and basses, for only 'two voices' from the contraltos (while the sopranos sing *sotto voce* before also being reduced to two voices), for 'not all' tenors and then 'others'. The waiting crowd in the last finale of *Rogneda* is handled naturalistically in the same way: 'one tenor', 'one bass', 'another bass', 'some altos', 'two or three sopranos', and so on, just like the crowd in *Boris*. The crowd jeering at the Pecheneg prisoners in the first act finale of *Rogneda* is quite as naturalistic as the chorus jeering at Khrushchov in Mussorgsky's opera.

When *Judith* was first produced in Moscow, a critic complained rather unreasonably of its lack of Russianness. That cannot be said of *Rogneda*. It abounds in Russianness of one sort or another: genuine popular melody (the fool's song in Act III and probably the women's chorus); imitated folk-melody (Rogneda's son's little song in Act IV); the *bilina*-type melody at the end of the opera, begun by the old leader of the Christian pilgrims:

Ex. 8

Andante maestoso assai

Po - ko - ris   krestu,   pro - sve - ti   na - rod,   Veru   pra - vu - yu

u - tver - di   v zem - le.

gradually taken up by the other characters, and finally by the chorus, in a really splendid climax which left its mark on more than one fine passage in Rimksy-Korsakov and perhaps on the end of *Igor*; and things like the girls' dance in Act II, with its final effective combination of the two themes:

[180]

Ex. 9

(Originally: G major, *Giocoso scherzando*)

which might have come straight out of *Life for the Tsar*.[1] Serov's techniques for the treatment of 'Russian' material are also derived from Glinka, though he seems at first to have found it hard not to harmonize modal melodies as major or minor. *Hostile Power* is, of course, full of folk or folk-like melodies which here compensate handsomely for Serov's normal weakness of melodic invention; it is hardly possible to distinguish the genuine from the imitation, and some of the most beautiful, as yet unidentified, must be—incredulously—attributed to Serov himself. Dasha's song at the very beginning of Act I sets the standard—and it will be seen that Serov had at last realized that the best thing to do with a folk-tune may be to leave it almost alone:

Ex. 10

Chu - st, chu - st, re - ti - vo - e, Ne k do - bru e - vo shche - mit

Her innocent admirer Vasya's song at the end of the act is even more beautiful:

Ex. 11

Ekh! vos - toskuysya, voz - go - ryuy —— sya, voz —— go — ryuy — sya Tï su - da —— rush-

- ka mo - ya! Uzh i sam li vstosko - valsya bolno ya!

[1] However, Karatïgin, who had seen the sketches for *Rogneda*, tells us that Serov himself had marked this dance 'imitation of Dargomïzhsky; similarly Rogneda's monologue in Act IV was inscribed 'imitation of Gounod', and the opening chorus of the act 'in Villebois's style' (i.e. of the popular choruses in Villebois's *Natasha* of 1861); see *Ezhegodnik Imperatorskikh Teatrov*, 1910, part iv, p. 108. Another effective combination, like Ex. 9, of contrasted themes previously heard separately, occurs in the odalisques' dances in Act III of *Judith*.

Serov had by now also hit on the idea of using snatches of these melodies to cover the caesuras in the vocal line and fill the gaps in recitative, so that a great deal of the score, like that of Tchaikovsky's *Voevoda*, sounds very '*kuchkist*'—at a date when the only *kuchkist* opera so far produced had been Cui's uncharacteristic *William Ratcliff*. (On the other hand, Peter's very Mussorgskian 'V polnoch, vo temnom lesu' ('At midnight, in the dark forest') was composed *after* the publication of 'Savishna'.) The fair-scene, not so much the *maslyanitsa* procession itself as the bagpipers, the cries of the sellers of bread, cakes, and drinks, and so on, is in the directl ine between such late eighteenth-century works as the Matinsky-Panshkevich *Sanktpeterburgsky gostiny dvor* and Mussorgsky's *Sorochintsy Fair*, a line which leads on to *Petrushka*.

In *Hostile Power* Serov also developed the device of sharp musical contrast which he had employed in the two earlier works. A purely musical combination has already been mentioned (cf. Ex. 9); there is a similar example, which it is tempting to call 'pre-Polovtsian', in the oriental dances of *Judith*. A striking passage of dramatic contrast occurs when Judith continues imperturbably singing of her intention to go to the Assyrian camp, against her maid's agitated recitative of protest. This effect is repeated and exaggerated in the Act I finale of *Rogneda*, when Ruald goes on imperturbably praying while the high priest of Perun and the people cry 'Death to him!' But the climax of melodrama is reached in the scene of the attempted murder of the sleeping Vladimir, where a solo violin plays an extended cadenza-like passage, recalling the scene in the witch's cave (X), over the solemn chords of the pilgrims' chorus from the previous act:

Ex. 12

But in *Hostile Power* contrasts of gay music with sinister action are used with fine irony: for instance, the distant music of the *maslyanitsa* and the drunken revellers in the pothouse as Eremka tightens his hold on Peter. Again, the light-hearted chorus of girls, first heard behind the scenes at the beginning of Act III, sounds again from the distance when Peter has been thrown over by

[182]

Grunya and the evil Eremka approaches him for the first time, and is heard in the orchestra in the last Act, when Peter, lurking in the ravine, hears his victim approaching ('Hark, here she is!'):

Ex. 13

Chu   o - na!!   o - na!...   Grunka s Vaskoyu   na sa-nyakh v dvoem

Coming here suddenly, as it does, after the *ppp* storm of whistling wind, suggested by an incessant chromatic semiquaver figure, with the occasional bark of a dog, it comes like a flash of ironic lightning.

Even in the Preface to *Rogneda* Serov claimed to be striving for '*dramatic truth* in sounds, although for the sake of this truth, for the *characteristic nature* of the music, "conventional" beauty, the "jewelled" elegance of musical forms had to be sacrificed'. He was far from achieving that in most of *Rogneda*, but he came near to it in *Hostile Power*. Asafiev contended[7] that, after all, *Judith* was Serov's best opera: 'Its stern, serious language and massively rough rudimentary construction have a flavour of archaism ... The score looks like the irregular but enduring and powerful stone-work of the walls and towers of ancient cities'. That is partly true, yet there is also a good deal of rubble-work and grouting. But it is something to have fashioned two such totally different works as *Judith* and *Hostile Power*, as well as the best pages of *Rogneda*, and to have breathed some real musical life into such puppets as the Jewish heroine and the evil Russian smith. These are surprising achievements for a brilliant, cantankerous, critical rather than creative, mind.

¹ *Izbrannïe trudï*, ii (Moscow, 1954), p. 336.

INDEX

[186]